To Kent   2012

I've a...
your m...
skills.
Find these courtroom snapshots
interesting. always,
Mel Harmon

BY THE SWEAT OF MY TONGUE

Profiles In Prosecution

MEL HARMON

authorHOUSE®

AuthorHouse™
1663 Liberty Drive
Bloomington, IN 47403
www.authorhouse.com
Phone: 1-800-839-8640

First published by AuthorHouse 8/27/2010

ISBN: 978-1-4520-6344-7 (e)
ISBN: 978-1-4520-6343-0 (sc)
ISBN: 978-1-4520-6345-4 (hc)

Library of Congress Control Number: 2010911768

Printed in the United States of America

This book is printed on acid-free paper.

Author's Note

"The wise know too well their weakness to assume infallibility; and he who knows most, knows best how little he knows." (Thomas Jefferson – from a legal brief submitted, July 31, 1810)

Speaking candidly ––

There's a practical point I wish to address. It's a disclaimer of sorts. When a Trial Lawyer's *tongue sweats* in the heat of Courtroom debate, his verbiage is <u>not</u> grounded in *personal* knowledge. It's important for a reader to keep this in mind. During my career I participated in the Prosecution of hundreds of felony trials. Over one hundred thirty of these trials were Murder Trials. However, I <u>wasn't</u> a *percipient* witness in a <u>single</u> case. <u>Every</u> time I've gone to Trial I've **believed** in the guilt of the charged Defendant, but I <u>never</u> **knew** he did it. That degree of certitude is impossible. I <u>didn't</u> see any of the crimes happen. I <u>didn't</u> hear them happen, <u>or</u> smell them, <u>not</u> perceive them with any other physical sense. My opinions were the product of hearsay.

Once assigned to a case I pursued my role as a Prosecutor with vigor and passion and honesty, but I **never** possessed *personal* knowledge of the cases! I <u>didn't</u> **know** if the crimes actually happened. I <u>didn't</u> **know** *exactly* what happened if they did happen. My data base was culled from witness statements, police reports, physical evidence, and sworn testimony. Beyond those evidentiary categories, I had to rely on intuition, common sense, experience, and a strong jaw. Attempting to draw just and reasonable inferences from what I'd read and heard. <u>No</u> all-seeing-eye gadget graced a wall in my office. I claimed <u>no</u> special powers nor skills of perception or clairvoyance.

My truth was case truth. But is case truth the whole truth and nothing but the truth? Or is case truth a parody of truth? The answer is relative of course. Yet, I believe it's important to be as objective as possible. Case truth is <u>not</u> infallible.

I'm well aware of the limitations of my Profession. Trial work <u>isn't</u> an exact science. On the twilight side of my Courthouse years, I've become somewhat more appreciative of a cold case fact. Trial Lawyers <u>don't</u> **know** what the truth is, they <u>only</u> **know** what the case evidence tells them it is. A crucial predicate to knowing is knowing how little you know!

Another important disclaimer: I discuss selected cases from my career in the book, but I <u>haven't</u> used **actual Transcripts** of Court Proceedings as a factual basis for what I've written. The references have been <u>my</u> case *outlines* and <u>my</u> *memory*. Naturally, both sources are subject to the not inconsequential limitation of human fallibility – though the *outlines* were meticulously prepared at the time the cases were tried. The precursor of Prosecutorial *tongue sweat* is <u>sweating</u> <u>fingers</u>.

As for my *memory* ––– well, it's certainly flawed. However, I'd say many things about which I've written *are* etched into my psyche. Many of the <u>names</u> mentioned within the text have been *deliberately* changed.

I've placed significant emphasis on **Closing Argument** in the text. I credit whatever small measure of success I've achieved in the Courtroom to a strong work ethic, thoroughness in preparing and presenting my cases, and the *POWER* of Summation. A word of caution is pertinent concerning the use of <u>quotation</u> marks in the Opening Statements and Closing Arguments highlighted. Obviously, if an author <u>isn't</u> using Court Transcripts it <u>isn't</u> possible to offer a verbatim recitation of his remarks.

Accordingly, this book contains a generous mix of literary license. There are two types of Summation: *Armchair* Argument and *Advocacy* Argument. The former is the way you'd like to have done it – absent the statutory and judicial restraints imposed upon a Prosecutor's remarks. The latter is the way you actually did do it. Since I <u>didn't</u> access Court Transcripts, I can only present *Armchair* Arguments that are loosely based upon my *Argument Outlines*.

I'll conclude these lines of candor with a further *expression of ethics*. I appreciate the following words. I believe the quotation accurately reflects my mind-set and my moral-intent each time I *worked a case* during my career –– whether inside or outside the Courtroom.

"The wisest man *preaches* <u>no</u> doctrines; he has <u>no</u> scheme;
he *sees* <u>no</u> rafter, <u>not</u> even a cobweb, *against* the heavens.
It is a <u>clear</u> sky." (Henry David Thoreau – emphasis added)

I can **truthfully** say I <u>never</u> had an agenda during my career, nor did I act from ulterior motive. I diligently tried to *see* things as they are. I never personally knew the parties, nor the witnesses, nor the victims or their families. I had <u>no</u> *personal* interest in the outcome of any case.

I'm **not** a racist. I <u>believe</u> in the brotherhood and equality of *all* human beings. <u>**Each**</u> of us is spiritually begotten by an Eternal Father in Heaven. I'm not preaching when I say this, I'm explaining **my** *personal* moral and spiritual *values*. They are the seed bed of my character and of my intention.

I *preached* <u>no</u> doctrine <u>nor</u> scheme in the Courtroom. I did <u>not</u> *perceive* the rafters – <u>not</u> even a cobweb of prejudice or personal interest. I <u>never</u> ran for public office, nor did I seriously entertain such thoughts. I <u>never</u> took a bribe, nor was I ever offered one. I <u>never</u> served the expediency of lobbyists. <u>No</u> outward <u>nor</u> inward pressures urged or pushed me into decisions or arguments I made. Each *case* assigned, to use Thoreau's metaphor, came to me as *a clear sky* –– free of preconceived opinion. Received by me with an open mind, inclined toward <u>neither</u> guilt nor innocence. Motivated by two objectives – determine what **is** *just* and **be** *just*, if you can.

I <u>don't</u> pretend to be a <u>wise</u> man, but I'd like to believe I've acted wisely with a modicum of consistency. I'm <u>not</u> a promoter of "snake oil" schemes. <u>Not</u> a Prosecutor programed to believe my service changed the nature of things. I'm just saying I tried to be fair –– ONE case at a time.

I'm a seventy one year old retired dude from the Clark County District Attorney's Office in Las Vegas. I <u>didn't</u> retire as an expert, and despite being blessed with the benefit of considerable hindsight, I'm most definitely **not** an expert now. I'm just a guy who believes *being* **a Prosecutor** <u>is</u> the greatest job in the world.

That said, I promise to be sincere about the things I write, but not impartial! I have an abiding *prejudice* <u>against</u> **Murder!**

Respectfully,
Mel Harmon

Preface

> "Lawyers earn their living by the **sweat of their tongues,**
> and they don't mind hard work." (anon.)

SOME LEGAL PUNDITS ESPOUSE THE USE OF <u>conversational</u> <u>tones</u> when addressing Jurors. They recommend a <u>friendly</u> <u>discussion</u> approach while arguing points to the Trier of Fact. These Courthouse virtuosos suggest that the sophistication of contemporary Jurors makes Courtroom <u>oratory</u> *passe*. **Excuse me!**

A PROSECUTOR has a sworn <u>duty</u> to <u>proclaim</u> the truth. Even the most casual Courtroom combatant *knows* that **facts** don't automatically prevail. **Justice** is often frustrated. **Truth** doesn't inexorably impose its will on a Jury. There is <u>no</u> magic *charm-wand* in the Courtroom. <u>No</u> *vaccine* for insulating undecided Jurors from the noxious effect of falsehood. <u>No</u> ambient *conditioner* to endow equivocal Juries with perfect discernment during their deliberations.

The cause of **Justice** must be championed by PASSIONATE ADVOCACY. The People's Lawyer must prosecute aggressively but prudently, and he must *speak* <u>dynamically</u>. Truth is promulgated by evidence, proper instructions, <u>perspiration</u>, and <u>eloquence</u>! *Manner of delivery* is a matter of personal style to be sure, but it's also a matter of *taking charge* in the Courtroom.

Let the Jury *know* by your <u>tone</u> of voice – by your <u>words</u> – by your <u>manner</u> – by your <u>gestures</u>, that this is <u>not</u> just a stroll in the park. It <u>isn't</u> merely a bull session. It's <u>not</u> party time. It's <u>not</u> theater. It's <u>not</u> a classroom lecture. This is gut-wrenching reality. What you're doing **is not** *conversational oratory*!

"Other sins only speak; **<u>murder</u>** <u>shrieks</u> out." (John Webster: *Duchess of Malfi* [1623], Act IV, Sc.2) A **Murder Trial** is unique. Like <u>punishment</u>, the *passion* of the Prosecutor's *rhetoric* should **fit the crime**.

A **Murder Trial** is *raw* and *real*. The crimes <u>are</u> solemn events with *actual* **consequences**. There <u>are</u> **dead victims** in the cemetery and **charged defendants** in the courtroom. There <u>is</u> **bereavement** and **shock**. There <u>are</u> *highly charged* **evidentiary issues** to be resolved. I'm unsure how the *passion of advocacy* finds fulfillment, through <u>conversational</u> <u>tones</u> employed in <u>friendly</u> <u>discussions</u>, within the **context** of a *First Degree Murder Trial*. A **Prosecutor's** <u>highest</u> <u>duty</u> in this setting is the *role* of **<u>dynamic</u> <u>advocate</u> <u>for</u> <u>Justice</u>**.

Contents

Vile Vengeance

"On Horror's head horrors accumulate..."
Even so my bloody thoughts, with
violence pace,...
Till that *capable* and *wide* **revenge**
swallow them up."
(Shakespeare, *Othello*, Act III, Sc.3, lines 371, 454)

CHAPTER 1

SOMETHING IS DIFFERENT. A STIFF BREEZE WHIPS the mimosa trees. The moonless night is warm and creepy. The shrill wail of sirens relentless in the distance. Those on the street sense a palpable tension building, expanding – intensifying. Volatile flames lick hungrily at the somber darkness. A sinister bluish-orange glow hovers over west Las Vegas. Large chunks of city blocks on the westside are burning. Many firefighters and police hurriedly respond to crisis points.

It's an extraordinary event. Multiple fires have been deliberately combusted by citizens in response to the acquittal in California of three Simi Valley police officers on charges of viciously beating motorist Rodney King. Widespread rioting has triggered arson and looting. The aura the rioters have created reeks with a spirit of reckless retribution. It is an ill-begotten omen of lawlessness that does not bode well for the immediate future.

The frenzied protest of hooligans in west Las Vegas is the night's lead story, but about one mile away a vile subplot will bedevil the diminished resources of the Las Vegas Metropolitan Police Department in this portentous gloom.

Perhaps, he is one among many. But within the borders of the city, on this 30th day of April, 1992, is a vain man with a bone to pick. He has a serious gripe. He carries within his heart a reservoir of bitter bile that infects his mind. He's been obsessed with a spirit of vengeance for months, and the poison spreads with the passing of each hour. He's been wronged by one he considered a friend. Seriously compromised. Threatened. And on horror's head horrors accumulate! What he now contemplates is horrible. Disgusting. Diabolic.

Yet, his bloody thoughts, with violence pace, malignant in his brain. He believes only cunning, cruel, complete <u>revenge</u> will swallow up his bloody torment. He's mistaken in his premise, of course. But how do we make sense out of nonsense? How are victims to be warned of impending catastrophe? How can one whose head is saturated with horror forgive the one who put the horror there?

There is no warning. It is a mission of stealth and subterfuge. The night continues to be enveloped by thick darkness. Natural cover for the perpetration of murderous mischief. A silver sliver of a moon will not rise until 2:19 am. By then the heinous deed is done. And the police have other fish to fry on the westside. They are preoccupied by a smokescreen of fire and rioting. The night seems ordained for perverted vindication.

There are six persons inside 532 Wardelle Street, Apartment D. It's almost midnight – the ominous witching hour. Though it's not the sorcery of witches that is imminent. The black specter of murder approaches. A car pulls up and parks. Two men with loaded firearms are inside. Both dressed in dark clothes. They linger in the car reviewing their modus operandi.

Mousey gets out, shrouded in the darkness. Quietly, fatefully he climbs the stairs and knocks. There's a brief pause. <u>He</u> is *known* by <u>those</u> inside. Or is he?

Lacy opens the door and goes to the bedroom. Mousey enters. He carries a concealed .357 magnum and a malevolent heart. Stuart and James are in the front room – apprehensive. There's small talk. They ask why he's dressed in dark clothes. He offers a flippant response. They sit down. More relaxed. Less vigilant. Disarmed by Mousey's manner and charming banter. Small errors in judgment can have calamitous consequence.

A few minutes later, Mousey excuses himself to go spit. It's a ruse. He unlocks the dead bolt and goes to the balcony briefly. When he returns he does <u>not</u> reset the dead bolt. Sadly, his treachery is unnoticed.

There's more conversation. Mousey stands up and goes to the window. He <u>parts</u> the drapes and <u>looks</u> outside. His actions are a sign of readiness. A green light. It's a go! The lights of the car blink menacingly. Message received!

Double R exits the vehicle. On horror's head horrors accumulate. He is strapped with a 9-millimeter – and by bloody thoughts that violently pace malignant in his brain. He is *known* by <u>one</u> who is inside. Or is he – really?

Step–by– step with measured stealth, Double R climbs the stairway to deliberate–murderous–mayhem. **Death** is at the door of apartment D. He enters unimpeded. His 9-millimeter in hand.

Stuart and James are blind sided. They say indignantly, "What is this?" Stuart reaches for his heat, but the intruders have the drop on those inside. The element of surprise is decisive. Stuart is told to take his cap off. He wants to keep it on, but the vicious intruders are insistent. He reluctantly removes his cap as his life passes in a kaleidoscopic flash before his eyes. He is literally <u>staring</u> into the gun barrel. A .357 magnum bullet crashes into his head, leaving a jagged wound of entry just above his left eyebrow. He <u>was</u> eighteen.

James is ordered to take his cap off. He pleads for his life. He says, "I won't tell." His appeal is denied. It falls on unhearing ears. The perpetrators aren't into listening. Dead men don't tell tales. He's told, in so many words, "No offense, buddy. But it's got to happen. Take your hat off." And he's shot in the back of the head by a projectile from the .357 magnum. He <u>was</u> nineteen.

A cassette player is playing. The volume of the music is jacked up – loud.

Things happen quickly. Mousey and Double R go to the back bedroom. Lacy is cowering on the bed. Terrified. Trapped. Sorry. Lamenting that she unlocked the door and let Mousey come in. Lamenting that she's here. Lamenting that she can't make herself invisible. Her distraught, imploring eyes beg for a reprieve.

To no avail. The hearts of the intruders are implacable. They relentlessly pursue their foul mission. Dead men don't tell tales – nor do <u>dead</u> women. They place a pillow over those desperate eyes. Double R callously discharges three 9-millimeter bullets into her writhing body. One round enters her upper right chest. The other two penetrate her upper right arm. Then also enter the right chest. She <u>was</u> twenty six.

It is time for deadly retribution. Bloody mayhem goes into the bathroom. Shannon is in the shower. **She's the target**. Helpless. Exposed. Frantic. There's an emotional melt-down. She acknowledges her transgression, and apologizes to Double R for betrayal. She'll make it up to him somehow. She begs to be spared. Don't kill me. Let me live. Please!

But the die is cast. She's made her choices. There is no pardon. No forgiveness. Only sadistic malice. On horror's head horrors accumulate. What happens in the bathroom is a venting of horror. It is **vile vengeance**.

"No beast is more savage than man when possessed with power
answerable to his rage." (Plutarch, *Lives. Cicero*, p.1054)

That would be <u>two</u> men in this instance. Partners in an unholy alliance. The deck is stacked. The playing field, the killing room actually, is <u>not</u> level. It is two versus one. Two strong men versus one weak woman in a shower. Two strong men with guns versus one woman without a gun. All she's got is a bar of soap, a wash rag, and tears for self defense. Poor – poor – Shannon. Naked. Vulnerable. She has no chance!

Their antipathy and their numbers and their bullets make them superior. These factors endow the assailants with the power of life and death. No beast is more savage than <u>two</u> **enraged** men possessed with the might and means and mentality to impose mortality's ultimate judgment.

They want to torture her. Make her suffer. Inflict pain for sport. They want her to die slowly. Knowing that she is dying as the pain consumes her being. A side of Shannon's head is pistol whipped. She sustains blunt laceration of the left temporal area and blunt force injury with ragged margins in front of the left ear. She is shot in the breast and in her hands. The assailants try to shoot her fingers off. A number of fingers are severely damaged.

Shannon screams and struggles, but there is no respite. Each firearm is used. <u>Both</u> men fire random rounds into her body. Multiple bullets pierce and graze her head, face, neck, breast, shoulder, forearm, hands, and fingers. There are <u>eight</u> points of entry, though some may be reentries. There are broad areas of gunpowder tattooing of the right thigh and lower leg.

Vengeance is mine say the home invaders. Pain, suffering, despair, and death – to the snitch bitch! They're devoured by rage. There is no empathy for Shannon. It's as though they've just butchered a sow in a slaughterhouse.

She <u>was</u> twenty four. The deed is done. They leave. Fleeing into the still moonless night.

But there is an intriguing circumstance. Is it an oversight? Did the sense of rage distort their thinking? Did they leave so hastily they left behind unfinished business? What is to be made of this?

Remarkably. Illogically, perhaps. <u>Two</u> little ones have survived the blood bath. They are Annie, who has just turned four, and eighteen month old Frankie. He sleeps through the debacle, but she *witnesses* a gruesome, despicable, real-life nightmare. All of it! She *sees* unabated cruelty inflicted in a way that <u>no</u> child should *ever* have to experience. She isn't shot, but she's the <u>fifth</u> victim in a very real sense.

Scared – shaking, pint-sized Annie runs to C, the other upstairs apartment, and begins banging on the door. She's afraid the bad guys will come back at any moment and get her too. There are four adults in C.

They've heard noises they believe are gunshots. They've called next door. No one answers, but the music is abruptly turned up loud. Understandably, they're jittery. Now, they hear nonstop pounding on their door. They hesitate. Alarmed. They hear a shrill little voice. "It's Annie. Let me in."

The door is opened, and Annie rushes inside like a little brown whirlwind. She exclaims, "They're all dead. They're all dead. <u>They</u> came and <u>they</u> shot them all dead...Uncle Ray – Ray came in, and <u>they</u> shot them all dead...<u>They</u> shot... [Shannon] in the bathtub."

Annie **testifies** at trial that "Little Ray and Scary Eyes came upstairs. I do not know his name. His eyes are scary. Both of them had black guns like cops have. They shot...[Stuart and James] in the front room. They shot...[Lacy] in the bedroom. Scary Eyes and Ray went to the bathroom to kill...[Shannon]."

Annie and her mother *live* at the crime scene. Her mother leaves to launder clothes prior to the murders. Mousey is also known as <u>Ray</u>. Annie is acquainted with him. Earlier he lived in the apartment for several weeks. They became friendly then. She calls him Little Ray or Uncle Ray. They've gone to the store together for ice cream and outside to play.

So, does this fact explain the survival of little Annie? Perhaps. It's been said that honor exists even among thieves. Does compassion exist even among stone-cold murderers? Possibly, when the issue involves little children. It's one thing to send a hail of bullets into the body of a <u>police informant</u>, and to preempt any likelihood of eyewitness evidence, from three <u>adults</u> present at the scene, by systematic execution to seal their lips. But it's something qualitatively different to *take out* little kids.

Human beings are complex creatures. They don't necessarily fit into some preconceived framework. I'm guessing, in this particular instance, that Annie's friendship with Mousey did *save* her. Frankie is asleep and he's only a baby. We don't know if the assailants even realized he was there. But assuming they did, he is obviously not a threat. He's much too young – and <u>asleep</u>.

But little Annie? She borderline. Bright. Alert. Articulate. <u>Awake</u>. A vivacious little *eyeball witness*. Potential trouble for the conspirators, rationally speaking. But suppose logic isn't the sole criterion.

I don't subscribe to blanket condemnation. I'm not fond of generalization. I don't often see things in black and white. I like to give credit where credit is due. The better practice is to concentrate on the specific evidence and reasonable inferences of <u>each</u> case.

The circumstances in the case at bar suggest that a measurable spark of redemption exists in Mousey and Double R. A sense of tender protectiveness toward a child is <u>not</u> a small matter. It's a major incongruity conceived within the madness of multiple murders.

Mousey likes Annie. She is his friend. They've gone to the store together. They've licked ice cream cones and played games together. They'd bonded. She calls him Uncle Ray. I believe he's unwilling to break that bond, and he persuades Double R to go along.

They've probably lived to regret their grant of amnesty to Annie. But for a few moments during this dark, malevolent night, when the beast within them is savage and their smoking guns are an awesome power answerable to their rage, there is a glimmer of light – of humanity in them. Mousy and Scary Eyes are compassionate to a child. They allow her to live – to breathe – to play – to chatter – and to *remember* the awful night when two murderers chose <u>not</u> to kill her. Their Prosecutor, as a barrister and as member of the human race, thanks them for their kindness.

Annie <u>is</u> now twenty! Still rejoicing in the privilege of being <u>alive</u>.

"Yesterday, *This* Day's Madness did prepare;
To-morrow's Silence, Triumph, or Despair..."
(Edward Fitzgerald, *Rubaiyat of Omar Khayyam of Naishapur*)

What is the motive? Why did Double R and Mousey want to kill Shannon? The madness and despair of April 30, 1992 is decreed almost *seventeen* months into yesterday.

Cocaine is a lie. It promises Paradise. It produces Hell. The Devil is a white demon inside a plastic bag.

Cocaine's lie seduces Double R and Mousey. They become drug trafficking business associates and friends. Shannon is part of the drug subculture and is familiar with both men. Double R considers her a <u>close</u> friend and confidante.

But she is arrested on theft-related offenses, and agrees to become a police informant to work off her charges. Not an unusual arrangement for a person with her connections. Though it is an extremely risky enterprise.

Shannon contacts her friend Double R. Desperate people engage in desperate and <u>imprudent</u> acts. They agree to a three ounce cocaine buy at a prearranged time and place a *short* distance from her residence.

It doesn't take a rocket scientist to appreciate the absurdity of this operation. Police surveillance is dutifully established.

Double R arrives at the rendevous point in a 1982 Cadillac on December 6, 1990 at 8:00 p.m. He's approached by Shannon who briefly gets into the car. She verifies his possession of cocaine. Signals to police that Double R is the person in the Cadillac and that cocaine is present inside the vehicle. Then she runs straight to her residence. I'll repeat that. Before God, the police, Double R, and the whole neighborhood – Shannon sets up her friend on a drug bust and runs straight home.

Police immediately converge upon Double R, and block his escape. He is ordered out of the vehicle at gunpoint. While he exits his Cadillac the three plastic baggies of cocaine, he'd intended to sell to Shannon, fall to the ground near his feet. The baggies are in plain view of law enforcement and are impounded as evidence. During an inventory search police find secret compartments within the vehicle interior. Solenoid-activated partitions are discovered in backseat areas on both driver and passenger sides. One and a half kilos of cocaine and $29,982.00 are found inside the concealed compartments. Double R's car is impounded. He is arrested for trafficking in a controlled substance.

The offense is punishable with a <u>mandatory</u> minimum sentence of twenty five years without possibility of parole and a maximum sentence of life in prison and a fine of $500,000.00.

It's enough to make a struggling drug dealer's blood boil – or turn *ice cold*, as the case may be. Shannon's complicity in the drug bust is easily deduced by Double R and his associates from the inception of the trafficking offense. Subsequent legal posturing leaves no doubt about the police informant's identity. Shannon's name is formally disclosed as the informant pursuant to defense motion in December 1991.

Double R and Mousey decide to smoke Shannon. The purpose of the hit is three-fold: (1) **Retribution** – Shannon's callous duplicity is unconscionable in their minds. The *snitch* bitch has to be punished. The issue isn't whether it will happen. The only issue is <u>when</u> it will happen. And they figure haste may be waste. It's often <u>patience</u> that makes a trail harder to track (2) **Elimination** – A *dead* police informant doesn't inform. She doesn't tell courtroom tales. She can't be subpoenaed. She can't be a witness. She's beyond the Prosecutor's jurisdiction. She's bye-bye! (3) **Deterrence** – They want to send a dark *message* to those in the drug culture. Do-not–inform! Don't cooperate with the police. You do so at your peril. Let Shannon be a stark warning to all who contemplate a similar course of action!

The drug trafficking charge still hangs over the head of Double R the moonless night of April 30, 1992. The plot to murder Shannon is still in force as well. Fires and rioting command large scale police presence on the westside. The conspirators decide these circumstances are perfect cover for murder.

"Evil is easy, and has infinite forms."
(Blaise Pascal, *Pensees.* Sect.VI, No.408)

The wheels of justice even grind slowly for quadruple murder, or perhaps I should say, <u>especially</u> for quadruple murder. Evil may be easy, but acquiring convincing evidence <u>isn't</u> easy in a climate of fear. The stakes are extremely high. Police and Prosecutors have to deal with a *youthful* eye witness and with the *Double Jeopardy* clause. A four year old child may <u>not</u> be a competent witness in court, and the Prosecution carries the <u>burden</u> of proving guilt beyond a reasonable doubt. Prosecutors don't obtain convictions with smoke and mirrors. Success requires sufficient *facts*. Premature prosecution may have drastic consequences. A defendant acquitted can't be resubmitted. When *jeopardy* attaches he is done!

The trial for Mousey begins two years after his horrendous crimes. By then little Annie is <u>six</u> and other evidence has been <u>added</u> to the mix. But a criminal trial is a succession of unpredictable events. It's always a roller coaster ride. It's hang on and hang in there, Buddy!

The darkest moment of the proceedings for the Prosecution comes the evening of the *first* day of trial. The zinger comes out of the blue and lands in the pit of my stomach. Then the news spews a dark, disconcerting haze into my brain. I feel only a hopeless sense of stress and immense frustration, *at first*. It's not always pleasant being a <u>prosecutor</u>.

It's not easy being a <u>witness</u> in a murder case. Particularly for a child. Annie has seen the holocaust of quadruple murder. Poor little Annie. The hideous sight of human beings cruelly dispatched to the world of spirits has been seared into her brain. Piteous images of Stuart and

James and Lacy and Shannon gunned down in cold blood still ravage her tender psyche. She is now six, but still encumbered by the frightful memories.

A court ordered lineup is scheduled at the Clark County Jail. A defense motion has been granted by the trial judge. The issue is simple. Can little Annie identify Mousey as he stands with six other men of <u>similar</u> stature, clothing, hair style, skin color, and facial appearance?

The judicial order is correct. The procedure is legitimate. The motion was not inappropriate. Defense Counsel would have been derelict in their fiducial duty had they not sought a lineup. Nevertheless, the process is hellish to Annie. Under ideal circumstances an unpretentious child should not have to be subjected to this.

Impressions of the lineup remain vivid in my memory. My focus is Annie. Her focus is **them**, and she's terrified. I sense the torment. Her little head is full of demons from the past. I see her gripping the Detective's hand as she stares apprehensively through the large glass partition at the seven men standing in the adjoining room. I hear her repeatedly ask the Detective, "Can they see me? Can they come into this room and hurt me?"

The answer to both questions is **no**. "We can see them, but they can't see us. They can't get where we are. You're safe." But Annie does not seem reassured. She's shaking now. Hanging back. She doesn't want to stand in the middle of the room directly in front of the lineup viewing window. She's afraid of being seen. She wants to linger off to the side in the shadows. Fearful of the unknown. Not really knowing what will happen. Not really knowing whom to trust. Residual fright dominates her thinking still. She doesn't want to be harmed by them – **by him**.

It's time. I see Mousey standing pensively with the other six. I see Annie tugging the opposite way as she's led by the hand to the center of the window. Hesitantly, timidly she's complies. But she refuses to stare at them. She glances briefly – then looks down. Her eyes sweep along the line – then she looks away again. She doesn't comprehend <u>how</u> she is able to see them and they are unable to see her. It's not logical to a six year old. She's thinking any moment someone will run into the room and haul her away.

And so, for a bunch of reasons. Annie **misidentifies**. She doesn't pick Mousey. She picks someone else. If she actually recognizes Uncle

Ray, she does not acknowledge it. Maybe because he *once* did her a big favor, she is returning the favor. *Almost* anything is possible. The bottom line: this is a serious setback for the Prosecution. Understandably, the Defense Counsel Ladies are gleeful.

So, the Prosecution Team is silently trudging back to the Courthouse. Deep in thought. Disheartened. Calculating. Concerned. This is not a propitious beginning for the trial. When your *only* eyewitness is a six year old and she can't <u>or</u> won't identify the bad guy, you may be in deep sh——t! But things will get worse. Oh, how true it is that a criminal trial is a *series* of unpredictable events. It's definitely not clear sailing for the Prosecution tonight. When it rains it pours. And the already foul weather of the evening, directly attributable to the lineup glitch, is about to take a definite turn for the worse.

We'd parted with the Defense Counsel Ladies a few minutes earlier. Just long enough for them to walk from the jail to their car, I suppose. Well, as we plod along the sidewalk through the darkening night, we suddenly have company.

A fancy Sports Coupe wheels up to the curb. The Defense Counsel Ladies have a surprise package for us, and they are anxious to make a special, albeit it tardy, hand-to-hand delivery. They cheerfully shove a packet of six envelopes and contents into my hands. Then brusquely explain that their packet of discovery consists of *love* letters written by Sherry to Mousey during his incarceration at the Clark County Jail.

The ladies are smiling. Barely keeping a lid on the sense of elation they feel. Their eyes inquisitively measure my reaction. The *unstated* message of Defense Counsel is enjoy your reading tonight, fella. Don't let the bed bugs bite, ya hear? See you in court, sucker.

Their mission accomplished, the departure of the ladies is hasty. Happily waving as they accelerate down the street. The Prosecution has been effectively sandbagged. <u>Withholding</u> their blockbuster secret until the beginning of the trial is a strategic triumph for the Defense. They enjoy the chagrin their disclosure has created, and leave us to wrestle with the evidentiary dilemma.

So, who is Sherry? Why are her *love* letters to the Defendant pertinent?

She is Mousey's girlfriend. He's confessed to her that he and Double R <u>are</u> the murderers of Stuart and James and Lacy and Shannon. Reluctantly, she's turned State's Witness.

End of the relationship, right? When a guy tells a woman he and a confederate have deliberately shot and killed four human beings, folks are entitled to presume such a revelation is the coup de grace that administers a sub zero, arctic chill to the romantic aspirations of his lover, correct? This guy is going to be immediately, *irrevocably* crossed off the list of eligible candidates for further amorous interest, true?

No, in this instance as goofy as it seems, those assumptions are wrong. Sherry continues to cultivate a relationship with the killer during his incarceration for quadruple murder. Really, think about the brain-dead incongruity of this action. He's told her that four people have been maliciously executed at his hands and the hands of Double R – appallingly shot dead in cold blood! And she's writing him *love* letters regardless?

It's certainly arguable that such behavior *casts* an ominous cloud over the credibility of the prospective witness and *conclusively* rebuts the veracity of the alleged confession. How is it possible that a sensible woman continues to be in love with a man who has committed these heinous crimes? What can she be thinking? Does she actually believe what he's told her? Has he really confessed to her or is the purported confession something concocted for reasons not readily apparent?

The first trial day zinger from out of the blue has found it's mark, and it knocks my prosecutive socks off. I struggle with the scenario for the rest of the evening. I'm fearful the evidentiary value of the witness has been decimated by <u>six</u> letters sent to Mousey <u>after</u> he's told Sherry he's a stone-cold killer. Further, another issue lingers in my mind, compounding my first night woes. Not to be forgotten is the misidentification by little Annie in the lineup.

It's a dark night for the Prosecution. But hey! Get a grip on yourself, Mr. Prosecutor. A trial lawyer learns to expect the unexpected. It's part of his job description.

"The nearer the dawn the darker the night."

(Henry Wadsworth Longfellow, *Tales of a Wayside Inn*, 1863)

Are things hopeless? <u>No</u>! A new day *dawns* two days later. The *flashing rays of light* consist of **two** additional letters. <u>**He**</u> **has written her!** They will become Court Exhibits 109 and 111.

My recollection of that pivotal Wednesday remains crisp. Sherry is scheduled to testify Wednesday afternoon. I want the Jury to have her confession evidence to chew on during the evening break. They'll need something substantive to decisively nudge their thinking toward conviction as the mid point of the first week of testimony ends. I'm hoping her testimony will begin to seal the deal. Accordingly, a pretrial conference is set for 12:30 p.m. in my office. This meeting is to occur during the trial lunch break.

It's worth noting that I've already met with Sherry several times in connection with my trial preparation. She's a key witness. No responsible Prosecutor waits until the day of testimony to review the relevant factual points to be presented by important witnesses. So, I know the basic content of what she's expected to say. She has provided a detailed statement to the lead Detective on the case, and she's personally confirmed her evidence to me. That said, it is a fact of Courtroom life that witnesses don't always testify the way they're expected to testify.

I know how apprehensive she is about being a trial witness. Her feelings of ambivalence run deep. Sherry is profoundly offended by the heinous nature of the crimes, but she isn't keen about testifying against a man with whom she has strong emotional and physical ties. It's axiomatic that in matters of love a person's heart doesn't necessarily listen to reason. Besides, this is a capital case. She does <u>not</u> want to have any complicity in Mousey's execution. She's into peacemaking not retribution. She's also scared. Almost frightened out of her wits, and her mother isn't helping the issue. She's adamantly opposed to her daughter's participation in the proceedings.

A significant paradox leading up to trial is that Sherry had remained AWOL for quite some time. She's hadn't been under subpoena until one of the Defense Ladies gratuitously provided information regarding her whereabouts some ten days before trial. Why was she so solicitous? Well, I'm not a rocket scientist, but I'd acquired substantial experience and sufficient Courtroom smarts to realize so-called gratuities from a Defense Lawyer are strategic. The Defense doesn't dish out freebies to Prosecutors. Every "freebie" comes with a price tag. I didn't know it at the time, but the Defense Counsel Ladies have Sherry's six *love* letters in hand, and they believe their <u>out</u> <u>of the</u> <u>blue</u> evidence will scuttle Sherry's credibility and dismantle the integrity of the Prosecution's case. The irony being: the Defense apparently figures they will be better off *with* Sherry than *without* her. Hummm, that's very interesting.

I've finished my sandwich and glance anxiously at my wristwatch as the time for the pretrial nears. I'm wondering at this instant, when push comes to shove, will Sherry actually make her appearance or will she be a no-show? Believe me, it's usually like pulling hen's teeth to get witnesses into the Courtroom in a murder case. A criminal trial is a series of unexpected events. What surprise waits in the wings today? .

As the world turns in the Clark County Courthouse, we are about to learn that Sherry has engaged in some trial gamesmanship herself. Cool!

She does show up for her pretrial conference. Arriving promptly at 12:30 p.m. I greet her in the foyer. Her hand is cold. I sense her nervousness, but her demeanor seems resolute. We walk together to my office and sit down. I engage in some friendly banter in an effort to put her at ease, to the extent that is possible, under these circumstances. I thank her for her willingness to testify. Trying to seem empathetic, I explain that I realize how hard this is for her.

I ask her how she's doing. Sherry glances down. For a short time, she appears a little preoccupied. There is a brief pause. Her hand eases into her purse, and she says quietly, somewhat matter-of-factly, "I have something for you, Mr. Harmon." At that precise second I don't appreciate the significance of what she's doing. But something momentous is happening. In retrospect, I'd say she carried the fate of her lover inside her handbag. I can only surmise, but I'm guessing that hours of soul-searching anguish and prayer preceded her decision.

Sherry continues. "You know about the letters I wrote to Mousey, but there is something you don't know. You need to know that he wrote <u>two</u> letters to me. I've brought them to you, Mr. Harmon. I think they'll be helpful."

Then she hands me two slightly soiled, inauspicious looking envelopes. How trifling and inconsequential they appear, but how large and portentous in their impact. The startling evidentiary value dawns swiftly upon me. It only requires a few lines of reading. Bingo!

This is today's unexpected trial event. The envelopes contain the double barreled surprise that has been waiting in the wings. They are a dual manifestation of Sherry's trial gamesmanship. She has spoken to the Defense Counsel Ladies. She could have given the letters to them. Instead, she gives them to the State. On this hump day of the first week of Mousey's trial, Sherry chooses justice over love!

She didn't have to do this. She could have stashed this stuff in a deep, junk drawer into perpetuity. But she's been subpoenaed. She is about to take an oath that she will tell the whole truth. Not part of the truth. Every bit of the truth and nothing but the truth. The law has imposed a personal responsibility upon her to be entirely truthful. That preempts her personal wishes and her safety.

Her **commitment** to the solemn duty imposed by citizenship to *come forward* to authorities with all the relevant criminal evidence she has – regardless of circumstance, and the personal responsibility imposed upon each witness in a trial to *truthfully testify* to all the relevant criminal evidence she has – is unforgettable to me. She has a personal interest in the outcome of this trial, but her offering is not strategic. She is a lover torn, yet in her soul a sense of duty has been born.

Consider the situation. This isn't cavalier jawboning in moot court. It isn't a robust UNLV classroom exercise in logical disputation. It isn't a carefree stroll in Paradise Park. It isn't a trip to a Wednesday afternoon matinee at the movies. This is a trip to the Clark County Courthouse with subpoena in hand. A capital murder trial is underway. A jury is in place. A young drug dealer faces a possible death sentence. The stakes could not be higher!

Four young human beings have been jettisoned into a faraway jurisdiction in a hail of bullets. Why? Because one of the four is a police informant. She's gone. The target of callous retribution. Mercilessly dispatched by eight bullet wounds of entry to her body. And the stark message is intended for all those wrapped in the garment of an informant.

These characters have proven their propensity to kill. The community knows what they're capable of. The community understands their desperation and their disrespect for the sanctity of life. The perpetrators have killed three of the four simply because they were present at the scene. Dead witnesses don't come to court. Dead witnesses don't do any singing from the witness stand. Their only singing is from the heavenly sphere.

So, it's perfectly understandable that a sinister ambiance of fear grips <u>each</u> witness. No, this isn't a sight seeing tour of the Courthouse. Sherry's not testing acoustics in the Courtroom. This is over-the-top grit. It's a profile in courage. This woman is a witness for the Prosecution. She's snitched off one of the killers. He's bragged about his inhuman sport and she's going to lay his *confession* out in <u>open</u> court. This isn't going to be *entre nous*, i.e., simply between me and you – a matter privately uttered.

It's <u>open</u> court. The Judge, the Attorneys, the Defendant, Court personnel, family members and friends of the Victims, family members and associates of the Defendant, curious onlookers, interested Courthouse groupies, the local press, and Court TV. They're all here. When Sherry spills her guts <u>everyone</u> will know that she is cooperating with the good guys in a deeply personal way. Everybody! She'll be anathema to the bad boys – and their associates. She'll have a bulls eye framed on her back. Which she knows.

When she surfaced, her initial persona was anonymity. She spoke several times to police detectives over the telephone, but anonymously. It took quite awhile for her to step from the shadows into the public eye. Only after weeks of tantalizing cat and mouse with the police does Sherry divulge her name and address and telephone number. Therefore, we may reasonably infer that she is well aware of the danger when she first contacts the authorities.

The point is – she did it anyway. Her conscience is pricked. Duty calls. She does it irrespective of personal risk! She gives up her **tell-tale** *love* letters and she reiterates her vow to publically testify. Sherry is a Criminal Justice System success story. She is a hero!

The darker the prospect for successful prosecution the *nearer the dawn*? Early afternoon cast the penetrating rays of a second dawning upon the Clark County Courthouse that memorable Wednesday. The brightest point in the trial, except for the Jury Verdicts, is dropping Mousey's <u>two</u> illuminating letters into the laps of the Defense Counsel Ladies. It happens on August 31, 1994 at 1:15 p.m.

The disclosure of two highly incriminating letters knocks the wind out of the Defense sails. Their cross examination of Sherry has to be passed until the next day. The letters incisively manifest an attempt by Mousey to **suborn perjury**.

Exhibit 109 is the *script* Mousey urges Sherry to follow in presenting her trial testimony. He concludes, "...Baby *these are the things* my attorney need you to say to help me come home...*this* is what we need baby, so you have to prepare yourself with *this*. Because we have to put on a Good show. One better than what the D.A. put on at my hearing, baby. I love you and *this* is going to work..." (emphasis added)

Exhibit 111 is the <u>inmate</u> *form* Mousey has drafted, complete with signature line, for Sherry to **retract** her previously sworn Preliminary Hearing testimony **implicating** him in the quadruple murders.

Now, do innocent people ask other persons to lie? Do they ask someone to delete damaging testimony? Is such conduct consistent with innocence or *guilt*? The words in these letters are the words of the Defendant <u>not</u> the words of the witness. When an accused person tries to put words into another person's mouth isn't that evidence of a consciousness of guilt? An innocent man doesn't attempt to *manipulate* a witness testifying against him! Yet that's precisely what Mousey does by proposing a <u>script</u> for Sherry's testimony in Exhibit 109. And he continues his effort to *manipulate* her role as a witness in Exhibit 111. He drafts an *illegal* <u>form</u> that implicitly asks her to <u>rescind</u> sworn testimony. He's urging Sherry to disavow and discontinue her incriminating testimony.

That conduct is criminal. It's called attempting to influence a witness, and it's called subornation of perjury. It's also called <u>not</u> believing in the integrity of the Criminal Justice System. It's saying, I want to orchestrate the outcome of my case. Tell lies for me and we'll live happily ever after. Let sleeping dogs lie.

"I cannot tell how the truth may be;
I say the tale as 'twas said to me."
(Sir Walter Scott, *The Lay of the Last Minstrel*,
[1805] Canto II, Stanza 22)

Let this procedural fact be unmistakably declared, she *does* testify and she *doesn't* delete the inculpatory parts. Sherry has <u>no</u> personal knowledge of the crime. She can only tell the tale as it was told to her. But what he's said she tells the Jury.

The Bailiff summons Sherry to the Courtroom. She enters, raises her right hand, solemnly swears to tell the truth, and tells the Jury that the same day she moved into the Harbor Island Apartments Mousey tells her, face-to-face, eyeball-to-eyeball, directly from his mouth-to-her-ears, that he and his homey murdered <u>four</u> people.

He tells her the unthinkable. It's surreal. Unbelievable. She's thinking, don't go there, Mousey. I don't want to hear this, please! It makes her numb. Disgusted. Sick to her stomach. She wants to puke. She wants to block out the unspeakable horror of his words. But the despicable litany flows unabated. Inconceivably, he appears to enjoy her discomfort and his capacity to gloat over the hideous blood-letting of *four* murders.

The confession has a rather peculiar beginning. They've been speaking generally about the crime. Mousey asks, "Do you think I'm crazy?" She replies, "Yes, I do think you're crazy if you were involved in this terrible thing." And he says, "Then you think I'm crazy!"

Sherry continues her account. Nervously averting his cold stare, she tersely lays it <u>all</u> before the Jury. Explaining what came straight from his mouth. Ponder the significance of her evidence. It isn't based upon rumor. It doesn't find its antecedent in idle gossip around the office water cooler. It isn't scuttlebutt from the street. She didn't read it in the newspaper. A television anchorwoman on the evening news didn't provide the story.

Mousey gives her the script. This is from him to her. Point-blank. There is no intermediary. Within the one-on-one privacy of her apartment, when his guard is down and his tongue is loose, he brags about what he's done. Somehow he seems proud of his deadly machismo. He tells her how it feels to put a .357 magnum against other human beings and deliberately fire bullets into their bodies – as they plead for their lives.

Bullets make holes in people. They hurt people. They make people bleed. Bullets penetrate skin and skulls and chests. They cause victims to scream in agony. They plow through tissue leaving bloody craters in vital organs. Bullets kill people. Innocent people don't deserve to die!

Death obliterates the promise of their mortal lives. Death leaves family members and good friends lonesome and inconsolably mourning.

But a bullet is inanimate. It doesn't think It doesn't make decisions. It doesn't plot murders. It doesn't pull a trigger. It can't discharge itself. It's simply an *instrument* in the hands of people. Ultimately, at the end of the day – after months of conspiring – when violent judgment is imposed – the bottom line is this: it's <u>not</u> bullets that kill. It's <u>not</u> guns that kill. **People kill**. People pull triggers. People send bullets crashing into other human beings. No right thinking person should ever lose sight of that irrefutable truth!

So, Sherry tells the loathsome tale in court. She utters her testimony sincerely, bravely, convincingly – and the Jury believes her. Media reps call *her* testimony and *his* letters a three run homer for the Prosecution. Touche. Conviction. Next case.

This tale of vile vengeance will be incomplete without briefly filling in the blanks with respect to Double R. He also pays a heavy price for mindless retribution. His drug trafficking case ends up in Federal Court. He's convicted and sentenced to time in a Federal Penitentiary.

Building a prosecutable case can be an arduous task. Fortunately, there is no Statute of Limitation for murder. The incarceration of Double R provides a window of opportunity for law enforcement authorities to collect additional evidence and to assemble viable murder charges.

His mouth is busy during his time in the slammer, and there are people listening. Too bad for Double R. When lips move killers lose.

"A fool's mouth is his destruction..."
(Proverbs 18:7)

Like his accomplice, a wagging tongue is the undoing of Double R. He's paroled from the Federal Penitentiary to the Clark County Jail. It's a remarkable tribute to the bird dog tenacity of the Criminal Justice System. Las Vegas Metropolitan Police Detectives are unflagging in their investigative efforts. Four years after my retirement from the Office of the District Attorney, I am a partner with an outstanding colleague in the Prosecution of Double R in late 2000.

He is convicted. *Eight and a half years* after his heartless, vengeful murder of a police informant, and the slaughter of three innocent bystanders, Double R is convicted of four counts of First Degree Murder for his complicity in the homicides of Stuart, James, Lacy, and Shannon.

Justice delayed is not always justice denied. Prosecutorial perseverance has its reward.

Judicial Sleight of Hand

"The time has come," the Walrus said, "To talk of many things:
Of shoes—and ships—and sealing wax—Of cabbages—and kings—
And why the sea is boiling hot—And whether pigs have wings."
(Lewis Carroll, *Through The Looking Glass*, Tweedledee's
recitation of a paragraph from a poem, "The Walrus and the
Carpenter," p.204)

CHAPTER 2

ENOCH POULSEN DIES IN A SYNCOPATED BURST of three bullets from
a Saturday night special. Curiously, Enoch's demise occurs on
Saturday night. His killer is his girlfriend. She and Enoch have been
living together for eight years. The late Mr. Poulsen is shot dead in the
house the "lovers" share.

An anonymous female calls a Las Vegas Police Department hotline
at 11:08 p.m. She reports that a man has been shot at 1217 Currant
Drive. Two patrol cars in the area are immediately dispatched to the
address in question. They arrive in tandem at 11:13 pm. There is no
ostensible evidence of foul play outside the residence. They check the
front door. It's unlocked. The officers enter the premises with guns
drawn.

They discover the body of an adult male lying face down in a pool
of blood. He's located in the living room. His head is four feet from
the doorway to a bedroom. The man isn't moving. Officers perform a
cursory examination for vital signs. There are none. No gun or other
weapon is observed in close proximity to the deceased.

A woman sits at the kitchen table weeping. Her face is buried in
her hands. While one officer remains with the female, his fellow officer

conducts a perfunctory search of the residence. No other persons are discovered inside the house, nor does the officer locate a gun or other weapon anywhere within the premises. The patrol officers promptly issue a call for backup. They request emergency medical technicians, crime scene investigators, homicide detectives, and a representative from the coroners's office.

The officer who has searched the house positions himself at the front door. The female continues to sit at the kitchen table. She's audibly sobbing now, and her shoulders are shaking. Her elbows rest on the table. Her face remains buried in her hands. She is wearing a loose-fitting pantsuit. She's instructed to stand. A pat-down search is executed by the second officer. The woman is unarmed.

She's asked her name. She replies, "I'm Sarah Cool." Not so cool on this particular night, I suppose. The officer wants to see personal identification. He asks about a driver's license. She tells him it's inside a wallet in her purse, which is next to the telephone. He searches the purse for a weapon. Finding nothing, he passes the purse to Sarah. She confirms her identity with the driver's license. She is a thirty seven year old, unmarried Caucasian. But she hasn't been unattached.

Ms. Sarah Cool is asked what happened. She pauses. Struggles, it seems, to get the words to come out. Then softly and tearfully murmurs: "I shot my boyfriend. I did it in self defense." She is immediately handcuffed.

Backup arrives. The deputy coroner examines the prone male. He is pronounced dead at the scene. An autopsy will be more definitive, but it appears to the Clark County Coroner's Office representative that the man has died of three bullet wounds to the chest. The victim's body is removed. He is forty.

The ID officers conduct their investigation of the scene. Photographs are taken, a crime scene sketch is prepared, the house interior is processed for the presence of latent prints, forensic samples are recovered from the floor where the deceased lay, and they look for the gun. No gun is found. Nor are expended cartridges discovered.

Homicide detectives interrogate Ms. Cool. She is responsive to questioning. Seems anxious to explain herself and agrees to make a tape recorded statement. This phase of the investigation lasts for approximately twenty minutes.

She appears composed throughout the process, although she continues to be highly distraught. She speaks haltingly, but by any objective standard, appears to speak <u>voluntarily</u> and <u>coherently</u>, She is articulate, alert, and unequivocal. Portraying an image of sound mind and body at all times.

Ms. Cool denies being under the influence of alcohol. She disavows the recent ingestion of drugs – prescription or illicit. Says she is not physically ill. Disclaims being under a doctor's care for any preexisting mental or emotional condition. She has only *one* problem: HIM. And that's been taken care of.

She says the relationship has been physically abusive for a long time. She's been periodically battered by her boyfriend for years. Yet, she loves him, so she stays with him. But love is a hurting thing, and earlier tonight the hurt became unbearable.

She says he came home about 10:30 p.m. He's been drinking. They argue, and as often happens, he becomes physically abusive. She begins yelling. He tells her to shut up. When she doesn't stop, he slaps her hard on the left side of her face. She isn't silenced. Her response is to ratchet up the commotion index. She screams obscene epithets. He grabs her around the neck with his hands, and digs his fingernails into her flesh. He says, "I'm going to put you out of your misery, Bitch. I'm going to choke you senseless, tonight. You're going to die right now!"

She says her reaction is swift. She lifts her knee and pummels his groin. He releases her. Doubling up in pain and chagrin. But he's much stronger than she is. When he regains his focus and his strength, she knows she'll need help. God didn't make men and women physically equal, but a firearm is a remarkable ally. A cold-metal equalizer.

She says she dashes into the bedroom. A gun is in the bedroom closet. She opens her attache' case and grasps the .38 caliber revolver she's recently acquired. It's cheap insurance. Nobody rapes a .38. Nobody manually strangles a .38 caliber.

She says she steps to the doorway with the gun in her right hand. Her index finger rests on the trigger. All six chambers of the gun's revolving cylinder are fully loaded with live cartridges. [She's ready for bear, or allow me to say in this instance , ready for Enoch.] And according to her account, he's ready for her.

She says he sees her reappear, and rushes across the room uttering vitriolic threats. She doesn't hesitate. She's afraid for her life. Gripping the gun in both hands, she extends the barrel toward his torso. Then squeezes the trigger in three sporadic jerks, and three separate slugs crash into his chest. He falls – dying. The .38 special has been more than an equalizer. It's become a killer!

She says she drops the gun to the floor. Kneels down, and tries to comfort her ex-lover. Enoch's bloods flows profusely from his chest. She is dazed by his plight, and stunned by her predicament. She picks the gun up. The barrel is still warm. She hurries to the bedroom closet, and places her firearm back inside the attache' case. Effectively hiding it.

She says she goes to the kitchen. Takes a deep breath. Sits down for a few minutes. Quietly mouths a short prayer. Then calls the Las Vegas Police.

A crime scene investigator goes to the bedroom closet. He locates the attache' case referenced by Ms. Cool. The .38 caliber revolver is discovered inside. The case and the firearm are processed for latent prints and impounded as evidence. The gun cylinder contains three consecutive chambers with expended cartridges and three chambers loaded with live rounds. It is totally consistent with the suspect's statement to detectives.

Sarah Cool is formally placed under arrest on a charge of open murder. She is transported to the station house. Several hours later she signs a typewritten copy of her taped interview with homicide detectives, and is booked into the Clark County Jail. During the booking process her neck is examined. No sign of injury is detected. Nothing is observed that is corroborative of her statement she has been forcibly grabbed around the neck by the deceased..

When an autopsy examination is performed upon Enoch Poulsen, three projectiles are removed from the his chest cavity. A crime lab firearms expert compares bullets recovered from his body with three test-fired bullets from Sarah Cool's .38 caliber revolver. A microscopic examination of projectile lands and grooves establishes a positive match.

Impressive. The police have a <u>corpse</u> and a <u>confession</u> and a <u>gun</u> and a <u>consciousness</u> <u>of</u> <u>guilt</u> [She hid the weapon. Comprehende?] and a <u>malicious</u> <u>act</u> [She fired *three* shots not a single shot.] and a <u>homicide</u> perpetrated *inside* her home and <u>she's</u> the *only* person still breathing <u>present</u> at the scene when police get there – and there are *no* <u>marks</u> on her neck.

Sounds like a cake walk, doesn't it? A slam dunk for sure. A can of corn. A gimme. A lead pipe cinch? Well, not really! When fiction becomes fact in the Clark County Courthouse, the case styled State of Nevada vs. Sarah Cool turns out to be an extremely slippery slope for the Prosecution. Or should it be written *when* fact becomes fiction? Hey, the evidence is here. Pooof, now it's gone!

So, let's have an eye-opening *Trial* experience together. Come with me as we stroll *Through The Looking Glass* of a Courtroom fairytale. Oh, tell me it isn't true, Charlie.

"The time has come," the Walrus said, "To talk of many things:
Of shoes–and ships–and sealing wax–Of cabbages–and kings–
And why the sea is boiling hot–And whether pigs have wing."(ibid.)

The stage is set. The Jury is empaneled. The charging document is called an Information. It's been read to the Jury by the Clerk of the Court. Sarah Cool is charged with <u>open</u> murder in the death of Enoch Poulsen. And in case someone is wondering, <u>open</u> murder doesn't mean it's an <u>open</u> season for *allegedly* abusive boyfriends on the star-crossed evening of the shooting. Or did it – on this sad occasion?

An <u>open</u> murder charge *usually* means the Jury has various crime options. Four in fact. Depending on their view of the evidence, they may find the Accused GUILTY of First Degree Murder or Second Degree Murder or Voluntary Manslaughter or Involuntary Manslaughter. Of course it goes without saying but I'll say it, the fifth option is NOT GUILTY. However, a zealous Prosecutor doesn't want to think about # five.

But moving ahead: the crime scene has been framed by the two first-on-the-scene patrol officers, and the pathologist has detailed his autopsy findings. The cause of death is three gun shot wounds to the chest.

Sarah's aim has been true. Two bullets penetrate Enoch's heart and the third lodges in his left lung. It is the opinion of the medical examiner that death did not result from any natural cause, nor is it accidental, or self inflicted. There is no disease known to man that creates bullets in a chest cavity, and the number of bullets surely eliminates the other two possibilities stated. A man doesn't get accidently shot three times and he doesn't shoot himself three separate times in the chest with a .38 caliber revolver. Not to mention the course the projectiles traverse as they plow through the chest. Nobody has an arm long enough to make suicide a feasible proposition in this instance. This is a homicide. It is a death caused by criminal agency, that is to say, Mr. Enoch Paulsen died as a result of action taken by another human being!

Let's set the courtroom cast. It is very pertinent, I believe, to the scenario that unfolds at trial. *First*, there's the reason we're in court. I have to start with the Defendant. A case becomes a criminal case because something <u>criminal</u> has allegedly occurred. The alleged criminal in this trial is the stoic, rather attractive ex-girlfriend, Sarah Cool. But of course she didn't act particularly stoical on the night in question. *Second*, there's Judge Ben. The veteran, somewhat pompous jurist, who is rumored to have a slight after hours problem of putting his beak to the sauce, and who certainly has his favorites in the barrister pecking order. *Third*, enter the high powered, folksy Defense Counsel gentleman. He's a friend of the Judge and he's glib and smooth and experienced. Perhaps, the most venerable member of the Clark County Bar. *Fourth*, there's me. The odd man out, so to speak. A relative greenie with no clout, and little chance in this case.

We could easily subtitle this matter. Various possibilities come to mind: the heavyweight vs. the lightweight, or the trial-seasoned gentleman vs. the rookie, or the crony, who is part of the inner circle vs. the non-crony outsider, or the juice guy vs. the guy with no connections, or the guy wearing a black hat vs. the fellow wearing the white hat. Meaning the Prosecutor.

I enjoy putting trial lawyer roles into an eschatological context. On the one hand of course, we have Defense attorneys vigorously plying their trade on the dark side, and on the other hand naturally, we have humble Deputy District Attorneys pursuing righteousness on the bright side.

Whatever! Because the so-called guy with the white hat takes a lickin here!

The homicide detective who conducted the tape recorded interview with the Defendant is called to the witness stand. Some preliminary and largely foundational remarks are offered. Direct examination approaches the major thrust of his testimony. We're poised to begin inspecting the red meat in our case.

I see it all in my mind now. Rather clearly in fact. The Defense Counsel gentleman raises his arm above his head in a manner not dissimilar to the Prophet Moses raising his arm to part the Red Sea. Well remember, I did say Counsel is venerable.

Then he stands and, in a deeply resonant and prophetic sounding voice, intones: "May Counsel approach the Bench?" The request is granted.

Oh Boy! Goody-goody gum drops. The stroll into Looking Glass Land begins. I'm thinking, I wonder what we'll find there. When we get to the Bench, the esteemed Defense Counsel gentleman says he has a motion. He is moving to *suppress* his client's statement. He says it has been taken in violation of the Miranda Rule and is therefore the product of coercive interrogation. He asks for a hearing outside the presence of the Jury.

Therefore, the Jury is excused by Judge Ben. He seems singularly unimpressed by my comments that the motion is being made in untimely fashion. The applicable Rules of Criminal Procedure require that such motions be made at least fifteen days in advance of trial. Actually, trial by ambush is <u>not</u> condoned in the Code. A fact I'm sure my esteemed Defense Counsel colleague considers a trivial matter.

Judge Ben explains, though there is a smidgen of validity to the Prosecutive complaint, he is over ruling the timeliness objection. The Defense Counsel Gentleman is a busy man, and the Court has inherent discretion in the interest of justice to proceed with a hearing on the *suppression* motion.

Aaarg! <u>Evidence</u> <u>suppression</u> is not something a Prosecutor likes to contemplate. Is it possible some *judicial sleight of hand* awaits in Looking Glass Land?

The homicide Detective and the Defendant are both questioned under oath outside the presence of the *official* Trial Fact Finder. I'm speaking of the Jury. I don't want any contextual misunderstanding. Unfortunately for the Prosecution and for the oft-forgotten principle of full disclosure, some *ex officio* fact-finding is occurring in their absence.

It is conclusively established that <u>no</u> Miranda warnings were given to the stoic, rather attractive female client of the esteemed Defense Counsel gentleman. Although the Defendant, by all accounts, **is** anxious to provide exculpatory evidence to police at the scene of the shooting, and **does**, despite her emotional state, present voluntary and coherent information during the interview.

Judge Ben hears argument from the parties. It's late in the afternoon, but he doesn't take the matter under advisement until the next court day. In less time than four judicial heart beats he pronounces his ruling. He doesn't cite any legal or factual basis for his decision. He says simply, "Motion <u>granted</u>."

Hey Baby, the *suppression* of a confession in a murder trial is a hot-button issue. It's not inconsequential. But Judge Ben casts a *confession* aside in a truly cavalier manner. He acts like he's trashing a can of spoiled chopped meat.

The high powered, folksy Defense Counsel gentleman flashes his toothy, trademark grin, and shoots a glance at me to gauge my reaction. Really. I'm green, but I'm not stupid. I'm not giving him the satisfaction of seeing how upset I am. I don't offer a hint of the churning turmoil boiling in my gut. I just sit there wearing my best dead-pan demeanor. But his look isn't cryptic. It says, "I've got you by the short hair, Buster. And there ain't a damn thing you can do about it."

Hel-lo! All of a sudden I'm sensing this decision has been choreographed before hand. Judge Ben and Mr. High Powered are merely following a script that's already been written. Hold tight, Man. It may be a wild ride.

I want to step back and survey the legal landscape. Can a Trial Judge actually EXCLUDE evidence? Yessiree! It's true, Winnie the Pooh. A

Judge can *undo* facts. What was – isn't! He has the power, and it's a power not infrequently employed.

There is a legal basis for such *judicial sleight of hand*. It's called the **Exclusionary Rule**. The rationale is a contrived ploy to deter police misconduct. It's a heavy-handed modus operandi <u>attempting</u> to compel respect for the guarantees of the Fourth, Fifth, and Sixth Amendments to the United States Constitution.

The prevailing view being that the only effective way to <u>police</u> the police is to remove their incentive to disregard constitutional rights by <u>excluding</u> evidence improperly obtained.

But legal postulation doesn't change the incongruity of *disappearing* evidence. It confers special properties upon a Court. Weird ones. The judicial robe becomes the cloak of a magician. He's a legal wizard plundering police evidence. He's doing the dirty work of the Defense. Lamentably, we're not talking about verbal smoke screens by Defense Counsel to *conceal* evidence. A Prosecutor expects that. We're talking about Judicial <u>fiats</u> that *eliminate* evidence. We're not talking show and tell. A Judge is saying, "<u>Don't</u> tell, and Mr. Prosecutor, go to hell!"

A Judge truly becomes The Man, in this mode, who decides what's real and what isn't real. Fully enhanced with the accoutrements of characters from *Looking Glass Land*, he becomes the ultimate authority whose grace blesses evidence with admission or condemns it to oblivion. A figurative wag from his *ruling wand* causes a confession to *evaporate* into thin air.

But what about the Jury in this manipulated scenario? Those persons, tried and true, who are expected to render a **just** decision without being privy to <u>all</u> the facts? What of the merits of full disclosure? What about a Trial being a search for truth? What of justice? What of reality? I held Ms. Cool's <u>confession</u> in my hand. It *was* real!

What of the Defendant's presumption of innocence? What of a Prosecutor's burden of proof? A Deputy District Attorney who *loses* his confession is cut adrift on a river of case-flow rapids. He's suddenly down stream without a paddle, unable to buck the current. He can't overcome the presumption of innocence and he can't meet his legal burden of proof since *key* evidence has been swept away!

When the homicide detective returns to the witness stand he'll be wearing *unseen* handcuffs. He'll be restrained by an imposed script.

Forbidden to tread the verbal path that leads to the Defendant's incriminating words. Testifying to an abbreviated version of the truth because his tongue is selectively *tied* by court order. He's promised to tell the truth, but the truth he'll discuss has substantially shrunk!

This isn't necessarily intended as a stump speech favoring dismantlement of the Exclusionary Rule. It's been in place for decades. But the underpinnings of the rule are deeply troubling. So I'm putting some random thoughts into print. Making my record and daydreaming. Doing some *what if* fantasizing. Wondering why a Prosecutor ever has to stroll into *Looking Glass Land*? Questioning why there are times when he has to play *make believe*? Believing in an <u>ideal</u> world there wouldn't be a rule that makes good evidence bad evidence because generally good cops occasionally make bad decisions. Really, what does that have to do with the enormity of the crime? What bearing do those factors have on the plight of crime victims? Prosecutors and victims need to have *every piece* of evidence available *every* time. Each trial combatant needs a level playing field, and big-reputation guys shouldn't be allowed to walk all over slight-reputation guys.

Personally, I don't like it much in *Looking Glass Land*. I've been there quite often. I'm familiar with the terrain. I've made the roller coaster ride <u>each</u> time inculpatory evidence has been arbitrarily *deleted* from my proof portfolio. Each time it happens I've felt gypped. Handicapped. It's analogous to a sprinter having some dolt scoot out and break one of his legs as he races to the finish line.

I'm not in to *make believe*. When I go to court I expect *reality*, not *fantasy*! I want a process that is plausible. I want results that are rational. You did the crime do the time. You didn't do the crime, you're out of here, until next time.

I'm much more comfortable in a world that tries to impose criminal justice in a logical way. The old fashioned say. The straight and narrow way. The way that focuses on PERSONAL ACCOUNTABILITY. The way that is <u>person</u> <u>specific</u> in *charging* and <u>person</u> <u>specific</u> in *punishing*.

It's a lot more credible that way. You see, a Criminal Trial isn't about sealing wax and cabbages and kings. Ya know what I mean? It's about life and crimes and suffering, death and due process of law – and punishments that **fit** the crime. No kidding, it's quite simple. The ocean isn't actually boiling hot and plump pigs don't really have wings. The Criminal Justice System is a **farce** <u>unless</u> it holds particular persons <u>responsible</u> for particular bad acts.

The Miranda Rule often misses the mark. It's a *judicially imposed litany* that has no explicit nexus to voluntariness. The issue is voluntariness, isn't it? This is the United States of America. We believe in the inherent dignity of every human being. An accused person is entitled to be treated with a measure of dignity. We do <u>not</u> condone torture. Accused persons have rights. Accused persons are accorded procedural safeguards. Coerced confessions are expressly forbidden. But we aren't against convicting guilty people, are we? We like <u>uncoerced</u> confessions! The Constitution isn't offended when a guilty woman stubs her toe. Ya know what I mean?

A salient truth being: departure from the Miranda litany is <u>not</u> , in reality, a per se exercise in *coercion*! That is, if we're unwilling to embrace the notion that what the High Court says a word means is exactly what it does mean to the exclusion of all other definitions. I'm sorry if this seems disrespectful, but that sort of analysis sounds like it came from a fairytale. It did. The same one.

"When I use a word," Humpty Dumpty said
in rather a scornful tone, "it means just what
I choose it to mean––neither more nor less."
(Lewis Carroll, *Through The Looking Glass*, p.238)

Saying, the only meaningful definition of *coercion* is the one ascribed to it in 1966, is to suggest that <u>every</u> confession obtained in this country <u>prior</u> to Miranda is coerced. Nonsense! A certain <u>activist</u> United States Supreme Court came along and decided they were a little smarter than all the others. So they plowed new ground. Revolutionizing the world of Police investigation and District Attorney prosecution. The vehicle employed, by this arguably flawed judicial activism, is the case styled Miranda v. Arizona. Miranda warnings have been mandated under a panoply of circumstances since the date of the decision.

Revolutionizing the world of police investigation? Well, it's not a revolution that works well. It's contrary to the nature of things. Police are trained to be crime investigators not constitutional law instructors.

Their call to service is gathering evidence not talking people out of giving evidence. By creating an unrealistic impediment to case solving from the get-go, Miranda tends to morph crime busters into liars. There will always be those who'll say they've complied to save their evidence, when in fact, they haven't complied. But moving right along.

It's highly problematic that society would be much more efficiently served if the *law* lived by the linchpin of *personal responsibility*. Blame should attach where fault lies. Where in the Miranda scheme is the <u>fault</u> of the victim? Where is the <u>fault</u> of families of murdered victims? What did the Jury do to earn hush-hush disqualification of compelling evidence? Wherein lies society's indiscretion? What of the need to protect communities from the terror of violent crime? How is that requirement met by arbitrary application of a court-conceived rule that can cripple the ability to prosecute bad guys – or bad gals?

If the police collect evidence in an *improper* manner, *sanction* the offending officers. <u>Reasonable</u> punishment is specific to culpability. It's not a scatter gun blast that sprays ricocheting salvos of non-specific *sanctions* into the distant horizon of innocent citizens. It's not forging an irrational doctrine that inflicts a wide swathe of repercussion which is heedless of specific wrongdoing.

Isn't the Exclusionary Rule a standing invitation for Miscarriage of Justice? Isn't it the wrong message under the wrong circumstances? Isn't *personal responsibility* the bedrock principle of any <u>successful</u> society? Especially in this time of high crime, doesn't the Criminal Justice System have to be grounded on a bedrock predicate of *personal accountability*? Otherwise, it lacks integrity!

We want Juries to hold criminals <u>personally</u> responsible for their offenses. Therefore, we painstakingly select Jury panels we think will render verdicts that are objective and fair. Decisions that are fair because they are objective. Then we subject them to a Trial anomaly featuring a venerable Jurist in a flowing black robe who frequently and selectively plucks up pertinent evidence that he puts in a *secret* closet somewhere. And these Jurors have an experience they don't know they're having. They *get* only *part* of the evidence.

The Criminal Justice System wants guilty criminals found guilty. Or does it? There are those skeptics who say the System isn't systematic and its Justice isn't just. So what's left is Criminal. Hey, that's one out of three. It's right on the money with the first word, they say. What it does **is** criminal!

The **exclusionary rule** is judicial sorcery. Tampering with the evidence. Make believe. The Court orders facts to *vanish* and we can't tell the Jury until it's too late, and the rest of us are forced to act like the suppressed evidence never existed. Hi Ho, Hi Ho. It's off the edge we go.

I'm sounding like a broken record. The illegal conduct, if such there is, during crime investigation is police action. So, penalize the police, not Jurors – nor citizens in the community. Don't scrap Society's bedrock principle of personal responsibility in favor of a Judicially contrived derivative evidence rule of suppression. Don't *stifle* evidence. **Don't suppress truth**! A Criminal Trial is supposed to be a *fact-finding* mission – a *search* for truth. In ideal circumstances we'd let the truth come into evidence! We wouldn't hide it. We wouldn't choreograph a scenario that becomes an open invitation for Jury verdicts, based upon *partial* evidence, that are *parodies* of justice.

And not to be lost in all this suppression talk is an undeniable fact. All the Court and the Parties and the Jury have heard is **her side** of the story. Any basis for exoneration is <u>exclusively</u> based upon what **she says** happened. There are no marks on the Defendant that confirm her allegation of a history of physical abuse and of being grabbed around the neck the night of the homicide.

THE INITIAL <u>SUPPRESSION</u> IS THE CRIME. This is all very *one-sided*. A guy who gets plugged three times in the chest doesn't do any talking in court. He can't tell his side of the story. His eyes are closed. His heart has stopped beating. His lips are sealed. He's in the ground. Period!

Actually, the Jury gets shafted *twice*. At the Courthouse <u>and</u> at Ms. Cool's house. There are really *two* venues <u>depriving</u> them of highly relevant evidence! And *four* instrumentalities – three bullets and one judge.

I get to the Courthouse about 8:15 the morning after. I need to interview the crime scene investigator who recovered the *gun* from the attache' case in the bedroom closet, and the ID officer who impounded the three fatal *projectiles* at the autopsy. These officers have been subpoenaed duces tecum, meaning their subpoenas direct them to bring their physical evidence with them. Unfortunately, the gun won't be needed today. It's not going to be used. Not today. Not ever!

A highly unpleasant surprise is waiting downstairs in Judge Ben's chambers. I'm just beginning the initial pretrial conference when I get a telephone call. It's Judge Ben's bailiff. His Honor requests the presence of my company. He and Mr. High Powered are waiting in chambers for me.

Immediately, I get *really-really* tense. It starts in my chest and radiates out and up and down. I'm thinking, wait a minute. This doesn't sound good. The *two* of them are already in chambers together. That smacks a little of ex parte mischief. Mr. High Powered may be doing some early morning missionary work on the case, as if he really needs to.

Now, it did occur to this Deputy District Attorney Lad to say something smart-alecky like, "Why are they bothering to wait for me? What I say doesn't make any difference. Trial isn't scheduled to begin for another hour. Just tell them to do what they've already decided to do. I'll see them in Court." But I didn't. Prudence being the better part of bar membership in good standing.

What I do is hustle myself to chambers. The Judge's secretary ushers me inside the inner sanctum. A spirit of merriment abounds that morning. Judge Ben and Mr. High Powered Gentleman are in the midst of belly laughs. My entry has surely been preceded by a hilarious comment of some sort. Something comparable to, "Here comes the little Sucker now. He's going to choke on his spit when he hears what's in store for his shit-ass case."

Judge Ben swings around to face me. He's still smiling as he says, "Sit down, Mr. Harmon. I've instructed my bailiff to call the Jury off until 1:30 this afternoon. The Defense has filed another motion. It's an application to suppress the .38 caliber revolver recovered at the scene as derivative evidence seized illegally. I'll conduct a hearing on the matter at 10:00 am. You may want to walk me through the procedure whereby the firearm was impounded. You may present evidence if you'd like. My secretary has your copy of the motion. Any questions, Sir?"

What I think is: "Well, of course I have some questions about getting sandbagged on consecutive days, Yer Honor. Why aren't the Rules of

Criminal Procedure applicable to this case, Judge? There's an *orderly* way to deal with Motions to Suppress. But the way it's being done here is *disorderly*, with all due disrespect! The Prosecution is entitled to proper notice. This is <u>disorder</u> in Court."

However, my head is spinning. And I'm feeling a little sick to my stomach. What I meekly say is: "No Judge, I have no questions. I'll see you gentlemen at ten." But I don't choke on my spit. My spit's fine thank you.

Mr. High Powered curtly nods. He is wearing a smug expression that says, "I'm engineering the Trial locomotive, Pal. Hang tight, Ya hear."

I put on evidence at the 10:00 O'clock hearing. For all the good it does. We submit oral argument. Mr. High Powered argues the revolver would not have been discovered by the Police <u>but</u> <u>for</u> his client's statement. She tells the coppers exactly where the gun can be found. However, the statement's now been stricken so the gun must also be struck. It is *fruit* of the poisonous tree.

I argue the Police enter the premises under exigent circumstances. A caller, presumably the Defendant, has reported the shooting of a man at 1217 Currant Drive. This is a Police emergency. They're summoned to the scene and they enter. Once inside they quickly confirm the shooting. A man is lying dead in a pool of blood on the floor. The Defendant sits weeping at the kitchen table. They are percipient witnesses to the aftermath of a crime. It is incumbent upon Police to conduct a thorough investigation of the crime scene. The gun would undoubtedly have been located in the regular course of the homicide investigation. They don't need a search warrant, they're already there at the request of the accused. The gun is attenuated evidence not directly linked to the confession. Therefore, it is <u>not</u> *fruit* of the poisonous tree.

After the attorney rhetoric has stalled, Judge Ben eyeballs me and condescendingly says, "The motion is granted, of course. The gun is inadmissible. Clearly, it's *fruit of the poisonous tree*." Ouch, that smarts. I'm thinking is the needle stuck or something? This is a reprise of yesterday. The sea isn't boiling, but it's certainly rough sailing.

The fruit of the poisonous tree doctrine is inglorious to behold through the lens of a Prosecutor. It's big time frustration. As the reader may have surmised, *fruit of the poisonous tree* is a legal metaphor. It is a principle that prohibits the use at trial of secondary evidence culled directly from primary evidence which is the product of an unreasonable search or an involuntary confession. That's probably about as clear as mud. I'll try again.

The metaphor is a creation of Judicial lexicon. The <u>primary</u> evidence in this instance is Ms. Cool's *confession*. When Judge Ben enters his order on the record that the *confession is suppressed*, he's also telling the record that the *confession is poisonous*. Since the *confession* is the primary evidence, it becomes the <u>tree</u> in the metaphor. However, the Court has said it isn't a healthy tree. It's a tree that's been spoiled by the misconduct of improper Police investigation. Gee whiz, our public servants were trying to solve a crime. That is bad, I say with tongue deep in my cheek.

Be that as it is, they're still guilty of a <u>toxic</u> sin of omission. They haven't said, "You have a right to remain silent. Anything you say can and will be used against you in a Court of law. You have the right to consult with a lawyer before you answer questions. If you can't afford a lawyer, a lawyer will be appointed to represent you free of charge." Or words to that effect.

This woman may have been willing to give a pint of blood as quid pro quo for the opportunity to get this dreadful experience off her chest. She could have been so anxiously determined to spout her mouth, about how straight she shoots a hand gun, she'd have given up her wisdom teeth to make her record with the cops. It doesn't matter. You get it, don't you? The voluntariness issue is incidental. It doesn't really make any difference in these matters if the <u>totality</u> of the evidence convincingly establishes that a statement is volunteered. What she's said <u>isn't</u> admissible because what she's said hasn't been preceded by an admonition that she doesn't have to say what she's said. Obviously, equating violations of the Miranda Rule with coercive confessions is a classic non sequitur. Shades of cabbages and kings.

Well, the king is the Judge. His decree makes the tree venomous. His pronouncement makes the trunk and the branches and the leaves and <u>all</u> the fruit corrupt. The <u>secondary</u> evidence in this instance is Ms. Cool's six shot, fully loaded *.38 caliber revolver*. This is outrageous. A MAN IS DEAD! But never mind. When the king, er – Judge, declares the tree poisonous <u>any</u> fruit of the tree is likewise poisonous.

Hence, it can't be fed to Jurors. They'll have to decide the case without the evidence. The poisonous evidence will defile and subvert their thinking, right? No. Not necessarily. In point of fact, the system could have been framed in a way that leaves the ultimate decision of voluntariness and trustworthiness of confessions to the Jury.

My experience tells me that Juror's are often just as <u>right</u> thinking as Judges – maybe more so. They haven't become jaded by the constant, daily, weekly, yearly bombardment of criminal trial issues. Notwithstanding their freshness, their simplicity of approach, and the innate sense of justice that many Jurors exhibit—after all it is their community, those who created the Miranda Rule evidently didn't trust Jurors enough to leave the decision of admissibility to them. Though it should be said in their defense, they <u>are</u> the triers of fact in a trial. Accordingly, some might argue it's imminently reasonable to leave to the trier of fact the decision as to what the facts are.

The bottom line is that police failure to pronounce the Miranda litany to Ms. Cool corrupts the tree. The tree is irrevocably contaminated, and its *fruit is poisonous*. The Jury doesn't get a single whiff of the <u>confession</u> and not a single hint of the presence of the hidden <u>gun</u> that made three holes in a man's chest. And when the Jury doesn't get a whiff <u>and</u> a hint, realistically, it is predetermined that the Prosecutor will whiff at the plate this time. You win some and lose some. If I hear a lawyer say he's never lost a trial, I'll be thinking, well you haven't had many trials then!

Now what is it I mentioned a few pages back about the Prosecution's IMPRESSIVE evidence? There were *seven power points*. The Police provided a <u>corpse</u> and a **confession** and a **gun** and a **consciousness of guilt** and a <u>malicious</u> <u>act</u> and <u>presence</u> at the scene and the <u>absence</u> <u>of</u> <u>marks</u> on the suspect's neck.

Not any more, Bubba. Here's the rub: when the Trial started my case was grounded in *seven connecting points of proof*. Now my case has come under the spell of too much legal abracadabra. It's significantly winnowed down. The ole Trial Judge has done some heavy *erasing*. The evidence is missing *three* key factors: the **confession** and the **gun** and **consciousness of guilt** are bye-bye!

As the world turns in the Clark County Courthouse – in this case on this particular week – yes sir, the sea is boiling hot and pigs do have wings. Duck, Mr. Prosecutor. Here comes another low flying porker. This has been a case mugging. It's become a death-of-the-criminal-case saga.

The case demise is a process. We proceed from one stage to another. The *impressive* case is weak now. It's hanging by *four thin threads.* Nevertheless, I'm a confident guy in court. I have faith in the righteousness of my cause, my preparation is fastidious, and I believe in my evidence – what's left of it that is. I actually think I *still* have a chance to win. I don't see the other flying porker coming. I get bowled over.

I try to be a professional. Additional witnesses are called. Direct and cross examination occur. I finish the State's *available* evidence and the State of Nevada rests. I'm going to share something. I hate Defense surprises, and resting isn't too restful sometimes. The trial is recessed by Judge Ben until the next morning. It is *presumed* the Defense will put on their case at that time.

It's 10:00 a.m. We meet outside the presence of the Jury, for some reason unknown to me. Obviously, there's been some ex parte chatter. Nobody's bothered to invite me to the rooster party, nor to give me a heads up. Ooooooh goody. What now?

The *what's now* is a <u>third</u> in-the-midst-of-trial motion by Mr. High Powered.

He's built quite a dike with his sandbagging, but he wants the whole shebang this time. He moves for an *advisory instruction of acquittal.* Gulp! This is a request that's calculated to make a hard working deputy district attorney really swallow hard. Let me explain.

Mr. High Powered Gentleman is asking the Court to tell the Jury *as a matter of law* there is insufficient evidence to convict his client. He's asking Judge Ben to advise the Jury to acquit. Sounds ominous doesn't it? But there is a saving factor. It's only **advisory**. The Jury doesn't have to heed the directive of the Court. They can say, "Go climb a frozen rope, Man. We'll do our job our way – the conviction way."

We argue our respective points of view. He's for the advisory instruction and I'm against it. The issue is submitted for decision. And almost before I've managed another hard swallow, the proffer is granted. Judge Ben tells us, in a manner of speaking, the ragbag assortment of factors that have survived his surgical cleansing are <u>not</u> sufficient as a matter of law to support conviction.

This development drastically changes the Trial time table. With a Judicial advisory instruction of acquittal in his hip pocket, Mr. High Powered Gentleman confidently rolls the dice. He elects <u>not</u> to put on a case. He's playing the odds. Relying on the presumption of innocence and the Court's admonition to find his client innocent. There's too much risk involved in adding to the existing evidence portfolio. The wily, venerable Counsel for the Defense decides against presenting evidence of his client's purported good character for peace and quietude. Further, he does not call the Defendant as a witness. Putting Ms. Cool on the witness stand subjects her to cross examination. That's a wild card. There's no telling where that might lead. The other Court Instructions are duly settled, and summation is scheduled for the following morning.

I'm dumbfounded by the ruling. Totally bowled over for the remainder of the evening by this judicial pig-on-the-wing to the solar plexus. The third in a trilogy of harsh setbacks. The Court's administered a triple whammy. I'm thoroughly stressed. The incredulity of the Court's advisory instruction of acquittal is appalling to me. Unexpected and unbelievable. It's as if Judge Ben has adopted a beat 'im into the ground mind set, "Let's make the rookie Prosecutor's thrashing complete." Where's the logic?

The Defendant's residence is a homicide scene at 2300 hours. The dead body of a forty year old man lies in a pool of blood on her living room floor. He's been shot three times in the chest by a .38 caliber special. Ms. Cool, sitting at her kitchen table weeping – though uninjured, her face buried in her hands, is the only person present who is still breathing. Positively, this evidence <u>cannot</u> be deficient as a matter of law. These facts and circumstances and reasonable inferences to be drawn from the facts are a Jury Question. You blew it, Judge Ben! This is atrocious. Why take it away from the Jury, Sir?

But I'm paranoid. Fearful that *four thin threads* of connecting evidence won't be enough to steer the Jury away from Judge Ben's advice to acquit. There's no way to know where Jury speculation about the <u>absence</u> of a firearm will take them. Thanks, Judge. Appreciate it, Yer Honor.

Further, no evidence of gunpowder residue or tattooing has been detected on the hands of the stoic, rather attractive ex-girlfriend of the victim by crime scene investigators. Of course, residue can be washed off and tattooing may not occur.

Finally – and this is huge, Jurors respect Judges. They are, generally, extremely deferential to their Trial Judge. It's a steep climb up a very tall hill to persuade Jurors to over rule the Court's rule.

I plow forward with my summation preparation. Daydreaming as I work. There's a single glimmer of hope that drives my effort. What if the panel happens to have ESP? What if the Jury solves the puzzle of this paucity of evidence? What if they crack the code? What if they figure out Judge Ben's role in hardball evidence censorship? What if, on their own, they recognize the irony that begs expression?

"The Judge is advising us there's insufficient evidence to convict Sarah Cool, but he's the guy who excluded the evidence. What's up with that? Can we trust His Honor's judgment? Where does Justice lie – really?"

It been a wild ride, and Mr. High Powered continues to guide the trial locomotive. But it can't get any worse can it? The answer depends on one's clairvoyance, I suppose. The Deputy District Attorney Lad has another cross to bear. It will be next to the last.

I get sick. The morning of final argument I have laryngitis. Wow! What does a Courthouse gladiator do when his gitis won't larynate? What does a Trial Lawyer do without his rhetoric? How does he sweat his tongue into a lather without his voice box? How does he earn a living?

<u>Writing</u> out my speeches won't test my tongue power. That only leads to writer's cramp. I'm stricken *with* a dilemma of cosmic proportion for a Trial Guy. Or is that the wrong phrasing? Perhaps, I'm stricken *by* the dark cosmos with the dilemma. And that's a truly spooky thought. I must confess I did <u>not</u> realize how influential Mr. High Powered really is. I had absolutely <u>no</u> clue his clout extends beyond the veil! Nor am I oblivious to the paradox that Judge Ben may be an apprentice of the cosmos.

Hypothetically, these two get together for some more convivial, ex-parte chatter after instructions are settled. They discuss a <u>troublesome</u> truth in due course. As the title of his instruction suggests – the Court's biggie, that ole Prosecution bugaboo – His Honor's **Advisory Instruction of Acquittal** is only ADVISORY. It <u>can</u> be disregarded by the Jury. This probably won't happen, **but** *possibly* – it will happen.

The hypothetical truth be known, Mr. High Powered is still a trifle worried. He doesn't want to leave any slack. There are to be no loose ends. The acquittal package has to be failsafe. But there's a minuscule problem. There's a loose end that's remains part of the mix. It's that little sucker, Harmon. What's worse, he's a loose tongue with the **rebuttal** argument. Harmon's loose tongue gets the last chance to waggle. That's unacceptable to the dark side. There can't be any wiggle room in this plot.

So hypothetically speaking, Mr. High Powered slyly submits one more mythological application to Judge Ben. This one's ex-parte all the way. His in-chambers proffer is indeed cosmic in scope. It's a petition to *suppress* the Prosecutor. Well, not all of him. The Court's *sleight of hand* has to be more precise. It needs to focus on the larynx. Done. A motion to *suppress* the Prosecutive larynx is granted.

Well Hell, it must have been granted. Something happened. There had to be some type of *nefarious* intervention. I don't have any history of laryngitis, and I'm not much of a believer in coincidence. Summation is set for 10:00 a.m. the next day. I spend two productive hours completing my argument outlines. I'm a virile, healthy, energetic, highly motivated, younger man. I'm feeling fine the night before the legal debate – albeit exhausted and stressed. Whatever.

That's a weekly occurrence for a Trial Lawyer. I'm a man who bucks the obstacles and speaks his mind! I believe summation time is my time. I believe a Prosecutor's highest duty is his *role* as a dynamic advocate for justice.

Anyhow, overnight I've come down with flu-like symptoms. The most conspicuous and debilitating symptom being that I awake *tongue-tied*. I can mouth words, but beyond having my lips read, all that exits my chops is a raspy whisper. I've been bamboozled by some *magical incantation* that's taken away my speaking capability. Is Judge Ben secretly honing skills in the occult? Is it the dark magic of voodooism?

Does he, at some point in the night, mutter a mystic chant before plunging a sharp pin into the neck of a deputy prosecutor voodoo doll labeled Mel? Possibly, that's a prescient hypothesis. What better way to fell a Prosecutor than through his larynx? Lawyers earn their living by the sweat of their tongues. Poor little Deputy D.A. Victimized at a time when he needs levitating eloquence.

I travel to the Courthouse and telephone Judge Ben's chambers. He suggests a meeting with Counsel at 9:00 a.m. The charmed conference occurs at the appointed time. I report my plight. My announcement is greeted with barely concealed mirth. I'm given forty eight hours.

Judge Ben says the Jury will be informed the Prosecutor is sick. Then he pleasantly inflicts a verbal knife twisting. His eyes twinkle as he quips: "We sure hope they don't get the idea you're *sick* of your case, Counsel." Very funny, Judge. You have a disgustingly cool sense of humor, Sir.

Forty eight hours isn't enough time for the evil spell to wear off. My voice is not up to speed after the two day recess. But the Court has other turkeys to stuff, and the Jury must be insulated against short term memory loss.

My speech capacity is a far cry from being restored. The Judicial hex holds. It's tough coping with a physical distraction that mutes logical thought. My volume meter is substantially diminished. What is barely forced out of my larynx is a scratchy mishmash having little resemblance to coherent summation.

The result is predictable for this star-crossed case. After a three hour Jury deliberation, it's ACQUITTAL. Oh the pain. It's the *last* cross I will bear in this Trial tempest. The coup de grace. The dread *fifth option*. Not First Degree Murder, not Murder in the Second Degree, not Voluntary Manslaughter, and not Involuntary Manslaughter. It's NOT GUILTY. No thrill of victory this time. It's only the grinding agony of defeat.

The Jurors try to mollify me afterward. They say they tried. They didn't really want to follow the Judge's Advisory Instruction of Acquittal. But there just isn't a lot of evidence. No beef in this one. In the end, they are forced to vote **not guilty**. However, I am assured that keeping them in deliberation for three hours is a *moral victory*.

Ugh! A moral victory, in a murder trial that springs a killer, is about as satisfying as planting a kiss on the lips of your one and only true love in her wedding reception line – on the day she's exchanged marriage vows with your first cousin.

Unenthusiastic congratulations to Ms. Cool. She catches lightning in a jug. She accomplishes something monumental – though not in a positive sense.

This is a negative outcome. She's killed a man and with the help of her friends – she's killed a case. I'm not expressing a specific opinion about the merits. I wasn't there. I don't know what happened. I don't know if a history of physical abuse existed. I don't know if the shooting was self defense or criminal homicide. All I know is what the Police reports and Witness statements and Trial evidence tell me. I don't know where Justice ultimately lies.

What I do know is this: The <u>Jury</u> deserved its day in Court and didn't get it. A Jury is entitled to all the evidence before passing judgment on the evidence. It isn't possible to be just without the facts. The <u>Victim</u> deserved his day in court and didn't get it. I'm wondering what Mr. Poulsen would have said about all this. But he's absentee. No Jury hears his plea. And adding insult to untimely demise, the Court deprives Mr. Poulsen his day in Court in absentia – by excluding the evidence against his killer. These factors constitute **procedural injustice**.

I also <u>know</u> that killing another human being should only happen when <u>all</u> other options have been exhausted. **If** Sarah's killing of Enoch is <u>not</u> her only option – that too is **procedural injustice**. IT'S CALLED MURDER!

Thus ends a bizarre snapshot of Courtroom doings. A tale of shoes and ships and sealing wax – of cabbages and Courthouse <u>kings</u>.

Mister Defendant Bye – Bye

"When he is best, he is a little worse than a man;
and when he is worst, he is little better than a beast."
(Shakespeare, *The Merchant of Venice*, Act I, Sc.2, Line 93)

CHAPTER 3

STEPHANIE – AN ORDINARY YOUNG WOMAN, MOST would say. If any young woman can ever truly be called ordinary. Personally, I'd rather think of Stephanie as *extra*–ordinary. Though we didn't become acquainted until she'd become a statistic. Just one of over a hundred in this mid 1980s year.

She is married, a diminutive sixty four inches and one hundred five pounds. She's friendly and efficient. Exulting in the privilege of being alive. A pretty clerk working a solo shift in the booth at a self service gas station near Caesar's Palace. Vulnerable it now seems. A work place is horrific when it's also a risk place. But then, Stephanie has no way of knowing.

"The Bird of Time has but a little way to flutter
——— and the Bird is on the Wing."
(Edward Fitzgerald, *Rubaiyat of Omar Khayyam of Naishapur*)

It happens with shocking suddenness. Stephanie doesn't know the Bird of Time flutters ominously in her direction this Thursday morning. Her name appears next on its itinerary. The venal Bird will intercept her day – and her life. But she has no idea what awaits as she steers her rattletrap, white over green pickup to work. Had she been privy to the ugly truth on the wing, she'd have made a hairpin U-turn and gone the opposite way. Pressing her ears back. Driving and driving, incessantly driving – as fast and as far as the old Chevy will take her. But, Stephanie has no clue. She continues along the route that leads to ground zero. While each block and each intersection and each moment bring her closer to infinity.

5:50 a.m. – It's a rather chilly early March morning. She arrives at the *rendevous site* wearing a sweater. She parks her pickup. A small market is part of the complex. She enters and speaks with the store manager. She says she isn't feeling well. An evil premonition possibly? She puts on some makeup in the ladies room and buys a coke.

6:04 a.m. – She relieves her co-worker in the pay booth. The Bird of Time is inexorably on the Wing now. Soaring in a direct beeline toward the pay booth. It lands. Arriving in the form of a pernicious assailant. She's gone minutes later. Abducted!

6:30 a.m. – The door to the pay booth is observed open. No cash is missing from the cash register. Stephanie's sweater and purse are seen, but she is missing. Gone without a trace, it seems.

7:40 a.m. – A grisly discovery occurs. It is ground zero for another victim of mindless, senseless terrorism. A Coca Cola sales representative finds the body of a young woman laying on a cement pad west of the loading dock to the liquor and beverage warehouse behind Caesar's Palace. The woman is lying on her back. The only garments she is wearing are a blue gas station smock, a brown blouse, and a bra. Otherwise, her bloody body is nude.

Her breasts are exposed. The bra has been torn apart between the cups. The blouse and smock have been pulled open. They simply cover her upper arms. Two dented, metal soft drink canisters are nearby. Each is stained with a blood-like substance.

3:45 p.m. – An autopsy is performed at the Clark County Morgue by the Chief Medical Examiner. The cause of death is multiple blunt-force trauma to the woman's head and face, manual strangulation, and aspiration of blood into her lungs. Death has been brutally violent and agonizing.

The woman has multiple lacerations and contusions of the scalp and face. A left basal skull fracture. Multiple facial fractures and a fractured mandible. Which is the horseshoe-shaped bone forming the lower jaw. There is multiple hemorrhage in the soft tissue of the neck. Submucosal hemorrhage of the larynx, and multiple defensive contusions on both hands.

A few hours past she was vibrantly alive. How quickly and with what callous indifference a human life is snuffed out. How frail and tenuous is mortality. Of course, the victim of this pernicious ferocity is Stephanie. Her husband is a widower now. The self service gas station needs a cashier. She is cold and stiff rigor mortis on a slab.

What sort of evil stalked the neighborhood a short distance north and consummated its criminal frenzy behind Caesar's Palace? What kind of perverse fantasizing, what unbridled animal lust, would do this to a beautiful, young female? Who is the abductor? Who is the craven murderer? Who – who – who?

Henry – An ordinary man, some will say. If any forty-ish man can ever truly be called ordinary. His father served as a Correctional Officer for many years. Henry has also been a Corrections Officer for a time. His sister is a Tax Attorney and a Certified Public Accountant. She says he quit school and joined the Navy for four years. Later he acquires a GED diploma. His sister says, "He is not capable of violence." Her children call him, "Uncle Butch." She says, "He is a good uncle." Several friends say he is a good man, "Not capable of committing a crime." A year ago he enters the waters of baptism, becoming a member of the First Church of the Nazarene. He embraces a gospel of love. But where's the love at the loading dock?

Which is it Henry? Where is your soul grounded? What were you thinking that early March morning behind Caesar's Palace?

The Apostle Paul may have a measure of empathy for your plight. He makes a scriptural confession: "...for what I would, that do I not; but what I hate, that do I...For I know that in me (that is, in my flesh,) dwelleth no good thing: for to will is present with me; but *how* to perform that which is good I find not. For the good that I would I do not: but the evil which I would not, that I do." (Romans 7:15,18-19)

Possibly all men should have a measure of empathy for your predicament, Henry. We all battle the proclivities of the natural man, don't we? Each of us is a bundle of contradiction. However, most of us don't cross the line to brutal perversion.

Oh Henry? ------

"When he is best, he is a little worse than a man;
and when he is worst, he is little better than a beast." (ibid.)

The evidence is what it is. Henry is proxy for the Bird of Time. He's the grim reaper who has intercepted Stephanie's day – and her life.

There are two great branches of evidence in a Criminal Case. They are **direct evidence** and **circumstantial evidence**. The meaning of direct evidence is as plain as the nose on your face. A first grader can easily grasp the concept. Whatever a person perceives with any of his physical senses is <u>direct evidence</u>. *Seeing* a nose on a face is direct evidence that the face has a nose. *Seeing* a dead body is direct evidence that the person is dead. If you *see* something happen that is direct evidence. And if you *smell* it or *touch* it or *taste* it or *hear* it as it happens – that is also *direct evidence*. Everything else is *circumstantial*. Therefore, the meaning of circumstantial evidence is easily comprehended and just as easily categorized. There's no need to ever be confused about the meaning of circumstantial evidence again. *If it isn't direct evidence it's circumstantial evidence*! And since we know the plain-as-the-nose-on-your-face definition of direct evidence, we know exactly what evidence is circumstantial. It's as easy as falling off a log. Which will be circumstantial **if** the witness testifying against you does not see you fall, but does see you sitting on your posterior next to the wobbly log dusting off your pants.

Further, it may surprise quite a few people to learn that circumstantial evidence is *not* qualitatively inferior to direct evidence. I repeat, circumstantial evidence is *not*, per se, entitled to *less* weight than direct evidence. This seminal concept of criminal evidence, as I understand it, rests upon an unequivocal premise: *both* direct <u>and</u> circumstantial evidence, <u>if</u> firmly established, are entitled to be given the **same** amount of <u>weight</u>; subject, of course, to the vagaries of evidence <u>credibility</u>.

The fact is: a *confession* is circumstantial evidence. Likewise, *fingerprint* and *bullet* and *DNA* evidence are <u>circumstantial</u>. Most evidence in criminal cases <u>is</u> circumstantial.

48

I'm very fond of Henry David Thoreau's classic example of circumstantial evidence. I've used it hundreds of times. Thoreau states, "Some circumstantial evidence *is* very strong, as when you find a trout in the milk."

I grew up on a dairy farm. I know the importance of having a herd of cows that achieves high-volume milk production. The more milk the cows make the more money the farmer makes. And although we never resorted to such measures at Harmon Farm, [Would I admit it if we did?] I fully appreciate this stubborn reality. Some dairy farmers *might* be profoundly tempted to increase their milk supply by dipping the milk can into a stream of water. Which, of course, is how the slippery trout in Thoreau's analogy got into the milk. Nobody saw the farmer dip his milk can into the stream, but we can be absolutely **positive** he did.

Why? Well, the trout didn't spontaneously generate in a can of milk. The natural habitat of a rainbow trout is *not* performing deft figure eights in a foaming vessel of fresh, warm milk. The fat rainbow didn't come from the cow's udder, she's a milk maker not a trout maker. Her udder *isn't* a fish hatchery, trust me on this one. So, since the squiggly rainbow didn't come from the cows's udder, it *had* to come from the farmer's stream of water. Hence, Thoreau's astute observation of record has withstood the passage of time. "Some circumstantial evidence is *very* strong, as when you find a trout in the milk." We didn't see it happen, but the circumstances are so compelling we **know** it did happen! The finned scrapper getting his first taste of milk is **irrefutable** evidence of dairy farmer duplicity!

How does this relate to **Henry**? It's elementary really. The nuts and bolts of the case are circumstance. No one *saw* Stephanie's **murder**. It is *circumstantial* evidence that convincingly connects Henry to her killing!

He drives a 1971 2-door, white over maroon, Lincoln Continental Mark III.

It's placed at the scene of the abduction for 4-5 minutes. Stephanie is placed inside the car with Henry at the self service pumps next to the pay booth· The eyewitness accounts of two witnesses, familiar with Henry and his car, **see** the Mark III at the gas station and **see** it zoom away at **6:17 a.m.**

She is "...laying back on the passenger seat. Her head...[is] tilted... her hair... [is] hanging on the back of the seat...She has "brownish, shoulder length hair. She ...[is] wearing a blue jacket the same as...[gas station] employees."

The station *sightings* are perceived by a physical sense. The witnesses have *seen* what they describe. The predicate to the crime is *direct evidence*. But there is <u>no</u> physical sense perception of the <u>actual</u> murder. The proof of the crime is found in <u>circumstance</u>.

Henry's Lincoln Continental has something in common with Thoreau's milk can. **It-has-contents** that do <u>not</u> claim Henry's Mark III as their natural habitat! Meaning they don't belong there. They were **put** there during the abduction, either deliberately or inadvertently. These items are undeniably incriminating. Out of place – out of bounds – and Henry's out of luck. <u>Each</u> of these items of evidence is a figurative *trout in the milk*!

First: **The presence of Stephanie in <u>the</u> <u>car</u>**. We wish it was only a trout in the milk. Instead, it's a cashier who in some way has been enticed out of the pay booth – and kidnaped. Trapped in a car that's speeding to the site of her savage demise. The door to the pay booth is observed open at 6:30 a.m. and Stephanie's body is discovered three quarters of a mile away on a loading dock pad at 7:40 a.m. It's a cruel chronology.

First and foremost, Stephanie is a married woman. She is not Henry's girlfriend. He lives in the neighborhood and as a customer he may be a casual acquaintance. **But** her natural habitat is <u>not</u> being in his car. There's <u>no</u> precedent for this. Absolutely <u>no</u> evidence she's *ever* been in his car before.

She's a cashier on duty. A responsible cashier doesn't leave her cash register unattended. A responsible young woman doesn't leave her money and the key to her truck unattended. She may like work, but at some point she needs a ride home. Stephanie would <u>never</u> voluntarily vanish from the pay booth to go on some frolic of her own with a virtual stranger, while leaving the cash register, her purse, and her sweater behind – with the door wide open. No way!

Second: **The presence of Stephanie's hair in <u>the</u> <u>car</u>**. Hair strands microscopically similar to and consistent with Stephanie's head hair were obtained from the right front passenger floor and the right rear passenger floor. It may come as a shock to some criminal offenders, but the incontrovertible fact is that human hair is an inanimate object. It does <u>not</u> have inherent mobility. It does <u>not</u> have little follicle legs that bestow prowess to move from place to place and from a woman's head into a killer's car. **If** her hair's in the car, she's been in the car!

Third: **The presence of Stephanie's buttons in <u>the</u> car**. Button – button, whose got the buttons? Why Henry has the buttons! Excuse me. More precisely stated, Henry's car has the buttons. But if it's Henry's car what his car has he has.

Four buttons are missing from Stephanie's brown blouse. A button with thread fastened to the button's four eyelets is found under the front seat in the console area, and a button without thread still attached is recovered from the right-rear passenger floor partially under a seat belt. The two buttons are microscopically compared with buttons left on the blouse. The buttons from Henry's car are <u>identical</u>. They have "... the same physical properties – same size, same shape, same number of holes, same hole configuration, and the same color." The dark tan threads from the first button are compared with those fastened to buttons on the blouse. They are identical. "Both are tan in color and composed of polyester and cotton fibers."

When Henry embarks upon his malicious enterprise he undoubtedly has no clue concerning the evidentiary value of *two* small buttons. This case clearly establishes that the best things often come in small packages. Henry has the buttons, so he has the guilt!

"Some circumstantial evidence is very strong, as when you find a trout in the milk." (ibid.) **Or** when you find *buttons* in the car. We didn't see him do it, but the circumstances are so compelling we **know** he did it!

Fourth: **The presence of a piece of Stephanie's belt in <u>the</u> car**. A four and a fourth inch piece of brown colored belt with a white metal tip is found under the driver's seat. It is <u>positively</u> identified by Stephanie's husband. Keep this factor in mind. Stephanie's lower garments were gone. Her pants have been *forcibly* removed.

What goes around comes around. If Henry hadn't messed with her pants the belt remains intact, right. There's no piece of her belt lying under the seat to *mess* with him. Poor Henry. What he wanted is offered on nearly every corner of the Las Vegas Strip. Why take a life to get your jollies?

Good cause I'd say, for the *forcible* removal of Henry from society.

Fifth: **The presence of Stephanie's blood on the car**. This isn't the figurative trout in the milk, is it? Actually, it's more like the figurative moss that adheres to the milk can when it's being used to scoop water from the stream – and the trout into the milk. Same difference. It's very strong evidence either way.

Blood spatter isn't part of those March showers that occasionally grace southern Nevada. If Henry has blood spatter on his car it isn't connected to a *natural* phenomenon. Nor is it manna from heaven. Henry's evil isn't heaven-sent. The urge to violate is conceived in a mortal man's head and confirmed in a mortal man's malignant heart. Murder is indisputably an *unnatural* phenomenon!

When blood spatter is present on a surface, something's been bleeding in close proximity. A beautiful young woman is the something that has bled in this case. The crime scene photographs graphically and grotesquely portray copious amounts of bleeding. Las Vegas Metropolitan Police Department Crime Lab analyses identify the source. Stephanie has shed blood behind Caesar's Palace and *some* of it got on Henry's car.

Spatter is to spray or splash mud, blood, or some other liquid upon a surface. Type O blood spatter is found on the exterior passenger door of Henry's car approximately three inches up from the bottom of the door and approximately one foot nine inches to the right of the door edge, and on the right rear hub cap.

Henry's problems with the blood spatter evidence are twofold. He isn't the person who did the bleeding and his blood type is B.

She-is-type-O-blood! It is Stephanie's lifeless body at the bloody crime scene, and blood spatter consistent with her blood type is found on Henry's car. Hey, dead people don't get up and walk around. Where she's discovered at **7:40 a.m.** is obviously where she's been killed. Therefore, we **know** Henry's car has been at the murder scene. We also have the smarts to know a car *doesn't* make the circumstances. A Lincoln Continental Mark III *doesn't* drive itself. There *has* to be a driver. Compelling testimony puts Henry behind the wheel at **6:17 a.m.**

as his car zooms away with a woman aboard . Ka-ching! Henry made the circumstances for which he stands trial.

"Facts are stubborn things."
(Alain Rene Le Sage, *Gil Blas*, Book X, Chap.1)

But the *trout in the milk* evidence doesn't end it. There is other strong circumstantial evidence. What a Defendant **says** is circumstantial. After the fact, Henry is afflicted with foot-in-the-mouth disease. He attempts to **fabricate an alibi**. Er – not a good idea in this instance. When a Homicide Detective assigned to the investigation asks him to *account* for his time between 6:00 and 7:00 a.m. on the date in question, Henry isn't the least bit inclined to be accountable. He tries to avoid accountability.

He says he took a friend who lives at Wynn and Spring Mountain Road to work at a cabinet shop in North Las Vegas near Cheyenne. The friend doesn't have the same recall of events. He testifies he didn't see Henry until his first break between 8:55 and 9:05 a.m. Henry asks for a favor at that time. He says, "I got in a fight with this broad. If anybody asks you, I gave you a ride to work."

Now is that comment pregnant with implication, or what? An innocent man doesn't ask another man to lie for him. Trying to fabricate an alibi is proof of a *consciousness of guilt*. What an irritatingly stubborn thing a fact is to those who lack self control.

But it gets better. Two weeks later Henry has a slight disagreement with a hooker. How much green she wants for around-the-world perhaps. She testifies, "I got a little rowdy. That's all there was to it. I got belligerent to a small degree. And I think this incriminated him or something, but he told me *he was going to do the same thing to me* **he did with the girl at Caesar's Palace with a coke canister.**"

Now, that is a chilling comment. And I'm thinking the young lady might want to consider changing her profession. Pronto!

After his arrest, Henry continues to shoot off his mouth. A cell mate relates, "He asked me for a cigarette. He seemed dazed... He couldn't believe he...got arrested...He couldn't understand HOW. He said he... got her to come out of the booth by telling her he had some good weed and to come look at it. He said he should have robbed the place to alibi his story. He said he held her down by using a sticker, an ice pick knife... He said she was pleading with him. 'Please let me go. Just let me go and I won't tell anybody.' He said HE COULDN'T LET HER GO. ...He didn't want to go to jail...he couldn't stand it in jail...He said she was a beautiful girl. He preferred white girls because when you get into one she's in your pocket...He said he had someone who was going to vouch for him. He said he went to his apartment, took his clothes off, and disposed of them behind the Sahara Hotel."

Well yes, Henry. You could have let her go. You could have cherished human life instead of destroying a human life. You could have had the decency to let her go – and face the music. Do the crime do the time stuff. It's called being PERSONALLY ACCOUNTABLE for the bad things you do. Dig?

"Facts are stubborn things." (ibid.) Death is stubborn too!

Summation is the time when attorney's *sweating tongues* get full aeration. A Jury Verdict must be unanimous in Nevada. Going twelve for twelve is not easily achieved by either party. This is the time when high powered rhetoric flies on both sides of the Courtroom. Most criminal cases have sticky points, and dissent is the rule not the exception during Jury deliberation. The Prosecutor and the Defense must pull out all the stops in final argument. He's the dynamic champion of truth representing the State of Nevada. They are the dynamic champions of acquittal. It's a simple division of responsibility really. The Prosecutor is the lawyer of the people and Defense Counsel is the lawyer for the accused. It's called the adversary system. Actually, it works quite well as the *sweating tongues* of courtroom gladiators wax eloquent on the issue of guilt or acquittal.

The proffer of evidence at Trial is moment to moment, day to day, point by point, witness by witness, exhibit by exhibit, and comes from here and there in no particular order. Summation is a phase in trial drama that occurs <u>after</u> the piecemeal presentation of evidence is finished. What's been offered by the parties has to be sorted and collated. Trial lawyers are the collators. The process is called final argument. It's that <u>pivotal</u> <u>point</u> when *the people's man* tries to pull it all together with elocution. He diagrams the facts, telling the Jury how to crack the evidence code and solve the case-puzzle!

There are <u>two</u> occasions in Trial when a Prosecutor must **truly** demonstrate his <u>passion</u> – his <u>tenacity</u> – his <u>energy</u> – and his <u>will</u> <u>to</u> <u>win</u>. They are **cross examination** <u>and</u> **closing argument**. During **cross** he's contending with Defense witnesses and during **closing** he's trying to dazzle the Jury.

The typical mind-set of a career Prosecutor, after the rigor and stress and unpredictability of introducing evidence, is the impulse to take a deep breath and murmur, "Praise the Lord, <u>summation</u> *at* <u>*last*</u>!" I don't think it *gets any better* for a Prosecutor than closing argument.

I don't like generalities as a rule, but here's one I put into my Prosecutorial Play Book. A Deputy District Attorney who *likes* winning and *appreciates* honing rhetorical skills, **never** waives <u>a</u> <u>closing</u> <u>argument</u>. **Never!**

It's said of lawyers, they *earn their living* **by the sweat of their tongues**, and they *don't mind* <u>hard</u> <u>work</u>! This is typically true as lawyers summarize evidence and verbally frame their theory of the case. It is <u>specifically</u> true of those who bear the burden of proof. The paramount responsibility of Prosecutors is convincing Juries their evidence has overcome the presumption of innocence and established guilt beyond a reasonable doubt.

Prosecutors must *work hard* during closing argument. They must make their *tongues sweat*. This is the time to <u>ratchet</u> up *intensity level*. It's the time for *appropriate* expression of **righteous indignation**. Most criminal cases *won't* be won because of closing argument – **<u>but</u>** every case *should* be **<u>argued</u>** as though **summation** is the *difference* <u>between</u> <u>winning</u> <u>and</u> <u>losing</u>!

Well, PERSONAL ACCOUNTABILITY for Henry is imminent. His crime is **random, brazen, impulsive** – and **<u>repulsive</u>**! He awakens with an urge to couple. His mind possessed by libidinous fantasy. Henry does nothing to restrain the destructive impulse. It could have been any pretty woman that March morning, however he exploits a situation in his neighborhood. He knows an attractive young lady who works an early morning shift. He's familiar with the business, and with her schedule.

He knows she'll be alone in a gas station pay booth nearby. He pulls between the pumps and the pay booth on the pretext of purchasing gas. But he has something else in mind, and it's not something he intends to pay for. He's stalking female prey. He wants a *personal* encounter. He's makes the circumstance, and triggers the scenario. Yet, Stephanie makes the circumstance feasible. For reasons known only to her and to him, the cashier leaves the safety of the pay booth. She pays dearly for those few steps. They cost her – her life.

Service with a smile? Henry said, "She was a nice, friendly clerk – who served me with a smile." Is it possible he thought his *coercive* effort at seduction would be rewarded by service with a smile on the loading dock? **It-was-not!**

She lays on her back, nearly nude – bloodied – and dead when she's found. Multiple cuts, contusions, fractures, and manual strangulation emphatically rebut a consent thesis. The aberrant reality is service with a scream. Stephanie's lifeless body is a hideous testament to her rejection of his seduction. Henry has a bizarre and vicious approach to foreplay. She is <u>not</u> a sex object, <u>nor</u> a plaything to be pawed and tortured and killed by senseless acts of depravity.

Her cries for help in the early morning isolation are stifled by sinister hands gripping her neck. The pleas for help fade to a feeble whimper, and then to an agonized whisper. Her frantic call goes unheeded. There is no deliverance.

When we juxtaposition autopsy and live photographs of Stephanie, the sheer repugnance of Henry's crime is indelibly burned into our psyches. Henry's dark legacy is vividly portrayed by BH and AH photos, i.e., <u>Before</u> Henry and <u>After</u> Henry. What emerges from the snapshots is a ghastly image of the capacity for violence that lurks within the handsome, composed, courtroom countenance of the Defendant!

"When the lamp is shattered
The light in the dust lies dead..."
(Percy Bysshe Shelly, *When the Lamp is Shattered*, [1822] Stanza I)

Murder *shatters* the lamp. **Murder** leaves the light lying *dead* in the dust. Like Shelly's lamp, how brilliant, how bright, how beautiful, and how full of purpose <u>was</u> Stephanie's life. Tragically, her mortal light and her shattered remains lay dead on a dusty concrete pad in early March 1985. Victimized by the cold, callous brutality of a killer. The crime also leaves a dark legacy to the living. When Stephanie is shattered – when her mortal light lies dead in the dust, the *light of all* who knew her is immeasurably dimmed. Those who love her can only feel empathy for her and enmity for her killer!

"Ladies and Gentleman of the Jury, you can sense Stephanie's suffering to a slight degree, but you're powerless to help her now. She's gone. However, there is something you <u>can</u> do. You <u>can</u> deal with her killer. You <u>can</u> send a clear and unmistakable message to him and to others who contemplate heinous crimes of violence. You <u>can</u> tell them that such conduct is unacceptable in Clark County. Not on March 7, 1985 – **not ever!** You <u>can</u> impose a judgment upon Henry that holds him *personally accountable* for his terrible deed. Not a judgment maliciously levied, but fashioned in fairness and a spirit of justice. You <u>can</u> force him to pay the **full price** for his cavalier disregard of the sanctity of human life."

"Murder is the ultimate selfish act! Anyone who murders is selfish to the core. Why does Henry kill Stephanie? What does she do to deserve such savagery? The answer is profoundly simple. What Stephanie does is be pretty and say no. Henry kills her because he's selfish. He kills her to avoid arrest. A pretty woman who is dead <u>doesn't</u> tell tales. She <u>doesn't</u> cry rape. She <u>doesn't</u> sign crime reports. She <u>doesn't</u> **testify**. She <u>doesn't</u> **identify**."

"Henry has sent Stephanie to another realm. She's beyond the jurisdiction of the State of Nevada. No subpoena nor process to compel her attendance from out-of-state will produce her as a witness. She's beyond the pale in mortality of due process of law. But what happened is succinctly tied together by the evidence."

"You've heard testimony that Henry seemed dazed after his arrest. He couldn't **believe** he got arrested. He couldn't understand **how** he got arrested. Now why does Henry say that? Why is he dazed by arrest? Well he says that and he's dazed because his selfishness has backfired! He's killed the <u>only</u> witness and that's supposed to be his guarantee. His grant of immunity for murder. His gold-brick-road free pass for this despicable crime. Oh, the irony – the cruelty of reality! Committing crime. Serving time."

"Ladies and Gentleman of the Jury, you have an awesome responsibility in this trial. You represent a cross section of the community. In a manner of speaking, you're the conscience of the community. Your decision will establish the standard of justice in this case – for Henry, for Stephanie, and for the community."

"During my Opening Statement, *I promised* the State's evidence would prove beyond a reasonable doubt that the Defendant is guilty of murder in the First Degree. During Jury selection, *each* of you impliedly *promised* that you would find the Defendant guilty *if* the evidence established his guilt beyond a reasonable doubt. I kept my promise! Now, I'm asking you to keep your promise. I'm asking you to return a verdict guaranteeing that the brute fury of the Defendant never makes another woman a corpse."

"Mr. Defendant, I have something to say to you. I've been waiting to say it for a long time. In fact, ever since you were first interviewed by a Homicide Detective the day following Stephanie's murder. You offered a series of evasive answers to the Detective's questions. Then you tired of the charade after about twenty minutes. Sarcastically, you told the Detective, 'I've said all I have to say. This is a waste of my time. The interview is over. I'm a busy man. Bye-Bye.'"

"Sir, each time I've looked at the crime scene and autopsy photographs of the young woman you bludgeoned to death, I've pondered what you said to the Detective. I've been mindful of those remarks throughout your trial. As witnesses have offered pertinent testimony, I've remembered your smug attitude. As exhibits have been admitted I've considered what might be an appropriate response. When the Jury Instructions were settled with the Court and Defense Counsel, addressing you was part of my things to do list. Summation is almost over. The stage is set. At long last, the time has arrived."

"Your choices got you arrested. Your choices made you the Defendant. Your choices put you in your Courtroom chair. Your choices mandate a particular Jury Verdict. If the criminal justice system has any meaning, it means those who commit horrific crimes of violence must be held *personally* responsible for their criminal acts. Now is the moment. These are the words: I've said all I have to say, Sir. I'm a busy man too. My argument is finished. I promise you I'm sincere, but not impartial. Mister Defendant – BYE-BYE!"

Where Is the Promise

"Where is the promise of...[her] years,
Once written on...[her] brow?...
Where sleeps that promise now?"
(Adapted from Adah Isaacs Menken, *El Suspiro* (*Infelix*) 1868)

CHAPTER 4

SHE IS CORN-FED MID WESTERN GROWN. A dusky-haired, nineteen year old wind blown daughter of the great plains. So young – so beautiful. A tender rose bud poised to unfold its velvet petals into a delicate symmetry of loveliness. Yearning to fulfill the dream of a joyful life every young woman carries in her breast. So sweet, so affable, so anxious to excel, so hopeful – so full of promise. Wistfully, emotionally, silently my lips form words that should have no relevance to the promise of one in her teenage years. Where sleeps that promise now?

She is about to finish her school year at UNLV in May 1983. Engaged in studying for and taking final exams. She's a teenager, but not a giddy teenager. She's a student, but not a playtime student. Going to college is serious business to her. She's an A student. Earnest about education and the pressing responsibilities of pending adulthood. She's a shining pillar of youthful maturity and sobriety. Thoughtful and honorable. She is not inclined to frivolous dalliance, nor binge drinking, nor teasing flirtation – nor casual acts of fornication. Prudent moral values are her code for college days – and nights. She has lofty goals and intends to achieve them. She's not a stereotype Jane College. If indeed anyone who pursues the vision of higher education can be rationally stereotyped.

Karen is extraordinary. The quintessential coed. Vivacious, pretty, personable, polite, punctual, diligent in class room attendance and in doing class room assignments. Wanting to be a scholar. Thirsting for knowledge. Striving for good grades. Attempting to impress and *please* professors – and graduate student *instructors*. Seeking a profession compatible with her personality – and her values.

Like many in this first measured step to independence, stretching her wings by attending an out of state university. Karen is a respectful daughter of a loving mother. She expects to see her mom soon. Spring semester is ending. Her mother has already begun the drive to Las Vegas to reunite with her daughter, and take the child of her womb back home for a summer break from the demands of college life. But sweet Karen won't be seeing mom soon. Mom's arrival will be too late!

Who? Why? What's the rationale? How can ugliness be allowed to cancel the plans of those numbered among the best? What is the sense of detours imposed upon those for whom the future seems brightest?

Sadly, **there's madness** loose in the world. However, it isn't God's madness. God doesn't choreograph the circumstance of madness. Mortality is crammed full of craven self interest, illogic, obsession, fantasy, aberrant sex, and gratuitous violence. Yet categorically, these things do not bear the hand print of God. Evil comes from mankind. Humans make evil circumstances.

"Cruelty has a human heart..."
(William Blake, *A Divine Image*, Stanza I)

The cruel heart isn't where an unsophisticated college coed is likely to expect it to be. This is enticement of a subtle nature. He's not a stalker. He's not a mentally deranged janitor waiting in a broom closet to pounce. He's not a transient deviant hanging out on campus. Not a prison escapee. Not a cross dressing female transvestite. Nor is he the pimply faced kid with horn rimmed glasses sitting across the aisle in her computer science class. Though we're getting warm. That premise is really close. He–**is**–in–the–classroom. The cruel heart thumps its sinister cadence during every session of the semester. **He's the graduate student instructor**! He teaches about computers, but his thoughts are about concupiscent connection. And his eyes often rest upon Karen"s buxom treasures. Sliding coyly from her face to her knees and beyond.

He bides his time until the stakes are raised. Semesters end. She'll want an "A" in his class. He'll adroitly imply such a result is possible – **if!** He wants to get her one-to-one so he can go one-on-one. A jug of wine, a loaf of bread, *a nice grade*, and thee – Karen.

Casual invitations to his apartment pave the way – and stoke the fire. She considers the offers. She thinks she understands what's at stake. But does Karen know how high the stakes really are? Does she know how tenuously she clutches mortality?

What happens is <u>not</u> destiny. Premeditated villainy intercepts the journey of the vivacious coed. Murder trumps the youthful maturity and the prudent moral values. It buries the fragile future of lofty goals and visions of higher education.

It happens Tuesday evening, May 17, 1983. A friend tries to contact Karen at her apartment the evening of the 17th. She doesn't respond when he knocks so he leaves a note on the door. It's still there the next day.

The studious coed from the mid west has two final exams scheduled Wednesday, May 18th. She has Public Speaking between 8-10 a.m. and Dance at 5:00 p.m. Karen is a **no show** for both occasions. Her absenteeism is a large red flag. It speaks volumes. *Cutting* classes is <u>totally</u> out of character for her – *especially* during finals week.

The hideous truth is revealed Thursday morning, May 19, 1983. Karen's partially clad body is discovered in a shallow ravine about fifty feet from Tonopah Highway. She has died of ligature strangulation. An assailant has deliberately tied a choking tourniquet around her neck in a grip of death. The binding compresses her windpipe with such force she is unable to breathe. She also suffers a fracture to the right 4th metacarpal bone of her neck. It is consistent with a boxer-type injury.

However, she hasn't been killed here. The shallow ravine a short distance from the highway **is** a drop-site! It's a spur of the moment get-the-body-out-of-my-apartment-as-quickly-as-possible measure. It's a camouflage. A decoy. An effort to conceal complicity in coed murder. No respect. No interment. No dignity. Just a cavalier disposal of human remains and a god-less prayer for reprieve.

This is a sex-murder. Rough sex is to be **his** quid pro quo for an "A." But that's a dead end street. Once he elects to employ sadistic force to overcome an emphatic refusal to consent, she's not going to be around to receive her "A." Grades have become a moot point. She's won't be needing a college diploma neither. When he's pleasured himself by force which crosses the line to an indictable felony offense, he has to take it to the next level or risk going to prison. And he does. He goes for broke.

"A dead man cannot bite."
(Plutarch, *Pompey*, p.795)

Nor does a dead woman bite. Karen doesn't bite and she doesn't bellow and she doesn't take her butt down to the police station. Her transportation is comped by the Medical Examiner's Office. It's a lifeless trip to the morgue. The Chief Medical Examiner believes death occurred 24-36 hours prior to the autopsy. Though he acknowledges this is only an educated *guess*. Numerous variables may stretch the time frame parameter he offers.

A sexual assault kit is collected. It includes vaginal samples. They disclose evidence of recent sexual intercourse. A Criminalist testifies to evidence of sperm inside the vaginal vault. Intact spermatozoa heads are observed. Is it rape? Of course. No other reasonable inference can be drawn from these circumstances. A bone in Karen's neck is fractured. The injury is consistent with being walloped in the neck. She's been strangled senseless with a ligature, and callously transformed into a piece of buzzard bait along a major roadway in northwest Las Vegas.

She's violated, sexually assaulted, and murdered. Then loaded into a car trunk like a bag of trash, hauled twenty five miles, and cast aside like a clump of road kill. This crime is despicable! No human being should ever – ever be *desecrated* like this. Certainly not the innocence, the sanctity, and the beauty of a young woman-child of nineteen. So, whose the trash in this scenario? Who is the guy who does the unthinkable?

"Man is the Only Animal that blushes. Or needs to."
(Mark Twain, *Following the Equator*. Vol. I, *Pudd'nhead Wilson's New Calendar*, Chap. 27)

He is twenty nine. He's a graduate student who subsidizes his education by being an instructor on campus. However, his job description doesn't include instruction in violent sex! His eraser is for the blackboard. He has no campus license to erase life.

He's into fantasy. His off-campus apartment is well-stocked with sexually explicit materials. Stacks of girlie magazines and Fredericks of Hollywood catalogs are recovered by police. Sex paraphernalia is abundant. These props provide combustion for frequent flights on fiery wings of eroticism. Class room lectures and strolls across campus provide a resource allowing him to personalize the objects of his lechery and ignite thoughts of passionate embrace. Karen becomes a primary target. He *has her* regularly in his mind.

The Computer Science final is Tuesday afternoon – May 17. *Seven* is a **lucky** number in Vegas if a patron of the temporal temples of casino gaming is tugging on the handle of a proverbial one armed bandit. However, the number of this fateful day is *seventeen*. There's no slot machine luck when the number is 17. Nor is *seventeen* necessarily lucky on campus in a temporal temple of learning. The opposite effect is true for Karen when the one precedes the seven. May 17 is decidedly **unlucky** for her. Perhaps her luck could have changed, if she'd been a little wiser in the ways of the world of men? If she'd been a bit more perceptive? A little more cautious? If only ––

Karen completes her final exam. She believes she's nailed it, but a student never knows for sure. Right? There are *variables* that factor into a final grade. The Instructor's mind-set being one of them. She's aware of this and wants to be sociable. So, she engages him. She pauses to thank the instructor for his teaching skills, and to wish him a pleasant summer.

Walter takes her hand. He compliments her on her classroom performance. While continuing to hold Karen"s hand he stares intently into her eyes and asks if she'd like to walk with him to his apartment to celebrate the end of the class with a glass of wine. She hesitates. Is it an inner warning? A prompting?

He interjects, "Please – it could make a difference. It gets a little lonely living in a bachelor pad. I'd enjoy your company. It would brighten my day, and it only has to be for a little while. It will mean a lot to me."

Please – it <u>could</u> make a difference? A difference for whom? Why can it make a difference? The message is coded. But isn't he *implicitly* saying, "It *could* make a difference for <u>you</u>. It *could* affect your <u>grade</u>. It *could* determine whether you'll get an **<u>A</u>** or a **B+**. Are you hearing me, Karen?"

She did hear him. She got the message. Sweet, studious Karen said, "Yes. I will walk to your apartment and drink a glass of wine."

Her **<u>yes</u>** changes her life. It makes it a whole lot shorter. Her longevity morphs from half a dozen decades into minutes. Further, the ending is very unpleasant, intrusively intimate, and violent! It will shock a University Campus and catapult a loving family into the throes of bereavement.

This is <u>not</u> the first casual invitation from the teacher to the student that she accompany him to his apartment for a glass of wine. Four witnesses testify Karen has spoken to them about her Computer Science Instructor. She's told them Walter has "invited her to his apartment to discuss her grade over a glass of wine." After the fact, it sounds extremely ominous, doesn't it?

Well, bright-eyed, hopeful, cherishing-each-moment-of-life Karen wasn't privy to after the fact. She <u>is</u> before the fact. She <u>isn't</u> after the fact. She's roadside litter afterward. And it happens because she <u>does</u> yield to his proposal and <u>did</u> go to his digs. She yielded to an enticement that impliedly offered: A glass of wine and an "A." She's an optimist and trusting. Yet, fate's door often swings on such an innocuous hinge.

Hey! This is dirty pool. It's isn't fair. An innocent young woman from the corn belt doesn't expect a sexual predator to be her college computer teacher. She is totally blind sided! Unaware she's stepped inside an ambiance that has a plentiful inventory of prurient libido stimulants, and is inhabited by a man who spends an inordinate amount of time steeped in sexual fantasy. She is unprepared physically and emotionally to fend off the amorous advances of an instructor turned seducer. A potent chop to her neck subdues her. Where is the promise of Karen's years now – once written on her brow?

Walter admits to a co-worker that *he does* share a drink with Karen at his apartment after the final examination. But he alleges, "She left sometime before

8-9:00 p.m." A next door neighbor testifies he <u>never</u> sees the girl leave.

Another witness testifies Walter told him, "He invited her to his apartment and that he had changed the sheets on his bed and other innuendos of a sexual nature."

A friend drops by Walter's apartment the morning of the 18th. He makes excuses and refuses to allow the individual to come inside.

Walter borrows a car late afternoon on Wednesday, May 18. He says he has some errands to run. Yeah – sure he does. Only it's not errands plural. It's <u>one</u> specific errand. It's about getting a dead woman out of sight so if the cops come calling they won't have him dead to right. And he can't do this by carrying the body of his victim to northwest Las Vegas piggy-back. He <u>has</u> to borrow a vehicle.

The car owner is a casual friend. He isn't anxious to loan his vehicle. He's a little skeptical. Concerned about how far the car will be driven. He reluctantly agrees, but checks the odometer before Walter leaves. The car is returned at mid morning on Friday, May 20.

It has been driven 50-55 miles. The distance from Walter's apartment to the *body* drop site is about 25 miles. That would be a round trip of <u>fifty</u> miles, correct? A coincidence? Not likely. There's little basis for believing crime cover-up events just inexplicably happen. Coincidence is generally man-made! Coincidence didn't drive the car. Walter drives it. Coincidence doesn't burnish the scrub brush off Tonopah Highway with a dead body. Walter does it. He makes the circumstances. Nor is it a matter of sheer coincidence that he just happens to add milage to the loaner vehicle odometer that will take him from his apartment to the drop site and back .Ya think?

There's inferential Trial testimony that Walter is *concerned* about changing his appearance following the crime <u>and</u> the disposal of Karen's body. He's worn a beard for a very long time. He *shaves* the beard right after the murder! His <u>timing</u> for dusting cobwebs off his razor to remove facial hair is intriguing and damning.

There is also trial evidence Walter takes a *soiled* <u>bedspread</u> to Al Phillips Cleaners the afternoon of May 19. An acquaintance drives him to the Al Phillips outlet on Tropicana Avenue. An acquaintance? Now that's a curious facet of the case. He still has the loaner car. Why doesn't he drive himself to the cleaners? Is it a matter of subterfuge? He's transported a dead body in the loaner car. He's lifted a dead body out of the loaner car. Perhaps, Walter doesn't want to risk being <u>linked</u> again to the *loaner car*!

Curious timing for a trip to the cleaners also? Sure and not coincidental. Has the item that needs cleaning been used as a make-shift body bag? Probably. Walter later retrieves his bedspread – freshly laundered.

Autopsy findings of the Medical Examiner are pertinent. There is evidence of *post mortem lividity*. Naturally, <u>post</u> <u>mortem</u> means *after* death. <u>Lividity</u> is descriptive of fluid *seepage*. Over time blood follows the law of gravity in a motionless body. Accordingly, blood often settles to the lowest points in a corpse. Pooling in areas where gravity has taken it. The tell-tale signs consist of areas on the body of a deceased person that exhibit a bluish leaden color, as if discolored by bruising. The presence of *post mortem lividity* conclusively establishes that the deceased has remained in a <u>fixed</u> position for a significant number of hours following death.

A woman left lying on her assailant's bed for close to *twenty four* hours, after being victimized by ligature strangulation, will likely display clear indicators of post mortem lividity. In Karen's case, the Medical Examiner concludes her body has *laid* against a fabric that is consistent with a <u>bedspread</u> for a significant period of time following death. He detects fabric *impressions* on exposed areas of her body that are consistent with the fabric of bedding. It seems the Bird of Crime has come home to roost, Walter!

A prior bad act is admitted. It occurs less than one year prior to sweet Karen's death. He uses a <u>knife</u> to forcibly rape another young woman on May 29, 1982. Possibly evincing a common plan, scheme, and intent to invite women to his apartment for forceful sexual liaison. The month of May brings out the worst in Walter, it seems. In Springtime a man's thoughts are turned to fancy? Well, conduct isn't fanciful, nor romantic, if what is taken is taken by force!

Evidence of an obscene call to yet another young woman is introduced. "Man is the Only Animal that blushes. Or needs to." (ibid.)

The connecting evidence is convincing. Inferentially, the factors leave little doubt. However, this isn't a rush to judgment. The Criminal Justice System isn't a poster child for speed. It's often damn slow. Less characterized by expedition than by creeper-condition. Much to the chagrin of those directly impacted by crime.

Yet, justice never sleeps. The Coppers <u>never</u> give up. Dedicated Detectives of the Las Vegas Metropolitan Police Department are unwavering in their efforts. These things take time. There are *lots* of cases to solve –investigations to manage.

Walter isn't indicted for the murder of Karen until April 1, 1988. That's almost five years of investigation. The Grad Student Instructor is finally in The System. And on April fools day! It's poetic justice. Walter's been skating for years now. Whose the fool now, Walter?

Enough said concerning procedure. I want to speak again of *sweating tongues*. **Summation** is the time a Prosecutor must <u>passionately</u> argue all the facts and circumstances that make the case **Murder in the First Degree**! He must speak of *the track marks* of <u>murder</u> and show the Jury where *the tracks* lead.

He doesn't do that by presenting a monotonous recapitulation of the testimony of <u>each</u> witness nor of <u>every</u> exhibit. Courtroom *time* is precious. The Prosecutor must <u>not</u> squander his opportunity before the Jury. A <u>boring</u> recitation of *all* the evidence is not a propitious way to make *his Prosecutive tongue sweat*. This practice **is** the *lazy lawyer approach* to **closing argument**. Its use clearly identifies that Prosecutor as an advocate who <u>hasn't</u> invested the <u>time</u> necessary to **selectively and effectively** <u>prepare</u> <u>and</u> <u>deliver</u> <u>his</u> <u>argument</u>!

The Prosecutor is The Dynamic Champion of Justice. He has to argue the **case truth** like a champion. Champions of the Courtroom are very selective in their choice of points to argue! Proper <u>selection</u> of **argument** points has its antecedent in proper <u>preparation</u>.

A dedicated Deputy District Attorney begins **preparing** his **closing argument** once he's settled on *a theory of the case*. He <u>continues</u> to

prepare <u>throughout</u> the presentation of evidence. **He-makes-his-fingers-sweat** too! He takes <u>detailed</u>, <u>legible</u> trial notes of testimony, unless the Court is supplying the parties with <u>daily</u> <u>transcripts</u>. He *always* keeps a notebook handy to write down **key points**, either as he hears them or at the end of <u>each</u> trial day. He categorizes and organizes these notes. He begins his **<u>list</u>** of points **connecting** the Defendant to the charges.

Most prospective Attorneys hear it in Law School. I did. **Well, it's true**! "The law <u>is</u> a jealous mistress." The legal profession demands earnest and energetic devotion from those who want to succeed.

> "I will not say with Lord Hale, that 'The Law
> will admit of no rival,'...but I will say that it
> is a jealous mistress, and requires a long and
> constant courtship. It is not to be won by trifling
> favors, but by lavish homage." (Joseph Story, *The
> Value and Importance of Legal Studies* -1829)

To which I feel compelled to add: **<u>each</u>** *murder case* a Prosecutor handles, in a sense, <u>is</u> a <u>jealous</u> <u>mistress</u>. During **each** journey to the *Trial Arena* the task at hand will require single minded <u>fidelity</u> as a precondition to winning. A **murder case** "requires a long and constant courtship." **Just verdicts** <u>will</u> <u>not</u> <u>be</u> <u>won</u> by "trifling" effort – only by "lavish" respect for the cause. Winning isn't an accident. **<u>Hard</u> <u>work</u>** makes winners!

Preparation is the *great equalizer*! A Prosecutor *may* not always be the smartest, the most handsome, the most analytical, or the most fluent, but **<u>if</u>** he **properly prepares**, that <u>effort</u> will *compensate* for a multitude of shortcomings. Trust me, I'm an expert on this point.

Further, a professional Prosecutor **never** <u>deliberately</u> <u>misstates</u> <u>evidence</u> and does his best to **never** <u>inadvertently</u> <u>misstate</u> <u>the</u> <u>evidence!</u> Misstating evidence in argument is the *quickest and surest way* to be **discredited**. <u>When</u> a Prosecutor loses his credibility he *loses* the Jury's trust, and <u>when</u> he *loses* trust his **chance of winning** <u>is</u> greatly diminished.

Facts are stubborn. Unyielding. The actual facts of a case do <u>not</u> change. A fact is something as it is. A fact is pure, unvarnished truth.

Lawyers may distort facts at will with self-serving *spin*, but what is fact remains intact. There is *infinite power* in **facts**. The people's lawyer never *embellishes* facts. Prosecutors need to repeat that expression frequently while looking at themselves in the mirror prior to **Closing Argument**. Accuracy is a stalwart ally of Prosecutors. **If** a Prosecutor <u>sticks</u> to <u>the</u> <u>facts</u> he'll be okay!

When the Jury comes to recognize that what the Prosecutor <u>represents</u> the evidence to be **is the evidence**, then things are really going well. That kind of **credibility** produces **credible** <u>verdicts</u>! A credible verdict is GUILTY **if** guilt is established beyond a reasonable doubt.

Will a credible verdict result in Walter's case? I argue the *track marks* of murder, but will the Jury be convinced the *tracks* lead to the Defendant? The Jury is the ultimate variable in every case! A guilty verdict is rarely a lead pipe cinch. The issue is usually in doubt until the Jury finally speaks its mind. This case is no exception. However, the State's *Rebuttal Case* gives the Jury a hefty nudge toward guilt.

"Ligature strangulation is a cause of death <u>horrible</u> to contemplate! The inability to breathe is terrifying – and agonizing. If Karen is conscious, she's struggling with all her might to loosen the cruel vise that digs a deep groove into soft tissue as it tightens around her neck. She gasps for breath. Her body thrashes from side to side, and her eyeballs seem ready to pop out of their sockets. The chilling grip of evil cuts off the flow of oxygen to her brain while she slips into ghastly darkness. This is the reality of Karen's last moments on earth. It is a murderous transformation from youthful beauty into a grotesque caricature of her essence. Nothing we do here changes this solemn truth."

"We can only <u>weep</u> for the anguish of a dear mother, who has excitedly driven hundreds of miles to Las Vegas in joyful expectation of a loving reunion with her daughter, only to discover when she arrives that her daughter is missing. And immeasurable worse, within hours to learn that her adorable daughter is dead! I'd say the depth of a mother's emotional travail in this context is almost beyond comprehension. The emotional high of expecting to see her precious child again, being swiftly swallowed up in the reality, that she is <u>never</u> to see her again in this life – not alive. <u>Never</u> to **hug** her and **talk** with her and **travel** home with her. *Not* in a few weeks, *not* after the next semester – *not* ever! Oh, the <u>unbearable</u> pain of such a loss! The <u>unforgettable</u> stain of such a loss each time she remembers how her daughter has died!"

"We can only <u>mourn</u> the loss of a wonderful, vibrant, young coed whose life is strangled by a man totally wrapped up in himself. An instructor who has betrayed the trust of his student to gratify his own licentious desire. Where is the promise of Karen's years once written on her brow? Where sleeps the promise of Karen now?"

"Criminal Trials often seem one sided. The Defense wants you to forget Karen. They want the whole focus to be on the Defendant. Let me make these *two* realities abundantly clear, the State of Nevada <u>hasn't</u> forgotten the nineteen year old "A" grade student who was murdered, <u>and</u> the State <u>doesn't</u> want you to forget Karen. **She's** why we're here – though she isn't here. She's six feet under at her hometown cemetery in the mid west. He's here though. He put himself here. The evidence proves beyond a reasonable doubt that he's the one who put Karen in the graveyard."

" The worth of Karen is great in the eyes of the State of Nevada. The issue being considered <u>now</u> is whether the members of the Jury have the courage, the determination, the intestinal fortitude, the resolve, and the sense of commitment to do their legal duty – based upon the facts and circumstances and law of this case. I believe you do!"

"Allow me to reference Walter's words as a witness. He *tries* to **alibi the car** when he testifies. He tells you *why* he borrowed it, and he tells you exactly *where* he took it after he borrowed it. He describes a series of errands that don't take him very far from the UNLV campus. Predictably, he says he never went anywhere on Tonopah Highway. Certainly, not anywhere near the spot where Karen's body was dumped. Walter is sort of behind a rock and a hard place on this car matter though. He doesn't want to have the car go too far, but he needs to have it go far enough, right?"

"Ooops! Houston we have a problem. Maybe Walter should have thought more about the State's right to refute his evidence. Perhaps, the former UNLV graduate student instructor kind of needed a crash course in Criminal Procedure 101. This is the way it goes for the parties at Trial, Walter. There's the State's Case in Chief and next there's the Defendant's Case in Chief. You testified in the Defense Case. But Trial Evidence doesn't end then, Walter. After the Defense Case there's <u>rebuttal</u>! It's not over until it's over. Possibly you should have given a lot more attention to what the Prosecution might present in its REBUTTAL CASE, Walter. Or maybe you should have just deleted the part about *trying* to <u>alibi</u> <u>the</u> <u>car</u>. But it is what it is, correct?"

"Deciding to testify on your own behalf was a big decision. It's not a matter of trifling consequence to waive one's Fifth Amendment privilege against *self* incrimination, is it? But then, there's a common denominator between testifying <u>and</u> murdering. It's–your–choice! Let's not forget that."

"You're certainly not the first. Many before you have gone to the witness stand in their own defense. Some successfully – some unsuccessfully. Whatever the result has been, each time there's been a constant. What's going to happen once a tense Defendant settles into the witness chair is <u>never</u> totally predictable. He can prepare for the occasion. He can rehearse the event with his Counsel. But no one, that's right – <u>nobody</u> on the Defense Team knows precisely what will be **asked** by the Prosecutor. Despite the inestimable skills of your Counselors, they <u>aren't</u> psychic, Walter. They don't read minds, and reading tea leaves isn't very effective neither. So all anyone can do is his best, right?"

"That's what I'm trying to do right now. I'm trying to do my best as the representative of the State of Nevada in this Courtroom. From the witness stand you told us <u>exactly</u> *where* you traveled with the car you borrowed. You said your **memory** of the series of errands you ran, that is, *where* you drove and the <u>precise</u> *route* you drove the borrowed car to perform them was still very clear in your mind. You swore under oath that the information you provided us was <u>true</u> and <u>correct</u>. And I listened carefully to what you said, and I methodically wrote down every one of your *true* and *correct* words. Then just on the off chance my note taking had been flawed in some respect, I asked the very capable and experienced Court Reporter who graces the Courtroom to provide me with a verbatim transcript of your *true and correct* testimony. "

"Well Sir, no offense intended. I suppose I'm a skeptic by nature or maybe I'm paid the lunch pail pittance they give me to be skeptical. Whenever a witness testifies I'm thinking, 'Yeah, but I don't <u>really</u> know what the truth is. I <u>only</u> know what this witness is telling me it is.' Hence, anytime the veracity of a witnesses' words can be confirmed or refuted, I'm interested in having more investigation conducted. Rebuttal case investigation, as it were. And since your *true and correct* words had been so precise, and I give you credit for that, it was really quite a simple matter to either confirm or refute your truths!"

"I gave the tireless Homicide Detectives assigned to this matter a copy of the transcript of your testimony, and I asked them to perform a **test drive** to determine the <u>actual</u> distance you'd traveled with the borrowed car. They were happy to oblige my request.

The Detectives used their police car. They checked at police automotive to verify that the vehicle odometer was correctly calibrated. Then – <u>starting</u> at the owner's residence where *you said* you acquired the borrowed car, and continuing from that point to <u>every</u> site *you said* you went to in performing your series of errands, and proceeding to <u>your</u> apartment after your business matters had been completed, as *you said* you did, and <u>ending</u> back at the owner's house where *you said* you returned the car the next day – the Detectives drove their car to the <u>same</u> places following the <u>exact</u> route *you swore under oath* to be true. Testing the **veracity** of what you'd said."

"Thereafter, the Detectives contacted me at my office with the <u>odometer</u> *numbers* generated by their **veracity test drive**. What constitutes a good number and what constitutes a bad number is a relative matter, I suppose. When I was growing up my mother used to tell me that 36-24-36 were good numbers for a woman to have. When I was in college if the test score wasn't at least 90 it wasn't a very good number for a student to have, and I had lots of numbers that weren't very good. I've heard when three 6's are linked together that's a Satanic symbol. So, I suppose 666 is a bad number to some. I'm also thinking if you're 54 and you'd rather be 35, that constitutes an example of good and bad numbers. But that's enough trivial chatter."

"There's only one <u>relevant</u> number in the context of the State's REBUTTAL CASE. That's the **number** on the cop car odometer when the Detectives end their test! Here's the irony of our predicament. Whatever the number happens to be it's going to simultaneously be a <u>good</u> number and a <u>bad</u> number for the Parties in this case. That's always the way it is in a criminal trial if we're looking *small* through the prism of the <u>adversary system</u>. There's a winner and there's a loser.

Of course, if we're looking *large* through the prism of JUSTICE, when **the verdict is <u>just</u>**, *everybody wins*!"

"That is the vision of the State of Nevada. The people want **Justice**. And I can ask no more of the Jury than to do your best to render a **true and <u>just</u>** verdict! I believe the **<u>number</u>** on the cop car odometer will greatly assist you in your quest.

The number is –– TWELVE. That will be easy to remember, won't it. There are twelve members of the Jury. Three of you are alternates."

"I'll say it again, when the Homicide Detectives finish their **<u>veracity</u> <u>test</u> <u>drive</u>** the number appearing on the police car odometer is TWELVE! It's a nice round number. I like the sound of twelve, personally. But I guarantee it's a **<u>bad</u>** number for the Defense, and they <u>don't</u> like the sound of it. Proof, I'd say, why liars need to have good memories. I don't think the Defendant was expecting that he'd have to provide a specific recitation of *where* he went and the *route* he used to get to his *fictional* places."

"He claims he has a good memory of where he went. I believe he does, but he didn't share it with us in this Courtroom. I truly believe he knows exactly where he went Wednesday night, May 18, 1993, but we didn't hear any of that slip through his lips. What we heard is a fairy tale. Something Walter <u>made up</u> on the witness stand in this Courtroom during cross examination. That's alright. We have <u>independent</u> evidence of where he *actually* went with the borrowed car."

"Remember Marley, Walter? He's the owner of the car you borrowed. He's a casual friend of yours. However, he didn't know Karen. He doesn't know me or the Judge or any of the other witnesses. Marley has <u>no</u> interest whatever in the outcome of this case. Yet, he did sort of put two and two together when he heard a news report about a young woman's body being discovered in a shallow ravine off Tonopah Highway, the day before you returned the car. So, he contacted the Police Department."

"He tells the Homicide Detectives this occasion was the first time you'd asked to borrow the car. He thinks it's a little odd, and he's skeptical about your motive. He's wondering how far you really intended to drive it. Therefore, he checks the odometer mileage before you take it <u>and</u> after you return it."

"He testified to these same circumstances. But Marley <u>didn't</u> ask to be a witness. He <u>didn't</u> want to be a witness. He's been <u>subpoenaed</u> to testify to what he knows. In point of fact, he doesn't *know* much. However, what he does *know* **changes** the landscape in this Trial. It explains how Karen got from where she is murdered to where she is found!"

"Marley is a credible *witness*. He's thoughtful, articulate, and forthright. He's a citizen doing his duty pursuant to subpoena. He has no axe to grind with anyone. He gets nothing out of his Court appearance except a bad case of nerves. Listen up, it's not easy or pleasant being a *witness* in a Murder Trial. A *witness* has to come out of the shadows into the bright sunlight of public scrutiny. A *witness* becomes a potential target himself. The Courtroom is a <u>public</u> forum. The Accused has a right to a <u>public</u> Trial. A *witness* never knows precisely what <u>part</u> of the <u>public</u> will be present to hear him offer his sworn, perhaps damaging, testimony. So, Marley's neck is stuck out. And all he gets is a possible case of the hives and the satisfaction of telling what he knows."

"<u>**It's the numbers, Walter**</u>! THE NUMBERS **prove** you're a liar. THE NUMBERS prove you *tried* to conceal your <u>crime</u> by hauling the <u>corpus</u> to a drop site off Tonopah Highway in a borrowed <u>car</u>. An innocent man respects the sanctity of life. He doesn't ruthlessly change a ruby into rubbish. THE NUMBERS <u>prove</u> your **guilt**, Walter."

"It's *about* 25 miles from your digs to where you dropped her, depending on the specific route you took, Sir. That's a round trip of *about* 50 miles, Sir. You said you took Marley's car a distance of **twelve miles**. Excuse me, you didn't say that, the cop car odometer said that. And that's after the Detectives had clocked the exact mileage of what you said in your *sworn* testimony. Your <u>true</u> and <u>correct</u> description of where you drove the borrowed car between May 18 and May 20, 1993. Well, we're <u>not</u> having any of that, Walter. The actual *rubbish* in this case is your attempt to **alibi the car**. Your *sworn* testimony in that regard is <u>untrue</u> and <u>incorrect</u>. But then you weren't concerned about odometer readings back then, were you? You had one, single, abiding concern – **dispose of the body**!"

"To bad for you, Walter. The guy from whom you borrowed the car had his *own* abiding concern. He wanted to know <u>how</u> *far* you were driving it. He <u>was</u> concerned about odometer readings. And the

74

odometer reading on the car you borrowed said **fifty** – **fifty five miles** – NOT – **twelve miles**, Sir. GOTCHA!!"

I'm adding a brief post-script. The Trial Jury **did** find Walter <u>guilty</u> of Murder in the First Degree. The Defense files a Direct Appeal to the Nevada Supreme Court. After briefs are submitted by the respective Parties and the Trial Transcript has been thoughtfully reviewed by the Court, Walter's appeal <u>is</u> denied.

But that <u>didn't</u> end the Appellate Process. What an amazing system we have in the United States of America. If any nay-sayer ever doubted the legal magnanimity and wonder of this great land and its procedural safeguards, then let him take a casual gander at Appeal Rights. We give these characters who run afoul of the law **two bites** out of the Appellate Apple. There's Direct Appeal and there's also something called Collateral Appeal. Which seems to go on ad infinitum, in certain instances.

I suppose the **second bite** stems from a latent disdain for and mistrust of **Lawyers** and **the-work-Lawyers-do**. Accordingly, the second phase in the TWO-HEADED Appellate Process is triggered when a convicted criminal concludes he's been *done in* by his scurvy Lawyer. The argument at this stage of the proceedings being: it's <u>not</u> the Jury's *fault* I was convicted, and it's not the Judge's *fault* I was convicted. **My Lawyer did it**. THE FAULT lies in my Lawyer. **He** <u>didn't</u> properly represent me.

Thus, every convicted criminal, who has the hankering to do so and nearly *all* of them have a hankering to do so – since nobody but a lunatic likes incarceration, **fires** his Trial Lawyer or asks the Court to **fire** his Trial Lawyer. Why? Because the convicted criminal dutifully explains: "I am going to allege INEFFECTIVE REPRESENTATION BY MY TRIAL COUNSEL." Wheee! It's a fresh start.

A <u>different</u> Lawyer is **hired** by the convicted criminal or by the Court if the convicted criminal is indigent. This clears the way for Collateral Appeal. The logic behind it all is impeccable. The Trial Lawyer is now behind the eight ball. The worm has turned. He's the one accused, and he <u>can't</u> be the one representing the convicted criminal when he's being <u>accused</u> of *professional misconduct* by the convicted criminal. There's a clear **conflict of interest**. Will the successor Lawyer step forward please?

Walter pursues the same course of conduct. He submits a Petition for Post Conviction Relief alleging ineffective representation. Hence, his Trial Lawyer is out and his Collateral Appeal Lawyer is in. His Trial Lawyer has gone from being the good guy to the bad guy in his Petition. The Defendant's Petition is scheduled for hearing at the Trial Court level. The District Attorney's Office file its Answer To The Petition For Post Conviction Relief. An evidentiary hearing is scheduled by the Court.

Various witnesses are called to support the Defense Petition, not least of which is Walter. He steps forward, imperfectly in sync with his successor Lawyer, determined to trash his Trial Lawyer. It matters not that Defense Trial Counsel is an advocate of renown who has tried hundreds of cases, an advocate of genuine integrity, and an advocate who has invested hundreds of hours in the defense of his client. That was then – he lost. Now it's the Collateral Appeal phase – which he hopes to win.

Grudgingly, I'm prompted again to give Walter a degree of credit for his performance in Court. He's intelligent, well prepared, and articulates his positions with a certain level of eloquence. I think the hearing was therapeutic for him. The Trial Process is an extremely frustrating experience to a losing Defendant. The Post Conviction Hearing gave Walter an opportunity to do some venting. He fully exploited his opportunity. What he had to say he said effectively. I'm convinced when he finished he believed his proffer had carried the day.

The fleeting encounter remains rather vivid to me. When Walter left the witness stand his stride toward Counsel Table carried him close to me. He looked directly at me. I could have averted my gaze, but instead I stared back. Our eyes locked for an instant. Two protagonists measuring the other.

Walter reached Counsel Table. Just before he brushed past me to his seat he gave me a slight smile – perhaps more grimace than grin, lifted his hand, casually extended his index finger, and said in a tone of vindication and so quietly it was little more than a whisper, "Mr. Harmon – GOTCHA."

It's a brave moment of braggadocio. Walter's Petition didn't prevail. But I admire his plucky persona, and appreciate him remembering something I'd said in Rebuttal Argument. Quite a bit of Attorney rhetoric bounces off it recipient like rain water off a duck's back.

Is There a Doctor in the House

"**There was** –– and O! how many sorrows crowd
Into these two brief words!" (Sir Walter Scott,
"*The Lord of the Isles*," Conclusion)

CHAPTER 5

MARI IS KANSAS BORN AND BRED – farm raised. A vintage product of the farm belt. Her core values reflect the environment of her maturation. They are deeply rooted in soil, family, religion, and compassion. She has a strong work ethic, and an abiding service ethic for her family, friends, and any person with special needs.

There's keen recognition of God's hand in the natural order of things when life begins in farming. A sense of partnership with the Almighty. A farmer's daughter may plant and cultivate, but she knows by itself that's not enough. A farmer's daughter acts from faith. She knows the elements must be temperate, and the heavens must be generous with abundant, timely rainfall to ensure bounteous harvest. There is a palpable interdependence between God and a farm family.

Grace is amazing on farmland. It's above and below and in every horizon to experience, to sense, and to enjoy. Farm days are full of simplicity and beauty and gratitude. Minds are full of truths of the soil, truths of scripture, and other great books. Hearts are full of love and respect for the implicit goodness of others. Stomachs are full of delicious, nutritious, home cooked meals. Prepared from traditional family recipes. The imagination of a farm bred child reaches high into the blue sky – and beyond.

There is paradox on the farm. A farm family may be poor yet well off. Life is both frugal and abundant – in the farmhouse and on the farmland. The total process imbues, shapes, and fortifies moral and spiritual mores. There's a richness, a brightness, and a perspective on the farm that is uniquely educational and tacitly expansive.

Mari is raised on a small farm outside Humboldt, Kansas. She's a cheerful, inquisitive, gifted, childhood sunflower in her formative years. Graduating as the buxom valedictorian of her highschool at age sixteen. She graduates from Kansas University School of Medicine at twenty four. Indeed, life brims with high expectation in her golden years on the plains.

She's a native Kansan with a Jayhawk diploma. Thus, it's not surprising that Mari's professional career begins at St. Joseph Hospital in Wichita, Kansas. She serves at St. Joe for more than ten years while specializing in emergency room medicine. Becoming a charter-member physician in Emergency Room and Trauma Center practice. Something fateful happens at St. Joe's. She meets Chuck. Is he heaven-sent or straight from hell?

Eventually, Mari partners with another doctor in opening a number of Emergency Medical Centers in Wichita. Life is good for Kansas Mari. She's establishes a nice professional niche for herself. The land of her birth is a land promising financial reward and a comfortable lifestyle that's been her dream.

She's off the farm. Early morning chores and the milk barn, planting and weeding, the sweat, the harvest, canning, quilting, and gentle merger of her soul with nature and changing seasons is past – though not forgotten. The golden haze of farm days will always lie tranquil in her remembrance. The connection to family is a tie that binds. Close association with her family is a necessary condition.   But it's not all bliss for Mari. Something **is** missing. The Doctor is *in* the emergency room for her patients when crisis beckons. The Doctor is there when family members want her loving care. But who takes care of the Doctor in the way she wants, no – needs to be cared for? Mari yearns for romance. The Doctor needs to be *in* for love! And when the Doctor is *in* is there a lover in the house?

Well, there's Chuck. It an on-going thing with Chuck. Sort of on-again-off- again with Chuck. They've dated for eleven months, and are twice engaged. However, it **is** on-again long enough for Chuck and Mari to be married in August, 1980. A union made in heaven, or an earthbound disunion of marital discord? A more dispassionate assessment than Mari is evidently able to render would have called for an even longer period of courtship. Long enough to really get to know this guy. Yet love chooses to be blind, it seems. I've always liked this sage advice:

"Keep thy eyes wide open before marriage,
and half shut afterwards." (Benjamin Franklin,
Poor Richard's Almanack, 1738)

Chuck is a mixed bag. But I suppose every human has his complexities. It's not particularly useful to press anyone into a mold of preconceived notion. We are what we are. It's the square peg round hole thing. Chuck is an ex-cop. However, he has a preference for the fast lane. He's not satisfied with the day to day grind of police work, nor with a police salary. His tenure from 1969 – 1971 with the Wichita Police Department lasts nineteen days short of two years.

He's charming, materialistic and, some would say, cunning. For example, there's a curious chain of events that occurs during a previous marriage. Is it an aberration or a declaration of his character? He purchases a large amount of life insurance and stages a fake drowning in a shallow Missouri river. The prior wife submits a claim to the insurance company. It would probably have been paid but for a slight indiscretion. Chuck is the insured and he *lives*. His arrest on another matter establishes the duplicity of the bogus insurance scheme. The ploy fails, but it's indicative of a sinister propensity.

What occurs in November 1979 is troublesome. Soon after he and Mari begin dating, Chuck either encourages her or, at the least, acquiesces in Mari's decision to apply for a personal life insurance coverage change. Two prior policies are converted into single coverage of $55,000.00. Chuck is a beneficiary. He *later* argues the conversion makes him an **irrevocable** beneficiary. Evidently, Chuck learns something from the phony drowning escapade. He comes to realize the *insured* has to be <u>dead</u> as a condition precedent to payoff. Therefore, it's a tad awkward for him to be <u>both</u> beneficiary <u>and</u> *the insured*. But now there's Mari –– poor Mari.

An event happens on Thanksgiving Day 1980 that contradicts what Mari is. It turns her life upside down. The Kansas farmer's daughter with the Kansas Jayhawk degree in medicine, endowed with core values rooted in rich farm soil, loving family, devout religion, and compassionate service, <u>moves</u> to Las Vegas, Nevada. It's a change of venue inspired by Chuck. His britches have grown too big for life *with* Mari in her native Kansas. That is too *close* to meddlesome in-laws.

It's undoubtedly a decision made contrary to her better judgment. But she's a married woman now. She's made her bed and she'll sleep in it out west in the glitzy desert terrain of sin city. She'll rue the day of this uprooting. She's like a fish out of water in the dry heat and tawdry casino environment of Vegas.

That said, there's service to be rendered anywhere on earth. Kansas born and bred to the art of medicine, Mari remains devoted to her profession. She follows the promptings of her professional Oath and of her medicinal skills by going to work in the Emergency Room at Southern Nevada Memorial Hospital.

> "I SWEAR...I will keep this Oath and this stipulation...
> I will follow that system of regimen which, according
> to my ability and judgment, I consider for the *benefit*
> of my patients, and *abstain* from whatever is deleterious
> and mischievous...With *purity* and with *holiness* I will
> pass my life and practice my Art..." (*The Hippocratic
> Oath*, Harvard Classics Volume 38)

Mari works unceasingly for the *benefit* of her patients. She pursues her task and her Oath with serene professionalism at the Hospital. She's tireless and adroit and empathic in the Emergency Room. Her associates at SNMH respect her and her patients love her. Mari *abstains* from whatever is deleterious and mischievous toward others. She practices her art and passes her life in Las Vegas with the optimal *purity* and *holiness* that is attainable by a mortal being.

Unfortunately, her compassionate service isn't destined to last long. There is a super-intervening incident. A trump card is played in Vegas. **Mari is <u>murdered</u>**! She thrives at work, but she <u>doesn't</u> thrive at home. She's short and overweight, she's over insured, she's thirty nine, and she's dead October 25, 1982 – long before her time. Her marriage has been terminal from the start. One party marries for love, the other marries for money. Crude, lewd, filthy lucre is not a nurturing bed for marital bliss nor marital longevity.

Is there a doctor in the house? **No**, the doctor lies dead on the floor of her master bedroom. She's <u>not</u> lying in the bed she's made now. Her body is sprawled on the carpet <u>next</u> to her bed.

ONCE **there was** a daughter – Kansas born and bred and farm raised. Once **there was** a time of amazing grace, above – below – within every horizon, for youthful rural Mari. **No more**. Once **there was** a cheerful, inquisitive, gifted, childhood sunflower. Once **there was** *imagination* that reached high into blue sky – and beyond. **No more – not ever again in <u>mortality</u>**!

Once **there was** a brash sixteen year old highschool valedictorian of her graduating class. Once **there was** a proud twenty four year old graduate of the University of Kansas School of Medicine. **No more**. Once **there was** *a mind* full of truths of the soil, truths of scripture – and great medical books. Once **there was** *a heart* full of love and respect for the implicit goodness of her patients. **No more**.

Once **there was** a skilled emergency room doctor at St. Joseph in Wichita and Southern Nevada Memorial Hospital in Las Vegas. **No more**. Her memory lingers, but she's gone. Vegas makes some. It is the downfall of others.

Once **there was** a hopeful wedding day in August 1980. **Not anymore**. Mari has been married for slightly more than two years. Reality drains the union from "I thee wed." Marriage pains obliterate the hope of wedding vows – and life!

> "**There <u>was</u>** –– and O! how many sorrows crowd
> Into these two brief words!" (ibid.)

HANDS: what amazing *facility* they have for grasping and lifting, for caress and comfort, for performance and creation. **Hands** are the *wonder* of artists and sculptors. **Hands** *script* the notes of great musical scores, they *write* classic books of literature, and compelling *words* of novels. The *grip* of **hands** produces fast balls and curve balls and knuckle balls. The dexterity of **hands** *empowers* gifted pianists to play Concertos. **Hands** *rock* the cradles of little babies. The **hands** of skilled neurosurgeons *execute* delicate surgeries with precision. **Hands** are the *tools* of miracles.

But LIFE is full of paradox. HANDS are paradoxical. **Hands** are instruments of *creation* <u>and</u> they are instruments of *destruction*. **Hands** *hit* people. **Hands** *swing* swords, *thrust* bayonets, and *shoot* guns. **Hands** *drop* bombs. **Hands** *steer* planes into tall buildings. Illegal *use* of **hands** chokes and murders!

A *pair* of cruel hands *choke* Mari to death. She dies of asphyxia due to **manual** strangulation. There are minor contusions, abrasions, and a one inch scratch on her neck. There is extensive injury to structures of her neck. The small muscles controlling elevation and action of the voice box have hemorrhaged considerable. The thyroid cartilage, commonly described as the voice box, is fractured. There is hemorrhage in the connective tissue between the trachea, or airway, and the esophagus. There are multiple flame-like or streaking hemorrhages of the inner lining of the voice box. Also, there are quite a number of small round hemorrhages in the epiglottis. That's the trap door structure that prevents us from inhaling everything we swallow.

Chuck is the immediate target of the investigation. He's detained briefly on the day of the crime. Then released. The Homicide Detective seeks additional connecting evidence. Successful Prosecution often requires endless patience. It's almost ten years before Chuck goes to Trial Court. But it's worth the wait. However, the *wait* will have been fruitless unless the **prosecution** is conducted with the proper *attitude* and the proper *preparation*

The great Harvard Psychologist William James said, "The greatest discovery of my generation is that **you can change your circumstances by changing your attitudes of mind.**"

I'm a firm proponent of that principle. *Proper attitude does change circumstances!* Being **an effective Prosecutor**, a <u>dynamic</u> <u>advocate</u> <u>for</u> <u>justice</u>, probably won't come from our Law School experience. It certainly won't come from a class textbook. It won't come from reading State Codes of Criminal Statutes, nor from a perusal of the Common

Law. It won't come from passing the Bar, as important as that step is in the progress of a fledgling Lawyer. It won't descend like manna from heaven immediately after a Deputy District Attorney has taken his Prosecutorial Oath. It's not something that can be conferred upon a rookie Deputy DA by an experienced Prosecutor who already has it. It doesn't come from a paycheck, though every Prosecutor wants to earn a comfortable salary. It won't come during the first day on the job, nor the second, nor necessarily in the first year. It *may* not come after years of advocacy. Some practitioners never become **effective Prosecutors**.

Some highly intelligent, highly qualified persons *never* realize their potential – *never* **really** capture the Spirit of Prosecution! Why? Because the indomitable spirit which makes a practitioner of criminal law an **effective Prosecutor** comes from inside! It comes from the Prosecutor's gut, from having a *PROPER ATTITUDE*. It comes from his heart and his core values. It comes from focus and deliberate prioritization. It's who the Prosecutor wants to become! Is it a matter of garnering a little Courtroom experience while passing through the system or is it a career – a passionate enterprise of the soul?

The Spirit of Prosecution is a burning *desire* to serve the community in which we live. It's a fervent *commitment* to achieve justice in the cases we're assigned – striving to truly be *servants of justice*. It's a steadfast *empathy* for our victims and our victim's families. An *appreciation* of the tragedy that lies in lives prematurely catapulted beyond the veil.

It's taking *every* case seriously and personally. It's taking *full* responsibility for being defacto counsel for the departed – those whose lips are sealed by murder. In a sense, it's *making* Prosecution our life! It's *acquiring* a solemn respect for the nobility of our Profession. It's having an abiding *conviction* that the cause of a Prosecutor is righteous.

This is the **attitude** that *changes* circumstances and **wins** the Cases that *should* be won! This is the **attitude**, after ten years of avoidance, that seeks to *change* Chuck's circumstance from scoff-law to inmate convicted of First Degree Murder. But it's NEVER easy!

I've mentioned that the Law is a jealous mistress. Well, she's a green-eyed monster and she's a **stressful** paramour too. In so many words, the dictionary calls stress a pressure or tension exerted on a material object; a demand on physical, mental, and emotional energy causing a degree of distress.

Trial work is STRESSFUL! I use the capital letters advisedly. A Trial Lawyer isn't involved in a powder puff profession. Murder Trials are particularly stressful. I won't speak for others. I see the Courtroom world through the prism of my personal experience. Murder Trials are damn hard – and indescribably stressful. I ought to know. For the last eighteen years of my tenure with the Clark County District Attorney's Office I handled Murder Trials exclusively – with a single exception.

During Trial the **tension** exerted on that material object called a Prosecutor is immense. I suppose we ought to get that from the word. A Trial in a legal sense is a Judicial determination of issues between parties by a Judge – with or without a Jury. A TRIAL in a life sense is a challenging affliction or experience that causes hardship or trouble, but may on occasion – produce growth and great satisfaction.

A Murder Trial embraces both of these aspects.

Responsibility weighs heavily on the People's Man. He's the representative of the State of Nevada and a valiant hedge between communities and crime. The Philistines of crime are, potentially, always at the gate.

He's the Victim's Man as well. In a very real sense, a Prosecutor represents the Victim in Murder Cases. Someone has to do it. Certainly, the victim is never around to have any personal say-so about the proceedings and about justice for the violently deported. The Prosecutor must necessarily fill the void. He must speak for the victim. He must advocate for the one whose lips have been sealed. He must prepare thoroughly, subpoena prudently, examine intelligently, be tactically astute, and passionately argumentative! He shoulders the *legal* burden of proof and the *moral* burden of proof for keeping the Jury mindful of the Victim.

The physical, mental, and emotional **demands** imposed upon the Prosecutor are grave. Perhaps, exacting a serious toll on physical and mental health. Most definitely, exacting a significant toll on emotional frame of mind. During Trial the hours are long and tedious. It's not nine to five. It's more like eight to midnight. And it's not forty hours a week. It's more like ninety eight hours a week. That's right, even a Prosecutor needs some time in the rack. It's not 24/7, though it approaches 14/7.

Furthermore, case thoughts always hover like scavengers within the inner most recesses of Prosecutive cognizance.

SUCCESS is the progeny of major investments in time. **Reading** Police reports, witness statements, pleadings, legal briefs, Defense discovery, transcripts of prior testimony, supplemental investigative reports, and daily Trial Transcripts is time consuming. **Writing** legal briefs, outlines of Direct and Cross Examination for Trial witnesses, and Summation arguments requires analytical thought and loads of time.

The jealous Mistress of Murder Trials is possessive – and petulant. Nothing about Trial work is effortless. It's like pulling hen's teeth. Which isn't surprising when you think about it. Nobody really wants to be in Trial Court. The Defendant sure as hell doesn't want to be sitting at counsel table as the Accused. Unless he's represented by a Public Defender, his Counsel doesn't want to be in Court. He'd much rather have the fee-meter running as he conducts business with clients in his office. Trial time is lost time to many successful Lawyers. They lose money when they're in Trial. As for Witnesses, they don't flock to the Courthouse because they're motivated by intellectual curiosity and altruistic hearts. Ninety five percent of witnesses are in Trial Court because they've been *subpoenaed* to be there. That's because they don't want to be there. They'd rather be anywhere than perched on the witness stand offering testimony in a Murder Trial. They're not stupid. They know being a State's Witness does on occasion provide reasons for retribution.

So, there's the on going petulance of **stress**. The Judge, the Jurors, the Witnesses and the Attorneys aren't addicted to stress. To the person they hate stress. Too bad, stress is endemic to Courtrooms. Trial terrain is stress terrain. And no one is more susceptible to stress than those *who earn their living by the sweat of their tongues.*

Trial stress certainly isn't less when a Lawyer stands to address the Jury. The pressure to speak appropriately and effectively is ever present. There are legal guidelines that put remarks made to Jurors within a particular framework of dos and don'ts. However, beyond that legal framework, the content of statements made to a Jury must be tailored to the facts and circumstances and nuances of a specific case. It's tough to generalize, and unwise to suggest there is a *canned approach* that works all the time. **One size** <u>does</u> **not** fit all. Consider the OPENING STATEMENT.

There is no *magic mantra*. <u>No</u> every–case–all–the–time–formula for success in an Opening Statement. Each case is unique. Each case is a clear sky composed of unprecedented facts and a different set of legal issues. Each case requires a *resourceful* response to the <u>particular</u> evidence and issues at bar. An effective Prosecutor isn't a copy cat. He finds a style of addressing juries that's comfortable to him. He tailors his **style** and his **words** to his *case* and his *personality* and his *skills!*

Good Opening Statements are relative. Yet, they are extremely important. An **Opening Statement** introduces the Jury to their Prosecutor and to his Case. A Prosecutor should **never** *waive* it and **never** fail to diligently *prepare* for it! Most successful Trial Lawyers say <u>properly</u> selected juries and <u>properly</u> presented Opening Statements <u>do more</u> than anything else to achieve successful case results.

The Jury Selection process will have been an emotional roller coaster for the panel of prospective jurors. Most will feel a sense of pride in having been picked to serve, but will feel somewhat intimidated by the responsibility of having to serve. They will be *extremely* anxious to learn about the nature of the case. <u>Never</u> <u>again</u> in the proceedings will their *interest* be so keen, their *focus* so intense, and their *minds* so impressionable! Their hearing will *hang* on <u>every</u> word of the Court and the Advocates.

DO NOT **disappoint them!** The Jurors need <u>proper</u> reassurance. They need <u>proper</u> information concerning the case. They need to have the issues <u>properly</u> identified. They need to know where the <u>proper</u> path to *justice* lies. The Jury needs to *know* to whom they should look for <u>proper</u> guidance – <u>who</u> to *trust*. And the Jury requires it at the beginning. Right out of the chute! The **Opening Statement** *keynotes* the trial. It <u>establishes</u> or <u>erodes</u> credibility. That is the Prosecutor's call!!

Actually, there is one sure-fire way to <u>erode</u> prosecutorial credibility. The path that *never – never – never* can be taken is OVERSTATING the evidence. An <u>effective</u> Prosecutor **does <u>not</u>** engage in <u>verbal</u> <u>hyperbole</u>! He **<u>never</u> exaggerates** what the evidence will show. A <u>credible</u> Prosecutor **doesn't deliberately** make *evidentiary promises* he <u>can't</u> keep. Further, <u>prudence</u> being the better part of Courtroom valor, he **refrains** from promising the introduction of evidence that has a *dubious predicate* for admissibility. Ordinarily, he **does** **not** promise the production of specific named witnesses *unless* they are crucial and cooperative to the Prosecution's cause.

If the Prosecutor promises the Jury something is coming, it better be on the case-in-chief locomotive! Otherwise, **the Prosecutive credibility** takes a serious hit at a time in the Trial when the Prosecutor needs to be standing tall!

The responsibility of passing judgment is not an easy task! An astute Prosecutor *always* keeps that truth in mind. It should be a *constant* source of motivation when he presents his Opening Statements. An ounce of prevention being worth a pound of cure, right? The "ounce of prevention" in this instance constituting the preparation and presentation of an effective Opening Statement.

The "pound of cure" being avoidance of the dreaded retrial when the job *isn't* done right the first time!

There are no guarantees, of course. Most veteran Prosecutors have experienced the gut-retching frustration of deadlocked juries. Abraham Lincoln wryly observed, "A jury too frequently has at least one member more ready to hang the panel than to hang the traitor."

There is some basis in fact to Lincoln's droll comment. The State of Nevada requires unanimity in it's Jury Verdicts. And it's never easy, regardless of the case, to get all twelve members of the Jury to *agree* on their verdict! That said, this Courtroom nugget is solid gold: A Jury is convinced of the *righteousness* of a charge in direct proportion to the *amount* of understanding and appreciation it has of the evidence at the precise **moment** it's presented. A cogent, accurately presented Opening Statement is the *case road map* that makes this feasible.

The Prosecutor must have the evidence and the issues succinctly set forth in a carefully crafted outline. This is not a time to be *perfunctory* in preparation nor *disorganized* in presentation. The Prosecutor **needs** to make a *dynamic* first impression. He **needs** to *demonstrate* firm conviction in the veracity of his case. He **needs** to show the Jury that the Prosecution is in control. A Prosecutor accomplishes this by exuding a confident manner. **Confidence is the product of preparation!** The Prosecutor must know his evidence and his issues. It's imperative for an

effective Prosecutor to have *relentlessly* studied and *absorbed* the facts of his case <u>prior</u> to delivering the Opening Statement.

There is <u>no</u> substitute for *thorough* **preparation**. *Every* **Opening Statement** must be predicated upon thoughtful, meticulous, meaningful **preparation!** Preparation is the *seed bed* of successful Prosecution. The hallmark of zealous pursuit of Murder Defendants is *a strong work ethic*!

The substance of an **Opening Statement** will typically have four parts: An <u>introduction</u>, A <u>statement of the evidence</u> the Prosecution *expects* to introduce, An <u>explanation of legal principles</u> *applicable* to the case, and *cogent* <u>closing remarks</u>.

A dynamic champion of justice **closes strong**. He stands erect, maintaining direct eye contact with the Jury Panel. He <u>tells</u> <u>them</u> *earnestly* and <u>without</u> *equivocation*, that the State's evidence **will prove** beyond a reasonable doubt that the **Defendant is guilty** of <u>Murder in the First Degree!</u> **He Makes that promise to them**. Then he *REVISITS* the issue in his <u>SUMMATION</u>!

Why? Because the Prosecutor is the people's man. Therefore, he needs to tell the Jury he's **kept** his promise to them. <u>And</u> because *a Dynamic Champion of Justice* wouldn't be standing before the Jury on <u>this</u> <u>particular</u> <u>case</u> **if** he didn't *believe* the Defendant IS guilty!

I often used **pertinent quotations** to provide a *rhetorical framework* for my comments to Jurors. I firmly believe in the imperative of **starting** *strong* and **ending** *strong*! I liked to start Opening Statements with <u>dramatic</u> <u>word</u> <u>pictures</u>!

It had been such a long wait to get *justice for Mari* and for *Mari's family*. I wanted *my tongue* to come out *sweating* from the **get go**. These are <u>some</u> of the words I chose for Choker Chuck –––

"May it please the Court, Counsel for the Defendant, Ladies and Gentleman of the Jury: **Life is frail**. Pascal once observed, 'Between us and hell or heaven –– <u>there</u> <u>is</u> <u>nothing</u> <u>but</u> <u>life</u>, which of *all* things is the *frailest*.'[Blaise Pascal, *Pensees*, Sect. III, No.213] Monday morning – October 15, 1982 – between *Mari* and hell or heaven – <u>there</u> <u>was</u> <u>nothing</u> <u>but</u> <u>life</u>, which of *all* things <u>was</u> the *frailest*. *Mari* <u>was</u> manually strangled to **death** inside the master bedroom of her home about 6:00 a.m. There was <u>no</u> evidence of breaking and entry.

"A murder case proves the *frailty* of mortal life. It <u>proves</u> life on this earth may end <u>abruptly</u>, <u>violently</u>, <u>unpredictably</u> – <u>senselessly</u>!! For life may end at the hands of a killer who has decided to *number* the days of his victim.

"Thirty nine year old *Mari* <u>is</u> a murder victim. She <u>was</u> a professional woman and a wife. She also carried substantial life insurance *protection*. [Now that's a misnomer if I ever heard one.] The morning of her death she <u>was</u> planning to fly <u>with</u> her husband to Wichita for a reunion with family and friends. Evidently, only <u>one</u> of them was enthusiastic about the trip.

"*Mari* awakened at 4:00 a.m. She showered, dressed, and had a bowl of cereal. Placed the suitcases in the trunk and the dog's cage in the back seat of their maroon Ford Thunderbird. But she didn't go anywhere in the T Bird. She didn't board a jet plane. She didn't get to eat lunch. She didn't get to see her family and her friends in Kansas. She <u>leaves</u> her house in a *hearse*.

"Chuck walks across the street to the residence of a Nevada Supreme Court Justice. He reports finding his wife lying unconscious in their bedroom when he returns from a trip to a neighborhood gas station. Police respond. They observe *Mari's* body lying on the floor in the master bedroom. She is fully dressed – wearing a blue blouse, a blue sweater, blue pants, knee high nylons, and brown shoes. Blood and mucous are coming from her nose and a white foamy substance is coming from her mouth. Her face appears red and flushed and swollen.

"Poor *Mari* is pronounced dead at 8:45 a.m. ....

"**Who** is the killer of *Mari*? –––the assailant who callously, maliciously, and abruptly ended a human life?–––**Who** is the man with the <u>cruel</u> hands who strangled a decent woman senseless in her home–––in **their** bedroom? **Who** is the man who violently <u>betrayed</u> his marital vows––––for **monetary** gain?

"The evidence in this case <u>will</u> <u>prove</u> beyond a reasonable doubt that **HE–IS–HER–HUSBAND**! 'Oh, how many torments lie in the small circle of a wedding- ring!' [Colley Cibber, *The Double Gallant*, Act I, Sc.2]

"**He** *thought* he'd gotten away with murder. **He's** *thinking* after ten years there isn't anything anybody can do about it. HE'S A KILLER——— **He** is in this Courtroom———I am looking at him———**He is Chuck D———**"

Chuck has been the *person of interest* from the inception of this investigation. He has *presence* at the crime scene, therefore he has *opportunity*. He has *motive*, and he has significant *gaffes* in his statement to Police. But he hasn't been formally charged. The years pass. It becomes almost a decade since the murder of poor *Mari*. Justice seems frustrated. Skewed by circumstances and long overdue. The fluttering Bird of Justice has had a lengthy, arduous flight from that somber day when *Mari* <u>missed</u> her flight.

Fortunately, there is no Statute of Limitations to abort a murder probe. The gig is up – finally. There's a breakthrough. Additional evidence surfaces. Police learn Chuck has committed a major *gaffe*. It happens 2-3 years after the crime. At last his Teflon persona has something *stick*. It takes only a few moments of indiscretion conceived by the equally lubricious tandem of *alcohol* <u>and</u> *arrogance*. Eventually, there's a call from Kansas. CHUCK HAS CONFESSED!

Chuck is charged with Open Murder. The case fast-tracks through the system. An eight-woman, four-man Jury hears the case. And the investigation that spanned almost 10 <u>years</u> doesn't take nearly as long to try. The Trial lasts 10 <u>days</u>.

The Prosecution has the burden of proof in a Criminal Trial. Naturally, Prosecutors <u>do</u> <u>not</u> shrink from their burden. It is <u>most</u> appropriate that the entity bringing a criminal charge bear the responsibility of going forward with the evidentiary proof! But a procedural *anomaly* follows as a result which is certainly not inconsequential. Because the Law imposes the **burden** of proving <u>each</u> criminal charge beyond a reasonable doubt, the Prosecutor has the *opportunity* to argue <u>twice</u> in SUMMATION. He opens final argument and be closes final argument. His last trip to the lectern is called <u>rebuttal</u> argument.

While the Prosecutive **burden of proof** should not be minimized it should not be maximized beyond reason neither. An important role for the Prosecutor during Final Argument is to <u>educate</u> the Jury that the Prosecution's **burden** is not proof to an absolute certainty. If a Prosecutor's feet are put to *that* kind of fire, there probably aren't many propositions he can ever satisfactorily prove. The Trier of Fact must understand that the Prosecutive burden is **Proof beyond a Reasonable Doubt**. No more! No less!

REBUTTAL ARGUMENT is a high point for me. And I'm thinking," **Is this a great profession or what**?" On what other occasion and under what other circumstance in this life is a person – dead bang, flat out, one hundred percent guaranteed – he will get the **final word** in an argument? Certainly, it ain't gonna happen at home with *the wife*. And it's not going to happen in an emotional tete-a-tete with a teenage son or daughter. The law degree doesn't cut any ice in such a forum. Oh, where is the respect for dear ole Dad?

However, there is *a time and place of refuge* for him **if** he's a Prosecutor. It's the Courthouse on the day he delivers his **rebuttal argument**. Ah, sweet mystery of life. This is living large. It's a chance to do some truly impassioned venting. On that day in Court for a few *shining minutes*, you're the king of the hill. No, more than that. **You're the king of the world**. Firing off the zingers you've saved, with a **Judge** enforcing the rule of rebuttal. **Sealing the lips of your opponents** – except for a few feeble, sputtering objections. Believe me. It's an idyllic experience! Better than a steak dinner. Better than a banana split. Better than dark chocolate that is 65 % cocoa. *Almost* better than ––– . Well, we won't go there.

"**Evil** is *easy* for a husband whose six feet two, two hundred forty five pounds and she is five feet two – IF he's alone with her, IF his eyes see only green backs as he sees her, and IF he chooses to be morally bankrupt. What happened to *Mari* is evil. She is murdered in her home, presumably her place of refuge and safety. Sadly, serenity at home is a *rebuttal presumption*. And it's a sinister rebuttal that frequently rears it's ugliness. Once **there was Mari**. What torment must be encapsulated in those *three* brief words.

"Murder is awful anywhere. But for a gentle, decent, god-fearing physician to be murdered in her home by the one who has sworn to be her protector is despicable! It's a circumstance that decent people find hard to conceptualize. **Her husband** wants to kill her. **His vow** to love and cherish and protect has become a wicked vow to destroy. He subdues her in the privacy of their home in the early morning hours. Then with the full weight of his massive frame pressing her into the carpet, he places his craven hands around her neck and begins to squeeze – tighter and tighter – until she's dead. Leaving her lifeless next to the bed where the *union* of hand and heart is – theoretically – consummated.

"It's shameful. He made his bed. Now he refuses to *lie* in it! This marriage has been a <u>sham</u> to him. But he won't be backward about *lying* to the Police.

"1. **A sham alibi** – There is <u>no</u> alibi for *Mari's* murder. It's phony. Make believe. Pretending – just like his marriage. Chuck says he was gone when the crime occurred. He says he went to an Exxon Station to gas up the Thunderbird and was out of the house for 15-20 minutes.

"He did go to the station. The issue isn't *whether* he went. The issue is *why* he went! Does he go for <u>gas</u> or does he go for an <u>alibi</u>? The owner often sees Chuck, and he confirms that he came by between 6:00 and 7:00 a.m. on the date in question. He's a retired New York law enforcement officer. He testifies that Chuck wasn't present at his station for more than *5 minutes*. The Station is 1/10th of a mile from the crime scene. It's a thirty second trip each way. Throwing in an extra minute of grace time makes Chuck *seven minutes* absentee.

"It's an upper middle class neighborhood that residents describe as quiet, peaceful, and crime free. There is no history of problems. Parents consider their children safe. A witness who has lived in close proximity to the crime scene for nineteen years calls it a "perfect neighborhood. He sleeps with the doors unlocked."

"Now really, what is the likelihood that <u>stranger</u> danger lurks in this quiet, residential area between 6-7:00 O'clock in the morning. The sun's rising. This is a Monday. People are rising and moving about. Walking dogs. Picking up the morning papers. Getting a few puffs on their coffin nails. Children are getting ready for school. They'll soon be headed to their bus stops. So, how likely is it really, that some stranger who is danger *randomly* breaks into a house and becomes so *randomly* enraged that he *randomly* strangles an unoffending woman to death. Then immediately leaves the *random* house and his *random* victim just as *mysteriously* as he enters. Leaving behind no evidence of <u>forced</u> <u>entry</u>, no evidence of <u>ransacking</u>, no evidence of <u>sexual</u> <u>assault</u>, and nothing

<u>stolen</u>. Everything inside is intact – except *Mari*. Where's the motive? It's like somebody's thinking, "I believe I'll just go into this house over here this morning. I'll kill somebody just for the hell of it, and after that I'll go to breakfast."

"Further, this dastardly act happens within a *random* time frame of 6-7 minutes when hubbie just happens to be gassing up at the local *self* serve petrol place. How convenient for Chuck. How inconvenient for *Mari*. But that my friends, is a very slender window of opportunity. And <u>nobody</u> is any the wiser. The *stranger danger* isn't sighted entering or leaving by a solitary soul. Nor do sounds emanate from the *random* house indicative of <u>foul play</u>. There are <u>no</u> startled, hysterical screams as the miscreant enters. NOTHING!

"Well, definitely there is *danger* present in the neighbor this October morning 1982. But it <u>isn't</u> stranger danger. It's much more deadly. More focused. More loathsome. It's *domestic danger*. It's home grown *domestic terrorism*. The *enemy* is inside the house. He's <u>strange</u> *danger*. A husband whose familiarity with his wife has bred contempt for her. A husband whose an ex-cop. Who has training in Judo and self defense, and who has taught these disciplines in an Academy. A husband who has converted the garage into an exercise room. Complete with a weight bench, bar bells, and other conditioning equipment – which he uses regularly. A husband whose fallen out of love if he ever was in love. A husband whose forgotten his job description. He's slithered from *protector* to *evictor*! It's a husband who <u>doesn't</u> need to go to Kansas this morning to visit his wife's family because there <u>isn't</u> a *Mari* anymore. A husband who <u>doesn't</u> need to put more gas in the car this morning because there isn't a trip to the airport anymore. It's all a pretext. A clumsy attempt to establish a BOGUS ALIBI. He's <u>made</u> himself a *widower*. A widower whose also a *beneficiary*!

"IS THERE A DOCTOR IN THE HOUSE? **Not anymore**. Her skilled, helping hands and gentle fingers are stiff and cold. Throttled into atrophy by a *pair* of hateful hands and *ten* foul fingers.

"2. **Incriminating demeanor** – Chuck's ploy fails because those hands that cruelly choked *Mari* fail him at Exxon. Well, more precisely stated, his <u>hands</u> with an untimely assist from his nefarious <u>brain</u> **fail** him. Chuck's *consciousness of guilt* causes his brain to *send* a message flashing through his sensory system that *tells* his hands it's *nervous* time. Thereby, triggering a bad case of *trembling, clammy hands* at the pumps. Just a bad break for bad boy Chuck? Or a smidgen of divine interdiction? He <u>betrays</u> his wife, and ironically it seems, his body <u>betrays</u> him. I suppose it's from such dilemmas that the phrase was born, 'The spirit is willing but the flesh is weak.' The spirit wanted to be cool, but Chuck's flesh is a fool.

"The owner of the self service gas station was formerly employed for three years with the New York State Bureau of Criminal Investigations. He's an observant type of guy. Plus, Chuck has been a regular customer for a year and a half. He comes in 2-3 times a week for gas, coffee and chats. He's not simply a face in the crowd. The station proprietor is very familiar with him.

"And on this fateful morning he's expecting Chuck. He receives a telephone call at the station around 6:15 a.m. Chuck says he's coming in to have the power seat fuse checked. Palpable nonsense. It's not a fuse that needs to be checked. It's Chuck's wife who is in extremis.

"He arrives between 6:40 – 6:50 a.m. He says the *fuse problem* has been taken care of. Hey, that's a big surprise. His perceived problem is a wife not a car seat. And regrettably, he has taken care of her! He also purchases *five dollars* of gas. Interesting. That's the equivalent of 3.8 gallons. Subsequent testing on the Thunderbird reveals, that after five dollars worth of gas has been siphoned from the tank, it still contains 26 gallons. It's well over half full. Chuck lives 7.8 miles from the airport. He doesn't need gas that morning. He can make several round trip airport swings with the fuel already in his gas tank. He doesn't need gas and he doesn't need new fuses, but he sure as hell <u>needs</u> an *alibi*. Obviously, the purchase of *five dollars* of gas the morning of the murder is simply a shameless ploy by a killer who wants to cover his tracks.

"Poor ole Chuck. He'd have been well advised not to try to pump gas under these circumstances. He's over-reached. He should've stuck with the fuse excuse. He's *unable* to do self serve. He requires the assistance of the station owner. **His hands** are *shaking* so much he has difficulty removing the gas cap, and can't steady his hands enough to insert the nozzle into the gas tank. Clearly, he <u>isn't</u> himself.

"It's a cool morning, but he's *sweating*. He's wearing a jacket and a hat with a rattlesnake skin band. Noticeably, he's *perspiring* around his temples. The owner sees *beads of sweat* coming down his sideburns and on to his cheeks.

"The ex-cop/station proprietor testifies, 'He was more nervous than usual... it was obvious that he was not himself in the morning. He was not himself with the conversation over the telephone with the fuses for his car and he wasn't himself getting the gasoline and paying for it.'

"Chuck tries to explain, 'I'm awfully *nervous* today, awfully *nervous* this morning. We're flying to Kansas to see my wife's folks.' Yeah, sure Chuck. The deed is already done. You don't have a wife anymore. Her next flight to Kansas will be to the cemetery.

"3. **Peculiar priorities** – Chuck returns to his residence. He claims he discovers his wife unconscious on the floor. But he's parked the car on the wrong side of the street and he's left the door open. Strong indicators he <u>already</u> knows before he enters that there's a problem inside.

"He hits the burglar alarm, and crosses the street to the house of a <u>Judge</u>. Naturally, he could have picked anyone in the neighborhood, but he chooses the Judge. Is this significant? Some wags might suggest the decision is a bit bizarre. Wouldn't a Judge be the *last* person a wife-killer would want to be messing with on the morning of the murder? Perhaps. But I don't think that rationale is apposite in this instance. I believe the choice is calculated. The cunning Mr. Chuck is using *reverse psychology*. He's trying to <u>deflect</u> *suspicion* by reporting his problem to the least likely individual in the area.

"Chuck bangs on the door. The Judge and his Mrs. respond. Chuck claims his telephone is out of order. He says, "**Help me**. Help, help **me**. Call the police and call an ambulance." An ironic use of words to be sure. There's no mention of *Mari*. Nothing specific is offered about the nature of the emergency. She's been dead for close to an <u>hour</u> now, and Chuck says nothing about his wife! All he says is HELP ME. And that's precisely why he's at the Judge's door. He wants help for himself! He has no concern for *Mari*. He's killed *Mari*. Chuck's call for help is abbreviated. What he really means is, "**Help me**. Help, help **me** –– continue to fashion a *false alibi*."

"The Judge calls the Police, but he and his wife have no particulars. Their perception: the situation is *very suspicious*. The first officer to the scene is dispatched to an 'unknown problem.'

"The Judge later testifies, 'I was curious to know what this was all about, because we had <u>no</u> indication before.' The Judge reflected: 'I didn't see an aspect of grief. I saw an aspect of *laboriously* explaining why they would not be going [on their trip]. Ultimately, he said his wife was dead!' The Judge's wife made similar comments. 'He was evasive. He seemed like he didn't want to say his wife was dead. It took a long time for that to come out.'

"Chuck asks the first responding officer to light his cigarette. His hands are *shaking*. They discuss CPR. Chuck's reaction is to suggest the *presence* of a stethoscope. He retrieves an attache case with a stethoscope inside from an adjoining room. But there is no evidence CPR has been attempted. Chuck says he tried to awaken his wife and used the stethoscope to listen for a pulse. Right Chucko. But you used it to <u>confirm</u> her passing after the strangulation, not from any sense of altruism.

"Chuck takes time for a little *housekeeping* as his late wife lies sprawled on the floor. He picks up contents of *Mari's* purse from the floor. Also, he mentions the need to procure a *refund* for their unused airline tickets. A legitimate concern in the near future? Sure. But is that a reasonable **priority** when the first Metro Officer has just arrived on the scene? The Officer states wryly from the witness stand, 'It seemed like he was more concerned about the refund than about his wife!'

"At some point a home security specialist arrives. The telephone works fine. However, he discovers the alarm system *panic button* has been disconnected from the telephone line. The disconnect site is behind a night stand in the master bedroom, but it's concealed. The night stand has been *conveniently* pushed to within 3-4 inches of the baseboard. Pushing a night stand back in place <u>isn't</u> something an intruder would do in his haste, but it's certainly something a malfeasant husband would do to prevent his wife from seeing his treason. Bingo!

"'Oh, what a tangled web we weave, When first we practice to deceive!' (Sir Walter Scott, *Marmion*. Canto VI, Stanza 17)

"4. **Motive** – What is the monetary value of a human life? Fifty dollars – one thousand twenty nine dollars – five hundred thousand dollars – a million dollars – billions – trillions? A foolish query, isn't it. The value of HUMAN LIFE can't be quantified in dollars and cents.

It's apples and oranges to suggest an equation between *money and life*. There is no equivalence. It doesn't compute. Wonderfully exhilarating, marvelous, miraculous, precious life is **incomparable**. It is one of a kind. *LIFE* is the summum bonum. *LIFE* is immeasurable – incalculable. *It is the highest good*. Reduced to reality's essence – **life is the only good**. Without it we have nothing!

"But I have a news flash. Give heed to my words. Chuck presumes to have the calculus. He presumes to know the formula. Ostensibly, he possesses the extraterrestrial acumen required for placing a price tag on *LIFE*. He has solved the insoluble. The unfathomable is fathomed. Some are skeptics? Hell, the value of human life must have been measured. The sickening, incomprehensible truth of this case is that **Chuck kills his wife for money**. So arguably, he knows the value of human life, right? NO, actually – terribly wrong! Ridiculous, Mr. Husband!

"But this is Calculus 101 according to the professorial Mr. Chucko. *HUMAN LIFE* is worth: [imaginary drum roll and stirring brass band fanfare] whatever sum of green a guy can finagle out of life insurance companies that have issued whole life policies on the woman he's murdered. AND THAT SUM IS: two hundred fifty four thousand thirty three dollars and eight three cents. ($254,033.83)

"So there you have it. He ain't Einstein and he doesn't have a doctorate in Philosophy or Math or Theology – but he's apparently deduced the precise monetary value of a HUMAN LIFE. She *dies* and he's *compensated*. Sometimes it's a strange world. And he lives high on the hog off the $254,033.83 insurance payoff for almost ten years. Decidedly uncool, Sir. In fact, Sir, it's unmitigated bull sh––t!

"*Mari* has loved you and trusted you. She's made you the primary beneficiary on various life insurance policies. And her reward for being loving and trusting and protective is an expedited exit from mortality. Chuck, you've got a weird way of saying, 'Thank You.'

"Emerson said, 'Happy is the house that shelters a friend.' (Ralph Waldo Emerson, *Essays: First Series*. Friendship) Unfortunately, *Mari's* house doesn't shelter a friend. It harbors an enemy. She's slept with an evil combatant. Chuck is living proof that "...the love of money is the root of *all* evil." (*Holy Bible*, 1 Timothy 6:10, emphasis added)

"5. **Voice from the grave** – There is an occasion when *Mari's* parents are visiting in Las Vegas. It's <u>several</u> <u>months</u> before her murder. Chuck is opening mail. A letter has arrived from an insurance company. He opens it. Reads it. Then quips, 'I don't want my wife to see this because she'll be wanting me to get some more insurance and one day I'll wake up dead in the desert.'

"Now that's a curious oxymoron isn't it. <u>Waking</u> <u>up</u> <u>dead</u>. But that's the testimony concerning his comment. However, my purpose in highlighting this specious declaration is not to criticize the word structure of the Defendant's prose.

"A short while later, *Mari* is out on the patio cooking with the barbeque grill. Her mother repeats Chuck's oxymoron: 'I hear your husband is scared to death of you and he doesn't want to take out any more insurance because he's afraid you'll kill him and he'll wake up dead in the desert.' And *MARI SAYS*, '**It won't be Chuck that wakes up dead in the desert**.'

"Now do those sobering, prophetic words make the hair stand up on the back of your neck or what? Pitiful, luckless *Mari* senses it's coming. But she doesn't act prudently on what an inner voice is whispering to her. She knows her husband. She knows of his insincerity. His deception. His materialism. His capacity for betrayal. But love <u>trumps</u> her judgment. Love clouds her vision. Love rules. Love is saying, 'Perhaps, if you patiently endure his indifference, he'll see your goodness, and eventually come to love you.'

"Vain wish. She makes a comfortable living at SNMH. Yet as a beneficiary of love she's penniless. Flat broke. 'Keep thy eyes wide open before marriage, and half shut afterwards.' (ibid.) Well, wise ole Ben Franklin only got it <u>half</u> right this time. Ben probably didn't consider murder a viable option. But Ben isn't Chuck! Since *Mari* didn't keep her eyes wide open before marriage, she certainly <u>needed</u> to keep *her eyes* <u>and</u> *her ears* **wide open** afterward.

"Nevertheless, the Doctor <u>isn't</u> speechless! And Chuck's glib bravado comes back to haunt him. Why? Because his words tell us that LIFE INSURANCE is on his mind. His words tell us that the **death** of his wife is on his mind. It's not a stretch at all to conclude that what he's saying to *Mari's* parents isn't about her – it's about him. He's the evil genie in this scenario. And her words uttered two and a half months before her death tell us that LIFE INSURANCE is on her mind. They tell us that **her own demise** is on her mind. Her words are a *powerful indictment*. Her irrefutable inference: SHE is the one who will wake up dead in the desert. And SHE DID wake up dead in a glitzy desert neighborhood in sin city.

"Still, there's an anomaly here. He kills his wife. He puts her in her grave. But she isn't silenced. *Mari* has a willing proxy. **The dead victim speaks** through her mother! In a sense, it's A VOICE FROM THE GRAVE!

"6. **Confession** – Please indulge me for a few minutes. I enjoy fishing. Though I'm not a proficient fisherman. I have the patience, but I don't possess the skills. I've sat for hours on the banks of fishing ponds waiting for bites on many occasions. Not infrequently, I've experienced long intervals of bite-less boredom as more gifted anglers are hooking scrappy speckled trout on both sides of me. It sort of bruises a guy's self esteem. Makes him wonder if he needs a different hobby.

"However, there's an upside to an empty creel. My futility as a fisherman gives me a chance to be reflective, philosophical, even insightful I think. It gives me a chance to ponder certain realities. For example, if I don't catch any fish I don't have to clean any fish. Now, that's a meaningful benefit. And besides, I'm a sensitive guy. I *could* catch fish if I *really* wanted to catch them, but I have a degree of empathy for the plight of the fish. Hooks are sharp. Hooks hurt fish. When fish are hooked they bleed. When they're caught, they get gutted and tossed into a frying pan. What a dreadful fate for swift swimming fish.

"That said, I remain a true devotee of fishing. *I'm hooked.* I love the scenery, the opportunity to relax, and the brisk tugs on the line when a finned fellow has swallowed my hook. So I'm thinking, well the fish has complicity in this debacle. Surely the fish bears some responsibility, right? It may start innocently, but there's no escaping this piscean truth of the waters, ultimately **the fault** lies with the fish. The fish is hungry and it sees something in the water that looks appetizing. So, it swims a little closer for a better look .What looks good from a distance looks delectable up close and it smells even better than it looks – to a fish that is. Presto. The adept angler's hook is taken. Wallah, Mr. Fish is outta there!

"Hey, the fish needed to put the brakes on. A smart fish is a cautious fish – and discerning. Questioning what this stuff is? Maybe it's not good for me. I really don't know what the ingredients are. I don't have the facts. I obviously need more information. I mustn't be impulsive.

"Impulsive fish don't live very long. They're fearless, and their stomachs are empty. They're confident, self assured, and bold. Given to glib rationalization. Like, what can be the harm in taking just a teensy, weensy nibble. Uuuuh – getting your throat ripped out!

"So, the impulsive fish makes a mistake that can be fatal. A mistake that gets it into a lot of trouble. **It <u>opens</u> it's mouth**. Now, that's a philosophical <u>keeper</u> isn't it? Slip that one into your creel of sayings to live by. *A fish gets into trouble by opening it's mouth*! It should have been more careful about the things it wraps it's mouth around. **If** it had only kept it's damn mouth shut it wouldn't have ended up in a pan of hot grease. Of course, it would be awful skinny.

"That's Chuck's Waterloo too. He's careless – and impulsive. It seems like such a trivial thing. It takes only a few moments of indiscretion. A snide verbal crack that finds it's genesis in *alcohol <u>and</u> arrogance*.

"During late spring or early summer 1985, Chuck goes to a watering hole called the Port of Wichita. He sits on a barstool. Orders a drink and begins to converse with the barmaid. A few minutes pass. Casual banter continues and another drink follows. Janine has seen Chuck before. She's heard things about him. Rumors that are intriguing and disturbing. She's curious. Business is slow. She decides to test the water. Maybe she"ll get a bite.

"Janine casually laughs. Then teasingly probes, 'You're Chuck D––– aren't you?' 'Yes, Ma'am, I am.' 'I've heard about you. Some people say you killed your wife. Did you do it?' Short pause ––

"A penny for your thoughts, Chuck. You didn't have to open your mouth ya know. You could have just kept it bottled up inside. Even a tavern isn't a suitable venue for venting about murder. But it seemed so harmless, didn't it. So tempting to flaunt your machismo before the pretty barmaid. She put the bait in the water and you took it. Hook, line, and sinker. SUCKER!

"A fish in a fish pond doesn't get into trouble when a fisherman's nearby unless it opens it's mouth. You're like the proverbial fish, Chuck. A killer in a bar doesn't get into trouble when a barmaid's nearby unless he opens his mouth. You didn't have to OPEN YOUR MOUTH. You could have abruptly ended the conversation then and there. Got up and stomped out of the Port of Wichita with your dignity and your freedom from criminal liability intact. This barmaid didn't pry your mouth open, did she? It's so foolishly imprudent to indulge in verbal strutting about a woman's murder – under any circumstance!

"It's your fault. You got yourself in trouble – on the day of your crime and on the day you <u>talked</u> about your crime. You wouldn't have been charged. You wouldn't be sitting here today on trial for murder if you'd kept your trap shut. If you had let a sleeping wife lie.

"But inexplicably, big – bad Chuck OPENS HIS MOUTH. He's asked if he murdered his wife. And he replies, 'YES I DID, and there <u>isn't</u> **anything <u>anybody</u> can do about it.**'"

Wow! Is that ever serving up a fat ole hanging curve ball to a Prosecutor delivering his Rebuttal Argument. It's pretty easy to hit one like that in the sweet spot of the bat. Back – back – back – <u>back</u>. Going –– going ––– GONE!

Is the case in need of CPR? Well, <u>it</u>––<u>just</u>–– <u>got</u>––<u>it</u>! Is there a doctor in the bar? A *healer* with an *admission of guilt* in his little black bag? No, only the Doctor's killer! But what's said will do quite nicely, Chuck. Thank you, Fella!

Did you kill your wife? 'YES I DID, and there <u>isn't</u> **anything <u>anybody</u> can do about it.**' Is that being boldly audacious, or what? Taunting law enforcement authorities. Implicitly issuing a challenge: BRING IT ON BOYS! It's <u>never</u> going to get any sweeter than this for a career Prosecutor. For a guy laboring with all his might to be a dynamic champion of truth. **Remembering** precious *Mari*. **Remembering** the *frustration* of almost ten years of delay. **Remembering** *justice*. **Remembering** you have the *last* word. **Remembering** that '**anybody**' is *all-inclusive*. Why that's the *whole world*.–– **Observing** the callous *arrogance* of the Defendant. Turning and staring at Chuck ––

"You told the barmaid you killed your wife and *there isn't <u>anything</u> anybody can do about it*. WRONG ––WRONG, SIR. You're present in this Courtroom charged with murder aren't you? Your fate is soon to be in the hands of the Jury, isn't it? Evidently persons like the Homicide

Detectives and the Prosecutor and the Judge and the Jury **can do** something about *Mari's* murder and about you. BELIEVE IT SIR. Justice will not be delayed any longer. Nor will justice be thwarted. You were WRONG when you strangled your wife to death. You were WRONG at the Port of Wichita to brag about what you'd done. And SIR, YOU'RE ON THE <u>WRONG</u> SIDE OF JUSTICE TODAY!"

After a delay of almost 10 years and after hearing 10 days of testimony, an eight-woman, four-man Jury deliberated for about **2 hours**, ate dinner, and announced their verdict shortly after returning to the Jury Room. THE VERDICT: <u>**Guilty**</u> **of Murder in the First Degree**.

Advisory Not Given –– Or Was It?

"A simple child,
That lightly draws its breath,
And feels it life in every limb,
What should it know of death?"
(William Wordsworth, *We are Seven*, Stanza I, 1798)

CHAPTER 6

IT'S THANKSGIVING WEEKEND 1987. ARTHUR IS SEVEN. He's traveling with his maternal grandparents and his mother. They make a pit-stop at a hotel-casino in Stateline. Their purpose is merely to stretch their legs, use the restroom facilities, and do a little casino gaming before departing Nevada and proceeding to their home in California. The agenda is so innocuous on its face. So tragic in its consequence!

Two *wild cards* exist inside, to borrow a trite phrase from the parlance of gamers. Adjacent to the casino is a *video arcade room*. It's not there by accident. Gaming laws don't permit children to loiter in gaming areas. The arcade provides a perfect place for a child to have fun while adults in his party indulge their appetite for gambling. At least, that what the designers intended.

Lamentably, the video arcade isn't a place for Arthur to have fun today. It's a very imperfect place for a child to play games on this date – on this occasion – at this time – under these circumstances. Arthur's only there for about twenty minutes. But at some point during that short twenty-minute interval, *wild card #two* is also there. **He's a child predator.** His prey on this day is little Arthur.

The arcade is included in the video surveillance system of the hotel-casino property. However, it is not definitive on this deplorable occasion. Trusting, inquisitive, joyful, unsuspecting, seven year old Arthur <u>disappears</u>.

Inexplicably, his decomposing body isn't found until a month later. He lies on the ground under a trailer located within employee housing on the complex. The site is accessible to the public, but it is not part of the hotel-casino business enterprise. Arthur has been strangled.

Choice, heaven-sent little Arthur. "Child of the pure unclouded brow and <u>dreaming</u> eyes of wonder..." (Lewis Carroll, *Through The Looking Glass*, introductory poem entitled, 'Child of the pure unclouded brow')

My youngest grandson is a vivacious seven year old as I compose these lines. When this matter went to Trial my youngest son, only slightly younger than Arthur, was full of brown-eyed radiance. I can relate to the horror of this crime. I have keen empathy for the shock, the emptiness, and the despair of the family for their little boy lost. Forced to wrestle interminably with the senseless riddle of his disappearance and the soul-retching guilt of allowing it to happen.

Murder is always terrible, but the shameless murder of an innocent child is unspeakably vile! A little boy doesn't dream of death. Why should a child of joy <u>dream</u> of death? What should he <u>know</u> of death? He's a partisan of life. A seven year old boy dreams of polliwogs and space ships and marbles and tarantulas. He dreams of flying kites and chasing birds and finding pots of gold at the end of rainbows – of running barefoot in the rain, of chocolate chip cookies and cheese pizza and fishing and gazing at bright stars on dark summer nights. His days are meant to be enveloped in the glow of celestial light and promise.

"Whither is fled the visionary gleam?
Where is it now, the glory and the dream
[of little Arthur]?" (William Wordsworth,
 Ode to *Intimations Of Immortality*
 From Recollections Of Early Childhood)

This case has troubled me for almost two decades. I think it's time to make **my record** – in a sense. I will preface my remarks with a caveat. This is <u>not</u> an expression of opinion concerning the guilt or innocence of any specific person. If I did possess such an opinion, it would <u>not</u> be pertinent to this treatise. There will be <u>no</u> *factual* allegation of criminal culpability for the tragic disappearance of the child. My thoughts <u>are</u> strictly *procedure* oriented. It's the *Judicial role* in this Trial during its most crucial and concluding stage that is truly fascinating. An experienced Advocate recognizes that procedure is often the precursor of outcome.

I've said it before in this book. I'll say it again, stress is endemic to Courtrooms. Trial terrain is stress terrain. And the emotional baggage of stress affects <u>every</u> participant.

However, this fact is especially apropos to the Prosecutor. *He is the one* who brings the charge. *He is the one* who bears the burden of proof. *He is the one* most cognizant of this trial truth: <u>every</u> Murder Trial is a <u>minefield</u>. His Case can *blow up* in his face a hundred ways every time he goes to Trial. He <u>knows</u> this and he <u>knows</u> he is vulnerable to the vagaries of *criminal procedure*. Will witnesses be no-shows? Will they be forgetful or inconsistent? Will they recant? Will evidence be accepted or rejected by the Court? Will objections to questions or answers be sustained? Will Jurors be attentive? Will they be objective? Will the Jury be convinced? Will they be properly instructed? And so it goes – ad infinitum!

Each Murder Trial is beset by case-changing variables that may implode at any moment! Yet, the parties–never–<u>know</u>–where–the–**mines**–are set, and what– will– **trigger**– the–detonation.

Therefore, what the Prosecutor needs <u>most</u> to succeed at Trial is an astute, objective, dispassionate Trial Judge. Every fair Trial requires the steady, even hand of a fair Judge. He's the Master of the Show. The major player in the cast. A Trial Judge calls the shots. He has the raw power in the Courtroom. If the Court is opposed to a party's position, that party's chance of success is greatly diminished. His Honor is a Major Trial variable – and he may be the greatest purveyor of Trial stress.

Will the Court strike charges from the pleading document? Will he grant motions to suppress evidence? Will he deny the proffer of evidence on grounds of relevance or redundance or reliability?

It is axiomatic to *Trial Procedure* that the **Judge** is the *Trier of the Law* and the **Jury** is the *Trier of the Facts*. The Judge decides the law and the Jury decides the facts. That's the <u>division</u> <u>of</u> <u>responsibility</u>. That's the <u>natural</u> order of things.

When the introduction of evidence by the Parties has been completed and <u>prior</u> to Closing Argument, the Court presents it's <u>legal</u> <u>instructions</u> to the Jury. Of course, there can't be a meaningful debate during Summation without <u>agreement</u> on the definition of terms. Any neophyte member of a high school debate squad is familiar with this *procedural* maxim.

The legal instructions constitute a series of statements regarding the law that is applicable to the case at bar. The **Court's legal instructions are the <u>law</u> of the case**. The Jury is required to decide the *facts of the case* within the framework of the Judge's *law of the case*. Hence, there is a pivotal linkage between the Court's legal instructions and the <u>outcome</u> of a trial that cannot be exaggerated.

A lengthy police investigation occurs. Herman is charged with kidnaping and murdering Arthur. He is a single occupancy, registered guest on the second floor of the hotel/casino where Arthur disappears at the time he disappears. The Trial begins. The Party's examine witnesses. Physical evidence is produced. The Court rules. Etcetera.

Up to a certain procedural point, the Trial is not a remarkable event. The murder is contemptible, but the Trial process isn't unusual. The Parties labor diligently into the *sixth week* with vigorous advocacy of their positions, and the Court expertly referees the adversarial offers of and objections to evidence. The format is firmly in place. The Prosecution has brought the allegations, it <u>must</u> prove them. The trial is hotly contested but amicable from its inception. In my view, the outcome remains a dead-heat issue at the end of the evidentiary phase.

However, don't fall asleep Mr. Prosecutor, the pock marked Trial terrain <u>is</u> still a hidden *mine field*. The Trial format is going to get shaky as hell. Check your seatbelt. Big time *stress* is in the wings. A debacle awaits you, Sir! Instructions and summation and deliberation and the *unknown* are yet to come!

In the final days of the proceedings, the Judge summons Counsel to his chambers for the purpose of settling Jury Instructions. This is the way it works. Each Party *prepares* and *submits* <u>proposed</u> instructions to the Court. The Judge reviews them. Counsel meet in chambers with the Judge to discuss and argue areas of disagreement. Applicable legal authority will be cited, reasons for the proffer of disputed instructions is explained, and <u>the</u> Court ultimately *determines* the actual set of legal definitions that will be read to the Jury. A record is made. The Court's instructions are given <u>prior</u> to summation in Nevada District Courts.

It's a critical juncture in <u>any</u> Trial. No other figure in the Courtroom is a recipient of the deference a Jury gives the Judge – that propria persona who presides with independence and neutrality over criminal Trials. No other figure is accorded the professional courtesy the Judge gets – and properly so. The Judge is the venerable embodiment of the Criminal Justice System. He wears the robe that is symbolic of his authority and his august position. He presides from a bench that is impressively elevated above all other persons in the Courtroom. He looks down at Counsel and the Jury when he speaks to them. Counsel are expected to respectfully stand before addressing him. As Court sessions begin, all persons present are directed by the Bailiff to stand until the Judge has entered and sat down. Likewise, all must stand as the Judge leaves the Room when the Court is recessed. Further, it's all by design. The Court has the final word and those in his Courtroom are *conditioned* to unquestioningly accept the finality of his word.

So, consider the <u>impact</u> upon the proceedings **if** somehow the *neutrality* of the Court becomes skewed. Suppose for some reason, never artfully nor astutely articulated, Mr. August Propria Persona acquires a view of the case that is *slanted* toward the Defense. And suppose in the <u>sixth</u> week of trial, this *proclivity* of the Court informally surfaces for the <u>first</u> time during preliminary discussion in chambers regarding settlement of the Court's Instructions to the Jury. How will this unsettling news impact the persona of the Prosecutor? Possibly, he'll become Mr. Impropria Persona. It'll be tantamount to a *procedural* train wreck won't it? The sh––t may very well hit the fan, right? The Judiciary has to be independent and neutral to insure the <u>integrity</u> of the case outcome! The Judge can't take sides, can he?

Well, there's a Biblical verse that reads, "...the Lord gave, and the Lord hath taketh away; blessed be the name of the Lord." (Holy Bible, *Job 1:21*) It's a sage expression of submission to adversity. Curiously, the same can be said of Judges in Trial proceedings. The <u>Judge</u> *gives* and the <u>Judge</u> *takes* away. Blessed be the name of the Judge? Hey, maybe the lid should be put over that last bit of verbiage. A Trial is an extremely partisan affair to the protagonists. There will seldom be universal acclaim for Court rulings. Typically, the Judge will be considered *blessed* only by the Party his rulings *bless*. That would be the party-beneficiary of evidence *given*. No adversary will cheer a decision taking evidence *away* – or taking a favorable verdict *away*!

But that's the thing about <u>Court</u> <u>Instructions</u> to the Jury. The Judge can't take sides, can he? Er – actually – practically speaking – yeah!! The Judge <u>can</u> take sides, and often does by the *manner* in which he instructs the Jury. What **he says** is the law **is** the law of the case. The Jury has sworn to swallow, excuse me I mis-spoke, I meant to say <u>follow</u> the Court's legal instructions. So, the Judge is in the extremely delicate position of being able to *give* and *take* away, at a time just before deliberation, when the impact is maximized! The Judge is telling the Jury what they can *legally* do and what they can't *legally* do. He's in the catbird seat. Imbued with the <u>judicial</u> <u>power</u> and the <u>judicial</u> <u>persona</u> to rock the Prosecution's case-boat so hard it capsizes.

What happens if the Judge gives the Trial Jury an **advisory instruction of acquittal**? There is such a woebegone creature in the world of Criminal Law. I've alluded to this legal phenomenon in a previous chapter. The Judge does have the statutory authority to ADVISE the Jury that in *his opinion* there is <u>insufficient</u> evidence as A MATTER OF LAW <u>to</u> <u>convict</u>. As the description of the Instruction implies, it isn't binding. It's merely advisory. **BUT –––**? What generally happens when it's given? Curtains for the Prosecution's case, that's what! The Judge to whom the Jury owes unquestioning deference is telling them in his opinion as **a matter of law** there is insufficient evidence to acquit. It doesn't take a rocket scientist to figure out what happens in a Court of Law, in most instances, when His Honor – in effect – tells the Jury they can't *legally* convict.

What happens when the Court does choose a side? Well, the Case is down the tube for starters, <u>and</u> churning eruptions in a prosecutor's belly are a sure-fire physiological phenomenon. Perhaps, a kaleidoscope of conflicting emotions rushing pell-mell through the poor prosecutorial brain is a point that also needs to be put on the record.

It can all slip away when the Judge instructs the Jury. Which is precisely why the Prosecutor must be vigilant and adversarial and at the top of his game when Court Instructions are settled. What the Judge has *given* during the Evidentiary phase, the Judge can deftly *take away* during the Instruction phase. Assuredly, a case hangs in the balance each time Instructions are selected. It can be, and often is, white-knuckle time!

And so, in the <u>sixth</u> week of trial the Judge delivers a bombshell! It was almost twenty years ago – in another century *actually*. But it remains etched into my psyche. The passage of time has not noticeably dulled my recollection of the scenario that unfolds. We're in chambers. It's a mild day in February 1989, though the climate in chambers is about to develop a sudden chilliness. The Judge has reviewed the submission of proposed instructions by the parties-adversarial. There's a measure of consensus concerning those offered by the Prosecution. The precise moment arrives inauspiciously. His Honor is announcing his mind-set regarding the <u>instructions submitted</u> <u>by the Defense</u> in slow, measured words. One of the instructions submitted in the Defense package is a *proposed* advisory to acquit.

It's inclusion hasn't surprised me, nor particularly alarmed me. Typically, given the high-profile nature of the case-at-bar and the evidence-at-bar, such an offer is summarily rejected. Often the Defense engages in procedural strategies at trial, not with the expectation of prevailing, but simply to make their record. Thus, preserving an issue for appeal in the event there is a conviction. So, the Judge is agreeing to some routine Defense offers and rejecting others. It's all been rather rudimentary, predictable, and of only slight trial significance to this seminal moment.

Then –– without warning the *unpredictable* happens. Things get really wacky fast. The bomb shell explodes. There has been no heads up – not the slightest hint. No testing of the terrain to gauge the reaction of Counsel to a dramatic game-changing instruction. This event is flat out of nowhere. A sizzling bolt of lightning from a serene blue sky.

His Honor picks up the proposed Defense Instruction and, in a nondescript, impassive, seemingly cavalier tone, says: "The Defense is asking the Court to advise the Jury to acquit because as a matter of law there's insufficient evidence to convict. I think I'll *give* that one."

Whoa! Excuse me! I must be day dreaming. I guess I'm more tired than I thought. Did he just say what I think he just said? This is incredulous. Yes, the case <u>is</u> circumstantial. I didn't produce any eye-witnesses to document the Defendant's physical complicity in the murder. However, <u>five</u> <u>witnesses</u> have placed the little victim in the company of the Defendant, or someone looking exactly like him, within the precise time frame of Arthur's disappearance. The two are walking together. The Accused or his double is holding his hand. A Pastor sees them upstairs in close proximity to the second story room registered to the accused.

I casually ask, "Judge, you inadvertently lowered your voice. I couldn't really hear what you said about the advisory instruction to acquit."

The Judge elevates his voice a little. His reply can't be misunderstood this time. "Counsel, I <u>said</u> I think I'll *give* that one." And I say, "You're kidding aren't you?" And he says, "No, I'm not kidding. I think I'll *give* that one."

The declaration is so tranquil – so casually expressed. Incredibly, it's as if the Judge is so completely convinced of the soundness of his position that he thinks everyone else will be of the same view – including the Prosecutor. Is the Court a visionary? Has an extraterrestrial event blessed him *alone* with the clairvoyance to decipher the riddle of little Arthur's disappearance? What *special* insight enhances the intellectual acumen and ego of a District Court Judge to the extent he's come to believe *he sees* what no one else sees? No one, that is, but the polished Counselors of the Defense – and of course, it's their job description to *see* acquittal.

The Investigating Officers on this case are among the top dogs of the Las Vegas Metropolitan Police Department Homicide Bureau. They have performed hundreds of homicide investigations, interviewed thousands of witnesses, and between them have approximately forty years of police work in their portfolios. They are resourceful men of integrity, of high intellect, of steadfast dedication to their profession, and they're tenacious as hell. They've been devastated by the death of little Arthur. Surely, they did *not* <u>deliberately</u> follow a trail that only leads to a rabbit hole! Aren't they entitled to some small vestige of deference?

I'm not saying the Homicide Dicks are necessarily right or wrong in their case assessment. There's case truth and there's <u>truth</u> <u>as it is</u>. The *two* may or may not converge. I'm just making a *pertinent* observation for the record. And also noting the slightest improbability, the slenderest chance, the p-p-p-possibility – unlikely as it may be, that the Judicial view is fallible as well.

Somehow, His Honor seems persuaded the State is looking for a way out of the ambiguity of this proceeding, and Mr. Harmon will do a back flip he'll be so thrilled to have this prosecutorial maze go away. Aaaah – such astonishing judicial naivete. So little understanding of the heart and the will of a career <u>courtroom</u> <u>cop</u>!

"I think I'll *give* that one." Random thoughts explode inside my head. It's a shooting pain. Instantly I have a headache. Ouch! What the hell? What's up with this? Hey Mister, let the Jury make an independent decision. Don't create this kind of tilt. Don't orchestrate. Stay neutral. Stay judicial. You don't decide the facts. The Jury is the <u>Trier</u> of <u>fact</u>! That is a sacrosanct truth of trial work. Do not encroach upon the province of the Jury. Don't upset the traditional trial format!

Besides, we didn't start this proceeding yesterday. This is the <u>sixth</u> week of trial. You *gave* us the testimony of these <u>five</u> <u>people</u>. These witnesses who connect the accused to the victim. You didn't strike their testimony sua sponte. You didn't grant any Defense motion to exclude the testimony as incompetent trial evidence. So, don't *take it away* now. In your heart you know this Defense Instruction is merely a toss-in for the record. They're not expecting you to grant it, Yer Honor. Let this proceed to verdict with a Jury decision unencumbered by advice from the Court. The Jury is the <u>conscience</u> of the community. Please, Sir, don't screw it up now.

A flurry of random thoughts is representative of my *thinking* before blast off. My *words* are a bit more circumspect. However, they are neither cavalier, impassive, nor nondescript. Hold on tight fella, here we go. You're an advocate aren't you – well start advocating. Let the Judge *know* by the <u>tone</u> of your voice – by your <u>words</u> – by your <u>manner</u> – by your <u>gestures</u>, that this <u>isn't</u> a casual stroll in the park. Just in case he needs reminding. It <u>isn't</u> merely an in-chambers bull session. It's <u>not</u> a tactical board game involving the Court and Counsel. It's <u>not</u> theater. It <u>isn't</u> a courtroom instruction-bee competition. A Prosecutor has a sworn <u>duty</u> to <u>declare</u> the truth, and the *procedural truth* is that the Judge's advisory instruction WILL BE patently inappropriate in this instance.

I don't remember everything I said. I do remember the *way* I said it. My nerve endings tingle. I raise my voice quite a few decibels, assume my adversarial persona, and loudly, passionately, and succinctly proclaim my **objection** to the ADVISORY INSTRUCTION. I'm like a wounded Matador in the arena. But this <u>isn't</u> a blood *sport*.

What has happened in the crime before this Court is *raw* and *real* – and *sickening*. A precious child that once lightly drew his breath and felt his life in every limb has been murdered. His body has been cast aside like yesterday's grungy newspaper, sans the dignity of interment. He has lain on top of the ground fully exposed to the elements. Discovered a month after his disappearance, he's doubly victimized. First, by the sadistic deviant who killed him. Second, by nature's callous indifference. Maggots now devour his once animate flesh. Little Arthur is simply a meal ticket to soft-bodied larva. What should a child know of death – or putrefaction? Dear little man, I grieve for you!

This Trial is a search for truth. It is gut-wrenching *reality* and it will have lasting consequences. It isn't a moot court experience, nor an academic exercise. This moment is – the rubber has just hit the road time. It's gut-check time. It's a portentous occasion calling for heated reaction from a dynamic champion of justice at a point when *procedural injustice* is about to be imposed! Will the Prosecutor in chambers answer the call? Aye Aye! Mr. Harmon hears the call and reports for duty, Sir. I'll do my best!

I've been blessed with a strong set of tubes. My vocal chords will resonantly hum when I enlist their service. On the day in question, I've been accused of *screaming*, of going *ballistic*, of being *enraged,* along with a few other unflattering adjectives, as I proclaimed my vehement opposition to the proposed Advisory Instruction. Obviously, words have different meanings to different people. Dictionary definitions represent an effort to arbitrate these differences with commonly accepted meanings. That said, I hereby offer a rigorous rejoinder to the referenced words. The modus attributed to me by the Court and Counsel for the accused are <u>not</u> words I consider applicable.

A Deputy District Attorney is a public servant. The public is <u>not</u> well served during murder trials by brown-nosing, meek, soft-spoken, hesitant, shrinking violet Prosecutors; whose first priority is sucking up to the Judge. Particularly, when that Judge has a devastating *procedural hatchet* poised to cleave asunder the prosecutive charges – when the Trial Judge has announced his intention to become the *thirteenth Juror* in the Trial even though he still wears the Judicial Robe – and when the effect of his *procedural anomaly* will be a <u>subversion</u> of prosecutorial due process. A Prosecutor who is a <u>true</u> public servant will not be cowed, nor intimidated, nor dislodged from his trial mission by anyone – including the Judge!

But *screaming*? I don't believe I've screamed at another person in my life. I'm <u>not</u> a screamer. A scream is a high-pitched, piercing cry expressing fear or pain, etc. Screaming is shrieking, screeching, squealing, wailing, howling, crying. What I did in chambers wasn't screaming. My voice was **loud** and **emphatic**, however, I–did–not–scream!

Going *ballistic*? Actually, not my style neither. Going ballistic is becoming frantically overwrought or furiously angry. I'm not a frantic or furious sort of guy. My reactive words are controlled and measured. Never frantically uttered in twenty nine years of **trial rhetoric**. The case at bar was–not–an–exception!

Being *enraged*? Ridiculous! Rage is fierce or violent anger. It is speaking furiously or madly. It is raving. It's having a tantrum or fit. Becoming hysterical. Going into a frenzy. My genetic code <u>isn't</u> programed for such a mind-set. It is programed for advocacy!

Which is all I did in chambers on that February day in 1989. **I advocated**! I performed my Prosecutorial Duty. Trial practice is the *practice of advocacy*. The *Adversary System* is the bed-rock premise upon which Criminal Trial work is predicated. Theoretically, it consists of three entities: the Prosecution – the Defense – and the Judge. He referees the battle between the opposing sides.

Realistically on this fateful day, the referee ends up joining the Defense. Making it three against one. There were two esteemed Defense

Counselors, the Most Honorable Judge, and ––– me. A poor little Prosecutor lost in a hostile heap of adversarial piling-on, needing to do more than just bleat. Not armed with the power to summon his own lightning bolt from the stratosphere to zap the Judge back into a more prosecutor-friendly orientation. No brass knuckles hidden in his jacket pocket to pummel His Most Honorable into acquiescence, nor another set of five connecting witnesses waiting in the hallway. No typed confession at his prosecutorial fingertips – <u>armed</u> only with his calling and the power of rhetoric. The power of the spoken word. Fortified by a sense of public duty and a tongue primed to sweat. And it had to be more than a weak, wavering, tentative plea.

So, I revved up my fortissimo. Shifted into my boom-box voice and passionately, succinctly, insistently, and vociferously **implored** the Judge, for perhaps, forty five minutes plus to give the Defense Advisory the <u>heave ho</u>. The atmosphere is tense and emotional. It becomes a contest of will. The two esteemed Defense Counselors mostly sitting on the sidelines. The Most Honorable Judge wanting to expedite the process and close debate, confronted by an unrelenting Prosecutor – tenaciously insisting on saying his piece.

The Judge later reports to the press that the Prosecutor tells him if he goes ahead with the *Advisory*, and the Jury heeds it, *the blood of little Arthur would be on his hands*. I did use such an analogy. However, I–didn't–put–it–<u>quite</u>–like–that. The little victim didn't bleed. The catapult for his premature flight to a heavenly venue is manual strangulation. There is no bleeding associated with the actual commission of the crime. The use of *blood* in my argument is allegorical. It <u>refers</u> to **death**.. The *death* of Arthur <u>and</u> the *death* of justice. I'm not equating what a killer has done with what a Judge says he's about to do. The Judge didn't kill the little boy. That isn't the point at all. A carnal man with cruel hands killed him – whomever that is. **The point being**, when a Judge *advises* a Jury to acquit in a Murder Trial, IF that advice happens to be erroneous, he <u>is</u>, in a sense, putting **justice** on the chopping block. Justice *bleeds* when criminal accountability is cheated.

I tell the Judge, in the passion of advocacy, that "IN A <u>SENSE</u>" the blood of the victim will be on his hands if he takes the case away from the Jury. The expression is <u>not</u> intended to be a <u>literal</u> assessment! It alludes to potential Judicial complicity by the **heavy hand** of *injustice*.

The Judge also reports to the media that the Prosecutor tells him if he gives the *Advisory Instruction* he won't be supporting the justice system and would be immoral. I believe this assertion needs to be edited.

First, I <u>didn't</u> say it like that. I neither said expressly nor inferentially that the—Judge—would—be—immoral. I would <u>never</u> have made the argument that way! I know this Judge personally. He's a fine man. I would <u>never</u>, per se, describe this good, *gentle* man as being intrinsically immoral. That would be foolish because it's untrue. We all make mistakes. However, a few flawed acts **do not** make the total man immoral.

There are two types of human relationships when such matters are reduced to their bottom-line essence. They are: VERTICAL and HORIZONTAL. It is through this contextual prism that I view the world. The <u>vertical</u> <u>relationship</u> refers to our *relationship with God*. The <u>horizontal</u> <u>relationship</u> refers to our *relationship with man*. Our relationships with The Holy Trinity are **spiritual relationships**. Our relationships with mankind are **moral relationships**. I *see* Murder Trial injustice as a moral issue. Accordingly, what I'm saying to the Judge is <u>not</u> that he's immoral, but that an <u>unjust</u> *Trial Procedure* <u>is</u> **immoral** IF it leads to an <u>unjust</u> *Trial Verdict*.

So —— is the Advisory Instruction to Acquit going – going – going —— gone? Or is it going – going – going —— given? It's high drama in chambers. The issue comes in like a lamb but it's a lion when we leave. There is no <u>final</u> <u>answer</u> yet. When we part company that evening the issue is *unresolved*.

It's about 7:00 p.m. I go to my office and place a call to the Homicide Bureau. I think they're entitled to know the case is in serious jeopardy. One of the two lead Detectives on the case answers. I ask him if he's standing or sitting. He informs me he's standing. I suggest he ought to sit down. There's a short pause. He's obviously concerned, says he's taken a seat, and asks me what's up. I tell him I'm sorry to have to break the bad news to him, but the Judge has indicated to Counsel in chambers he intends to give an Advisory Instruction of Acquittal.

The initial reaction on the other end of the line mimics my initial reaction in Chambers. The Detective exclaims, "You're kidding!" And I say, "No Tom. I wouldn't kid about something like this. The Judge has indicated he intends to give an Advisory Instruction of Acquittal. I just came from Chambers. We've been going at it on this issue for close to an hour. I don't think I convinced him to change his mind."

The Detective is stunned! He tells me he's going to call the Judge. I tell him that wouldn't be a good idea. He says, "No, I'm going to call him, and give him a piece of my mind." I say emphatically, "Don't–call–the–Judge. *My advice* to you is **not** to call the Judge. This is a matter between the Attorneys and the Court. I have to deal with it. I realize it's hard. You've invested a lot of time and energy in this investigation, but you <u>have</u> to stay out of this. I just called to inform you, not to enlist your help."

The Detective didn't heed my advice. He called anyway.

I don't remember what day of the week the *Advisory Issue* surfaced. Was it an end of the Court-week Friday afternoon that went into the evening? Or was it a week day to be followed by a recess from formal Trial proceedings? I only know the following day <u>wasn't</u> a Trial day. The lights were out in the Courtroom, and some would argue – in Judicial Chambers. I just remember the Courtroom being dark the next day, and of course, it's a rather dark, bleak day for me and for Metro. And I'm not speaking of weather conditions.

I have a vivid recollection of going to lunch with my wife across town at a soup and salad diner. I can't say whether this was the next day after the intense rhetoric in Chambers or the second day after. I know we went. We needed time together and I needed a distraction. It's about 11:30 a.m. I'm expecting a healthy, dietetic lunch, but I get a surprising appetizer on the way in.

We pass several local newspaper racks. What is plainly visible to all eyes just sort of jumps out at us. The front pages each depict a good sized, close-up picture of me, of all people – **arguing**. Evidently they're file photos from a previous trial. My jaw is jutting out. I seem to be getting into somebody's face. Emotionally jaw-boning with somebody – or <u>at</u> somebody. The words **intimidated** and **threatened** are boldly featured. It's there for the whole city to see.

Now is that a conversation piece for lunch, or what? The newspaper head lines are as startling to me as the Judicial disclosure concerning the *Advisory*. What happens in Chambers <u>usually</u> stays in Chambers. I'd supposed the volatility of the in-chambers argument was *entre nous* – only between us. The *leak* isn't from me. I hadn't said anything to the media about the in-chambers tete-a-tete. Not one little peep. I <u>don't</u> do things that way. BUT SOMEBODY HAS! By the way, I haven't mentioned this so far. The Trial Jury is <u>NOT</u> SEQUESTERED.

Our curiosity is certainly piqued. We buy both newspapers, and continue into the restaurant. While we eat we peruse the print. We get a mouthful in addition to our expected fare of soups and salad entrees. Enough to make an ever-suffering Prosecutor choke at the lunch table.

Incredibly to me, the newspaper stories are reporting the Trial Judge had concluded he would give an Advisory Instruction of Acquittal to the Jury, since he's convinced the Defendant is innocent. <u>However</u>, he's now unsure what he'll do, because he believes the neutrality and independence of the Judiciary has been compromised by words and actions of the Prosecuting Attorney and a Homicide Detective. The Judge asserts he's been INTIMIDATED and THREATENED by the abusive tone and language of Prosecutor Mel Harmon's argument in Chambers opposing his declared intention to advise the Jury to acquit, and by a coercive telephone call from a named Metro Detective.

My wife and I leave the restaurant. I feel chastened – and empowered! Hey, that's a heavy dose of public Judicial reprimand. Enough to give a guy indigestion. Pass the Rolaids, Dear. Yet, it's a kind of left handed compliment too. A Trial Lawyer often feels as though his arguments simply sail over the heads of those to whom they're directed – or that they're simply spaced. Heard, felt, discarded, and forgotten. Like the proverbial rain off a duck's back.

Not–in–this–instance! The community is presented with the spectacle of a Judge, the revered man in the black robe, the embodiment of the Criminal Justice System, the so-called master of the Courtroom show, who alleges he's been **intimidated** by a measly little ole Prosecuting Attorney's *sweating tongue*. What's up with that? How did this happen? And <u>if</u> it did happen, why in the name of heaven would any self-respecting Judge admit it happened? Wouldn't he want to maintain his persona of public respect?

Be that as it was, it does seem apparent this time that a Prosecutorial message has not only been heard, felt, internalized, and remembered by him to whom it has been directed – but memorialized for the entire community to contemplate. Uh – that would be <u>anyone</u> who has an interest in the proceedings. That includes the un-sequestered Jury, maybe?

The print media revelation of this day is probably only the <u>initial</u> splash. It sends shock waves reverberating though the legal community. It creates a rising surge of verbiage that may have significantly impacted the <u>INTEGRITY</u> of the Trial Verdict. To hell with the personal dilemma the Court perceives. The sixty four dollar question is: Does this *gratuitous* <u>publicity</u> compromise the neutrality and independence of the JURY?

The eight hundred pound gorilla is out of his cage, so to speak. The emotional fulcrum, that didn't stay in Chambers where it should have quietly reposed, has become a firestorm of speculation. Will he or won't he?

But does it really matter anymore? Whether he does or doesn't has lost it's relevance, hasn't it? Every person who reads, and who hasn't been living in a bubble for the past few days, <u>knows</u> His Honor believes the Defendant is innocent. Hasn't community insight into the Judicial mind-set already molded public opinion? More importantly, how much is the Jury impacted if one or some or all of them have been exposed to the revelatory news flashes that Mr. August Propria Persona has a view of the case that is *slanted* toward the Defense? Is it unreasonable to conclude that as the Man on the Bench goes – so goes the Jury?

Whatever —— . In due course, His Honor summons Counsel to Chambers again. It's not a reprise of the previous barrister follies. This occasion is reflective and subdued and contrite. The Court wishes to make *his* record. He will rule on the proposed *Advisory Instruction to Acquit*, however he wants to preface his ruling with an explanation for his ruling. He makes a lengthy record of *his* impressions of what happened in Chambers when the sh–t hit the fan, and what has happened since.

Nobody has perfect recollection. So, the Court is probably, inadvertently, indulging in slightly revisionist history-making. It's impossible not to. I'm doing the same thing now – though encumbered by a twenty year interval rather than a several day interval.

The Judge explains his belief that this must all be part of the record for Appellate purposes in the event the Defendant is convicted. He speaks of many things during the **second session**, but I'll cut to the chase. His Honor says he has been *personally degraded* by the verbal outbursts of the Prosecutor on the occasion at issue. Further, His Honor says he feels *threatened* and *intimidated* by the remarks and manner exhibited by the Prosecutor. Mr. Harmon's rage has had an unsettling effect on him. *Threatened* and *intimidated* – the Court suddenly feels a heavier burden that he'd ever anticipated. He regards Mr. Harmon as one of the best Prosecutors in Nevada, but he'd considered having the Bailiff arrest him for contempt of court as a result of his verbal abuse. He also says he feels *coerced* by the call he's received from a Metro Homicide Detective he names on the record. He states the call is *highly inappropriate* and he took it as a *threat*. Conveying to him that the Detective or Metro or whoever he felt the Court would think he was representing, did not feel it was appropriate that the Court give an Advisory Verdict of Acquittal. –– Well, duh! He really thought Metro would be in agreement when he trashed their murder case?

Therefore, the Judge observes, I *don't dare* give the Advisory Instruction of Acquittal now. And the reason I don't is that I don't think the Court should have the burden of responsibility in this community for any decision that comes back from the Jury.

Uh – EXACTLY, Your Honor. You try the *law* and they try the *facts*! Isn't that the *procedural format* for a Criminal Trial, Sir? Why would any Judge ever want to take such an awesome responsibility *away* from the Jury and *put* it on his own shoulders? Seems a bit unorthodox doesn't it?

The Court says his burden of responsibility weighs heavily in another sense as well. In the hours after Mr. Harmon's outburst, **word of the exchange** has been *leaked* to the local press. Accordingly, he feels yet another reason to abandon the *Advisory Instruction*. Given the existing circumstances, the Jurors, who have not been sequestered, **might think** that the Court's urging of acquittal is motivated, at least in part, by *vindictiveness* toward the Prosecutor.

Ooooh, an image of *Judicial vindictiveness* could be bad. That could totally undermine the Judicial intent to orchestrate justice. The Jury might turn on the Court and go for the Prosecution under that *threatening* scenario. That's a hot button issue. A catch-22 of sorts. So, I'll punt. –– And there you have it. The firestorm of speculation is laid to rest. *NO ADVISORY.* The Judge punts on fourth down. The Prosecution wins? The Defense loses? Well –– no! There a ringer embedded here. A humongous wild card hovers over the proceedings.

It's interesting, very interesting. Even the Court seems to have a *tacit* **belief** that the UN-SEQUESTERED JURY, <u>despite</u> being admonished by him to <u>refrain</u> from reading or viewing or listening to any newspaper, television, or radio coverage of the case, **nevertheless**, <u>WILL</u> read and view and listen to news coverage of the case. Thus, becoming **fully apprised** of *his* Judicial Opinion regarding the case!! That, my friends, is a very telling observation. One of the two pegs that constitute the basis for <u>not</u> giving the <u>Advisory</u> is anchored in the *Court's presumption* that the Jury is cognizant of the extraordinary case coverage in the press.

The Judge concludes his record by declaring that the *delicate balance* of an independent and neutral Court has been badly tilted. Therefore, His Honor invites the esteemed Counselors for the Defense to move for a mistrial, which he says he will grant, if that is their wish.

That isn't their wish. They decline the invitation. They're not stupid. They can read the tea leaves. The handwriting is on the wall. Even the Judge believes the Jury has disregarded his admonition. The Twelve Tried and True have become The *Thirteen* Tried and True. The other twelve know the score. They know His Most Honorable believes their client is innocent. Why would the esteemed Defense Counselors want to have a mistrial granted, so they can do all this over again – under these circumstances? They really like their odds now? They believe their client is about to grab the gold ring and get the whole shebang this time out of the chute!

Besides, **if** the "delicate balance of an independent and neutral Court has been badly tilted," WHOSE responsibility is it for such a mishmash anyway?

Who is it that, arguably, blew the **passion of advocacy** within the privacy of Chambers <u>way</u> out of proportion? Isn't this a JUDICIALLY CREATED ISSUE? Why does a Judge take adversarial comments of a Prosecutor so <u>personally</u>? If a **public servant** believes an injustice is about to occur, isn't he under a *sworn* legal obligation to take **exception** to the miscarriage? To ask for right – to petition the Judge TO DO RIGHT – to **Petition Rectum Rogare** is inappropriate? Since when? Why is **arguing** that <u>the</u> <u>Judge</u> <u>Do</u> <u>Right</u> a proper basis for <u>severe</u> chastisement?

Where does the buck stop in this matter, really? Isn't it the Judge who has declared an inclination to *substitute* his opinion for the Jury's opinion? He's admitted as much. He subsequently acknowledges to the print media that **he** was prepared to *Advise the Jury to Acquit* BECAUSE **he** was convinced the Defendant was innocent. He says, "He believes that the *real killer* was right in my Courtroom – that it was one of the witnesses against...[the Defendant]." (emphasis added)

The Court's point of view evolves into a decision to *shepherd* the Jury to the "right" decision. His original <u>intention</u> is a departure from the norm. Typically, Judges don't step into the arena of fact-finding. The <u>declared</u> **intention of the Court** is the *hair trigger* that fires a fusillade across the Prosecution's bow. Arguably, it is an inappropriate example of *Judicial meddling*. Did a <u>subversion</u> of Due Process for the Prosecution result? **That** is <u>not</u> precisely measurable, of course.

It is an undeniable fact that BOTH sides in a criminal case are entitled to a *fair* trial. It is also undeniably a fact that the Judge is <u>supposed</u> to be an *impartial* arbiter in criminal proceedings. So, what happens to *Procedural Due Process for the Prosecution* when a Judge <u>abandons</u> his *neutrality* and becomes **an advocate** for the Defense?

The Highest Court of the Land provided a perceptive pronouncement many years ago: Tumey v. Ohio, 273 U.S. 510 (1927) – "The question in this case is whether certain Statutes of Ohio, in providing for the trial by the mayor of a village of one accused of violating the Prohibition Act of the State, deprive the accused of due process of law and violate the Fourteenth Amendment to the Federal Constitution."

The Court states in pertinent part: "**Every <u>procedure</u>** which would offer a *possible* **temptation** to the average man as **a judge** to *forget* the burden of proof required to convict the Defendant, <u>OR</u> which *might*

lead him __not__ to hold the *balance* nice, clear, and true between the State and the accused, __denies...due process of law__." (emphasis added) – at p. 532

Did a SUBVERSION OF PROSECUTORIAL DUE PROCESS happen here? On that February 1989 day in Chambers – the nice, clear, and true *Judicial balance* between the State and the Accused became **blurred**! That is a fact. To what **end it led** can't be determined. That is solely a matter of troubling speculation.

Events unfold to a disposition of the Trial. Stung by the *Judicial spin* that has labeled my advocacy **intimidating** and **threatening**, and not wanting hard feelings to linger, I go to the Judge and *personally* apologize for my untoward behavior. My what? I'd previously acknowledged on the record, "That although I disagreed with parts of...[his] assessment of our exchange in Chambers, I..[wasn't] going to disagree with...[his] conclusion that my conduct was contemptuous. It was ugly. It's not something I'm proud of."

Yeah, but my contempt is __not__ for the Judge. I honor his position and I like him as a man. I'm **contemptuous** of his intention to deliver the *ADVISORY INSTRUCTION* – given the totality of the *Trial Circumstances*! What is **ugly** is his intention to *encroach* upon the province of the *Trial Jury*! I'm **not proud** of the *Procedural Anomaly* of a Judge wanting to be **both Judge and Jury**!

The Jury is dutifully instructed – absent a declaration of *Judicial Mind-set*. The cadre of *sweating* tongues deliver their Summations. The Jury deliberates for slightly more than a day. Their Verdict is NOT GUILTY.

My purpose in this piece is __not__ to second guess the *veracity* of the verdict. Their Verdict may very well be the *right verdict*. I wasn't at the crime scene. I didn't see the abduction of little Arthur. I didn't see cruel hands compress his neck and strangulate his body and dispatch his spirit to a place beyond the veil. I didn't see those cruel hands drag him to the spot where vermin feasted on his precious little remains. The only truth I knew was case truth.

I want to make something **absolutely clear**. THE SOUL of the *fabulous* Profession of Prosecuting Attorney is NOT about numbers.

The number of guilty verdicts and the number of not-guilty verdicts accumulated is NOT germane. PROSECUTING–IS–ABOUT–JUSTICE! When *Justice Wins* a Prosecutor wins.

If the Jury Verdict in February 1989 is a *Just Verdict*, then everybody's a winner!

–– The killer, whomever he is, will get his comeuppance from THE COURT OF FINAL JUDGEMENT at a time to be named. Make book on it!

What concerns me is not THE VERDICT per se. What *troubles* me is the extraneous, unsolicited hullabaloo swirling around an **un-sequestered** JURY. And it's all so unnecessary – so contrived. It's not **contemptuous** to be wrong, to err comes with the territory of being mortal. Human judgment is error prone. It's not contemptible, in my view, for a Judge to be wrong. It's **contemptible** for a Judge to be *indecisive*. And it's **contemptible** for a Judge to berate others for being *decisive*.

When a Public Servant has made a *conscientious decision* he believes **is** RIGHT, he shouldn't wilt under pressure. He shouldn't abdicate the moral strength of his conviction because he's decided he's been **intimidated** and **threatened**. RIGHT IS RIGHT – regardless. A Judge who is truly serving the public stands by his guns. His resolve doesn't crumble before the insistent rhetorical clamor of opposing view. He stands tall and true and resolute. He lets the chips fall where they land. He's not concerned about his public image or his tenure, nor about those who question his judgment or his intellect. His sole concern is the PUBLIC INTEREST. The public wants justice. JUDGING IS ABOUT JUSTICE! A Judge's abiding issue is: AM I RIGHT – IS THIS DECISION JUST? If the answer **is** YES, the true public servant is unbending. He's immune to **intimidation** and **threats**. Further, he will never – never – never *acknowledge* vulnerability to such reprehensible tactics, nor will he ever *make public* his PERSONAL OPINION regarding guilt or innocence during the pendency of a Trial over which he presides!

I've spoken *twice* on this page of Their Verdict. What concerns me is whether it *really* was THEIR Verdict? Or was the **integrity** of The Jury Verdict tainted by the corrupting influence of unfortunate News Media Publicity?

Sure, the *Advisory* <u>wasn't</u> **formally** given –– but <u>was</u> it **INFORMALLY** RECEIVED?

"JUSTICE, though due to the accused, is due
to the <u>accuser</u> also. The concept of **fairness**
must **not** be strained till it is narrowed to a
filament. We are to keep the balance true."
(Benjamin N. Cardozo, in a Supreme Court
opinion, *Snyder* v. *Commonwealth of
Massachusetts*, 1934. Emphasis added)

What About Bob's Ladies?

"Let's talk of graves, of worms, and epitaphs."
(William Shakespeare, *King Richard II*. Act III, Sc. 2, Line 145)

Chapter 7

They are, then suddenly they aren't. Bob's case is a dilly. It spans nineteen years, three hundred sixty one days. A *significant* part of my tenure as a Prosecutor in southern Nevada runs concurrently with the mystery of Bob. I went to work for the Clark County District Attorney's Office two and a half months *before* Bob pulls his first caper. I'm not licensed to practice law in the State of Nevada when Bob goes off the deep end. I'm in the process of establishing legal residency in the State as a predicate to taking the Bar Examination when Bob gets ballistic. I'm mostly confined to the DA library on the fourth floor of the Courthouse laboring as a law clerk when Bob commits the ultimate bad act. I will retire eight years, six months, and ten days after Bob is *retired* to the Nevada State Penitentiary.

Actually, the mystery of Bob is a *trilogy of mysteries*. He's a sly one – subtle, cunning, and diabolic. Bob believes it's possible to commit *perfect* crimes. He believes he's found a *loophole* in the laws of homicide. Prior to making Las Vegas his domiciliary city, Bob has spent time in the lone star state. He does some reading in Texas, and whether justified or mystified by what he's read, comes to the conclusion that murders are **un-prosecutable** without bodies. Which is a rather convenient concept for an incipient murderer whose a tidiness freak.

"Of all the creatures that were made he [man] is the most detestable. Of the entire brood he is the only one – the solitary one – that possesses malice...He is the only creature that inflicts pain for sport, knowing it to be pain." (Mark Twain, *Autobiography*, Vol. II, p.7 – 1924)

Katherine is a thirty four year old divorcee, the mother of four daughters, when she *vanishes* into the ethereal vapor of the sapphire Nevada sky. Gone without a trace. Katherine is simply – bye-bye! It is a Friday – April 26, 1968. Two days later her sleek black Cadillac Limousine is found abandoned in the Tropicana Shopping Center parking lot near Office Liquors. The vehicle is empty, no keys are in the ignition, only latent print smudges are detected, the doors are locked, and no forensic evidence is collected suggesting foul play. Of all God's creatures man *is* the solitary one that possesses **malice**.

Laura is an attractive forty seven year old realtor. She is single but engaging – intelligent and sophisticated. Urgently interested in becoming a twosome with the *right* kind of guy, when she *disappears* into the balmy haze of a melancholic southern Nevada night. Like Katherine, almost twelve and a half years before, she is gone without a trace. Laura is also simply – bye-bye! It is Sunday – October 5, 1980. Four days later her vintage black 1969 Lincoln Continental Mark III is discovered abandoned in the Caesar's Palace Parking lot. There is no sign of its owner. The vehicle is clean – inside and outside. It bears fabric marks, suggesting it has recently been wiped down. Several smudged latent prints are lifted from interior surfaces. The keys are missing from the ignition. Both doors are locked. *No* forensic evidence is recovered that establishes criminal conduct. Nevertheless, of all God's creatures man *is* the only one that inflicts **pain** for sport, knowing it to be pain.

Latisha is a lovely San Diego nurse. She is one hundred thirteen days past forty two years, yet whose counting. She's a bachelorette but recently engaged – dedicated to her profession and *wanting* nuptial bliss. It's a Saturday night, April 5, 1986, when she seemingly drops off the planet. *Evaporating* into the evanescent beauty of a southern California evening. Like Katherine, almost eighteen years earlier – and Laura, five and a half years prior, she is gone without a trace. Latisha too is simply –

bye-bye! Her white 1984 Pontiac Fiero is also abandoned. It's recovered from the parking lot of the Hanalei Hotel on hotel circle. Missing from the vehicle are its owner, the ignition keys, identifiable latents, and any *speck* of criminal mischief. The doors are locked, the windows are up – and intact. Of all God's creatures man *can be* the most **detestable**.

Sounds like a tough case, doesn't it? Or is it <u>cases</u>? No suspect. Or is it <u>suspects</u>? ––– No crime scene. No corpse. No autopsy evidence. No photographs. No forensics. No percipient-witnesses. No weapon. No prints. No motive.

No ghoulish stalker of women, active in his avocation for the better part of two decades but now abstinent, his penitence manifest by a halo hovering above his ears – bearing the sign, "I did it." No *plausible* psychics – anywhere. No pie in the sky. No hope? No time left? Remembrance fading.

Well, I suppose we could have tried dart boards or a Ouija board. What a tempting tactic – if only! A no-lose situation – if only! <u>Ouija</u> is a trademark for a board marked with the alphabet and various signs, used with a planchette to obtain *mediumistic messages*. A <u>planchette</u> is a small board supported on casters at two points and a vertical pencil at a third point, said, when lightly touched by fingers, to move of itself, the pencil thereby tracing words.

It's a thesis of the *seance crowd* that extraterrestrials communicate from the dead in this manner. Well, *if* that's a fact such an approach becomes an everybody- wins situation, doesn't it? IF **Katherine** and **Laura** and **Latisha** <u>are</u> among the dead, they'll happily come to the assistance of frustrated Law Enforcement Authorities. And IF the Ladies <u>aren't</u> dead we won't hear from them. A resolution is at hand, right?

Under such a scenario the Coppers and the Prosecutors can take a shortcut. Smooth this out. Conduct a *seance* in lieu of an arduous, tough, hard-nosed investigation. Or is it <u>investigations</u>? Go right to the crux of the issue. Or is it <u>issues</u>? Summoning the victims back. Learning IF the vertical pencil will trace a name. Or is it <u>names</u>? – **Bob** perhaps? Or **Tom** or **Dick** or **Harry**? Oh, hell, it slipped my mind. I've already rejected the <u>psychic</u> solution as *implausible*. Seance and psychic are based on the same *fallacious* system of **hocus-pocus**! The Criminal

Justice System doesn't have a *conjuring apparatus,* nor any certified <u>Conjurers</u>. Though esteemed Counsel for The Defense do enjoy <u>trying</u> to CON JURORS.

There is NO shortcut available to the Coppers and the Prosecutors. It's grunt time all the way. The hard way is the ONLY WAY. But *fantasy is fun* to think about. Wouldn't it be grand IF we could summon departed homicide victims back for some cogent input concerning their killers! What tales the ole vertical pencil might sketch.

Back to reality now. Sounds like a tough case? It <u>is</u> a tough case. Some Courthouse wags suggest it is a mission impossible. **Not** something that is <u>plausibly</u> <u>prosecutable</u>. Made that way, primarily, as a result of *two factors*: TIME and CORPUS.

Time – There is no Statute of Limitations to deal with in charging murder. Murder Prosecutions aren't calibrated by the calendar. The law absolutely imposes <u>no</u> set time within which murder charges must be brought. A filing can come within two days, two months, two years, twenty years, or theoretically after fifty years. Based simply upon the passage of time, there's <u>never</u> a *legal deadline* for the initiation of a murder charge.

However, many *factual* considerations hamper cold-case prosecution. The <u>availability</u> of witnesses, the <u>memories</u> of witnesses, the <u>integrity</u> of physical evidence, and the inherent issue of <u>credibility</u> in an old case are just a few of the practical problems relating to the Prosecution of stale murder cases. Such factors *always* figure into the calculus of *cold case* decision making.

Something stale is often something spoiled. The "...dim seen track-marks of an ancient crime..." (Sophocles adaptation, *Oedipus Tyrannus*) are often difficult to distinguish from irrelevant tracks – or clues. **Time** often *spoils* the dim seen track marks of *stale* crimes.

Corpus – means *body*. **Delicti** – means offense or *crime*. Thus, **corpus delicti** refers to the *body of the crime.* That is to say, <u>the proof of the crime</u>. *The body of the crime of murder* is **proof** **beyond** **a** **reasonable** **doubt** that murder has been perpetrated. An actual *corpse* is <u>not</u> required in Nevada criminal law. However, proof of the **corpus of murder** becomes <u>much</u> more difficult without human remains. Which is precisely why killers often try to dispose of the bodies of their victims. Such a strategy is not novel, but accomplishing the objective can be challenging.

The problems most of these self-centered characters experience usually stem from being *too lazy* and *too hasty*. A surprising numbers of murderers don't possess the wherewithal to bury their corpses deep enough, or hide them good enough, or burn them long enough, etcetera. And naturally, every murderer has a fervent wish to expeditiously *distance* himself from his foul deed. Consequently, the body remnants are discovered, and the **corpus of murder** is *conclusively* established. Like Mama always said, "Haste makes waste."

When a body is *never* found, death can *never* be proved to an absolute certainty. Further, the Police lose their best physical source for the detection and preservation of forensic evidence linking a <u>specific</u> suspect to the crime. If there is *no* body there can be *no* autopsy examination. Hence, a medical examiner has *no* way of determining and documenting: (a) whether a victim is truly dead, and (b) *if* the victim is dead; whether he or she died of natural, accidental, self inflicted, or criminal means.

Additionally, *if* there is **no** body there will be *no* autopsy photographs, *no* victim exemplar prints, *no* body fluid specimens, *no* hair samples, *no* clothing to impound, and *no* collection of foreign residue for subsequent comparison to and possible match with a suspect.

There's also the reality of dealing with trial juries. The lay persons on a jury will want to be given absolutely *conclusive* evidence of death. They are confronted with an onerous moral burden under the best of circumstances. It's neither easy nor pleasant to be called upon to impose judgment upon another human being. Trial Jurors *need* to know there actually **is** a murder! It is a well documented fact that *most* jurors are ill prepared to take the leap of faith required to *presume* there is a murder in the absence of a murdered *body*. They may sense in their guts from the totality of the circumstances that murder has occurred, but the **convincing power** usually comes up short without a physical body. *If* Jurors aren't sure there's been a murder, they can't *realistically* be expected to convict someone for murder. That fact is undeniable. The failure of a homicide investigation to locate a body <u>is</u> *always* a serious impediment to a successful prosecution! It is harbinger to a failed prosecution.

But —— in rare cases it–is–possible. **Murder is the ultimate act of selfishness!** It's not surprising that a resourceful killer will seek to deprive his victims of dignity in death, their loved ones of closure in life, and police of murdered bodies in their investigations. Therefore, it is highly imprudent to insulate clever killers from conviction because they have *disposed* of the bodies of their victims. **Murders are complete when victims die!** Mutilating or burning or burying a *corpse*, for example, is *evidence* of premeditation, but these acts of concealment are **not** elements of murder. The *disposal* of bodies is a hideous addendum to murder! That's all. Remember this legal imperative. Those who murder are not entitled to freebies under any circumstance!!

Successful prosecution of a <u>bodiless</u> case is directly proportional to the degree of *trust* the Jury is willing to bestow upon their Prosecutor. A certain amount of capital is generally available to the Prosecution. They wear the white hats, right?

The Prosecutor comes to Court in a *unique* position. <u>He is the representative of **the People**!</u> Theoretically, the Prosecutor <u>is</u> the *unbiased* <u>seeker of truth and justice</u>. He has NO axe to grind. He <u>doesn't</u> know the accused or the witnesses. He has <u>no</u> pecuniary nor familial interest in the outcome of the case. The Prosecutor *personifies* the "justice" role in Criminal Justice System. He's the good guy – the <u>Courtroom Cop</u>. The *point-person* defending a cowering public against crime's vicious onslaught. Every case is styled, **People** v. John Doe, Defendant or **State** v. John Doe, Defendant. During a criminal trial **The Prosecutor** <u>is</u> the <u>People's Man</u>!

It is a salient feature of the Adversary System, that in *close cases* – all other things being equal, the Police and the Prosecution <u>are</u> *usually* given an **<u>edge</u>** in *credibility* by Jurors. Due to the tasks they perform in the Criminal Justice System, the Police and the Prosecutors <u>are</u> *usually* given the benefit of a doubt. Evidentiary *gaps* are plugged by an *amorphous factor* called **trust**. This <u>resilient truth</u> shouldn't come as a surprise to those with a little Courtroom sophistication. The only question being: Just how *white* does the Jury believe those hats are? And the answer is <u>never</u> more important than in a *case without a body*!

So, this is my advice to the guys and gals with the white hats: **Don't** <u>smudge</u> them. **Don't** <u>squander</u> the *trust* the system gives you. **Exploit the "trust" factor!** <u>Nurture it</u> – <u>enhance it</u>. *Always strive* to <u>project</u> a

positive prosecutorial personality! Be professional – **Be** honorable – **Be** objective – **Be** articulate – **Be** credible – **Be** *trust –– worthy* – and **Be A Winner!**

Of course, the Prosecutor's hat isn't going to seem very white, and the *trust factor* will be negligible if he's got the <u>wrong</u> Jury. It's all for naught if the Jury is composed of the wrong chemistry and the wrong people.

There is no more *important* nor *unpredictable* stage to any Trial than Jury Selection! No one whose tried cases will minimize the significance of the Jury Selection procedure. <u>Every</u> *insightful* trial practitioner in the Courtroom battlefield will express the opinion that Jury Selection is the <u>most</u> crucial phase of a Trial.

If a Jury is impaneled, which *favorably* views the position of a particular party, that side is in a good position to win. But when the majority of Jurors are unfavorably disposed *against* a party, then tons of evidence and rising tides of rousing rhetoric *won't* make any difference in the decision. The die *is* cast from the get-go, and the evidence and the eloquence will likely fall on deaf ears.

Many trial advocates publicly express a *desire* to select Jurors who will be *open minded* and arrive at *just* decisions. However, <u>most</u> trial practitioners *aren't* really looking for open minded Jurors. They *don't* really want *justice*. They want to *win*! <u>Each</u> side in a Trial wants to be a *winner*. The advocates are *actually* looking for Jurors who are *close minded* rather than persons who are *objective* in their analysis. When the *facade* of philosophizing is peeled away, *what Lawyers want* are Jurors who, because of their experience and their propensities, are most *likely* to vote for the position of their clients. Whether that client is the *State* or the *Defendant*.

The overriding *need* of <u>each</u> adversarial party in a Trial is to get the type of Jurors they *want* to serve in the Jury Box. Every *ploy* will be utilized in this endeavor. Defense Lawyers will strive to *precondition* the prospective juror panel by hammering away at their twin towers of presumption of innocence and burden of proof. Prosecutors will hammer away at the heinous nature of the crime. All the forensic skill and all the acquired wile for *suggestion*, for *persuasion*, for *pre-*

indoctrination and *predisposing* minds of Jurors <u>will</u> be employed by glib gladiators of the Courtroom arena in an unflagging effort to be *winners* in the Jury selection sweepstakes.

<u>Both</u> sides recognize this abiding verity: **if** you don't *win* early you'll probably *lose* later. Trial Lawyers don't give a hill-of-beans about *quality* Jurors. What each side wants are *biased* Jurors. Those <u>predisposed</u> to their position.

It isn't realistic, but Lawyers want to confound the ordinary flow of events. They want to know the *ending* at the *beginning*. Will the end result be winning or losing? The key to a HAPPY <u>ENDING</u> is the Jury. Therefore, the Trial Lawyer wants special insight, keen perception, and yes – clairvoyance at the *beginning*. That is to say, he wants his sharp prescient gifts during Jury Selection. The Trial Lawyer's fondest wish is having the ability to *look* into the minds of prospective jurors. Unfortunately, despite self perceived powers of discernment, Lawyers don't have the wherewithal to crawl inside the heads of those summoned to the jury pool. They don't read minds. They aren't seers. They don't actually possess the spirit of clairvoyance.

So, given the *crucial* importance of securing a Jury having the <u>right</u> chemistry and the <u>right</u> people, it's not uncommon for Parties to hire a surrogate. These surrogates are the so-called Jury Selection Experts. They are expected to do *mind reading* **for** the Lawyers – so those best fitting the preferential Juror profile might be identified. These well-pedigreed experts fill the vacuum that remains after the more *finite* denizens of the legal profession have exhausted their piteous getting–inside–the–heads–of– prospective–juror skills. The "expert" juror consultant, presumably vested with *extraterrestrial perceptive prowess* and a degree in psychology, assumes the role of a courtroom *soothsayer*.

Intense analytical sessions involving Counsel and the "expert" are *spent* outside the Courtroom examining information gleaned from prospective jury panel members, and I do deliberately use the word *spent*. Time is money to a courtroom *soothsayer*. Their <u>fee</u> <u>meters</u> constantly hum in overdrive. What happens outside the Court is supplemented by numerous huddles with Counsel inside the Courtroom as *voir dire* procedure unfolds. Prospective Juror response purportedly <u>empowers</u> these *primates of a higher realm* with the *Alpha and Omega* capabilities necessary to **identify** the *beginning and the end* at <u>**the beginning**</u>.

Do the statistical charts and the psychological methodologies and the sociological profiling of Jurors help or hinder the selection process? Or is their behavioral science – *junk science*? **No one** really knows! The only tangible *indicator* is: Did the Party that employed the services of the juror *selection* consultation "expert" win or lose! However, that fact alone isn't totally definitive.

Every Criminal Trial is infested with a subtle cornucopia of variables which are *unique* to that particular case. The *act* of winning or losing *cannot* be explicitly **linked** to a specific *cause*. Being a *winner* is never **proof** of why you won!

During my Prosecutorial years I avoided the additional Trial expense of a Jury Selection Consultant. Being a public servant I fed at the public trough, but I wasn't wasteful. That would have been contrary to my nature. Hopefully, my career has been guided by a solid set of values. For instance, I'm a *fiscal conservative* and I'm a *factual skeptic*. I believe in facts, but I recognize that many things witnesses convey as fact don't even remotely represent the truth. Therefore, I like to wrap my mind around evidence and analyze corroborative or conflicting circumstances before I accept a proffer of testimony as fact. In point of fact, I'm skeptical of the "art" of soothsaying. I don't really believe anyone can tell the Parties at the beginning of a Trial what a particular Juror's Verdict is going to be at the end of the Trial. The best anyone can do is offer an educated *guess*. Hence, I've never been greatly enamored of the role juror consultants perform in the selection process. Of course, there is a fiscal dimension to every criminal proceeding. Trials cost money. Lots of it. But that's not an excuse for squandering public funds. It doesn't justify extravagance. I consider the use of Jury consultation "experts" to be extravagant.

My innate factual skepticism has led me to conclude that the contribution of "expert" Juror consultants is not sufficiently meaningful to justify their use by the Prosecution. There aren't any shortcuts in this business. With all due respect, nobody sees past eyeballs and gets inside Juror heads. I don't like to generalize, and I don't want to be too severe in my judgment of psychological skills. Which are certainly consequential in many situations. However, based upon the negligible impact, I believe, Jury selection consultants hired by the Defense have made in Trials I've handled, I think their so-called expertise is <u>highly</u> over-rated.

During nearly twenty nine years in the Courtroom I interviewed thousands of witnesses, questioned thousands of prospective Jurors, and personally engaged in the *selection* of hundreds of Juries. Through it all, I think I've won most of the cases I should have won – with a few notable exceptions. And I <u>don't</u> attribute any of the losses to the absence of advice from an "expert" Jury Selection Consultant.

I've acquired a few insights about human nature from my experience, and what I <u>know</u> came from *living* it and *witnessing* it – *not reading* about it! I *want* Jurors who are connected to the community. People who have accepted ownership of their community. People who appreciate the stake they and their families have in Police and Prosecutive efforts to maintain law and order. I *want* Jurors who are productive, law-abiding citizens. Their ethnic background or race or gender or religion or occupation or financial status <u>doesn't</u> matter one iota to me, but I <u>do</u> *want* them to appreciate and to have a sense of responsibility for their *citizenship* in this great Land of Procedural Due Process of Law.

I *want* Jurors who *want* to serve. Persons who believe it's an honor and a duty to serve their community in the Jury Box. I *want* Jurors who will devote their <u>full</u> attention to the proceedings when the Court is in session. I *want* Jurors who will base their decision <u>solely</u> upon the evidence introduced at Trial by the respective Parties and the Law of the Case as it is provided by the Court. Persons who will not allow public opinion nor media publicity nor personal trepidation to influence their Verdicts. I *want* Jurors who are willing to demand personal responsibility for the commission of violent crime! I *want* Jurors who will <u>find</u> the Defendant guilty **if** they are convinced beyond a reasonable doubt that he is guilty. I *want* Jurors who will be as focused and as diligent and as analytical as it is <u>possible</u> for them to be until their service has ended. Persons who can leave the Courthouse with heads held high, with clear conscience, and without regret – because they have <u>done</u> <u>their</u> <u>best</u>. And I **didn't** need a Jury Selection Consultant to tell me **what** I wanted and **who** the ones I wanted were!

The Jury **is** the *ultimate variable* in every Trial. The Jury **is** the *wild card*. Jury Selection **is** the <u>most</u> important *stage* of every Trial. And when your Jury consists of the wrong chemistry and the wrong people, your tongue can *sweat* buckets, but ALL the *perspiration* will be to no avail. And the Lawyer never knows for sure until it's over.

<u>**Nothing** changes this truth</u>: when we get to the bottom line – to the end of the Trial after all the evidence has been received and formal written Judicial Instructions have been given – to summation – to the submission of the case to the Jury – to the Jury Room – to emotional Jury argument and agonizing deliberation, NOBODY on the face of this earth is <u>actually</u> <u>able</u> <u>to</u> <u>predict</u> with any degree of mathematical certainty how the deliberation of a particular panel of twelve Jurors on a specific case *will end*!

Until the Jury Foreperson announces the Verdict in open Court, NO ONE knows *for sure* what it will be. **Not** the Judge, **not** the Accused, **not** Defense Counsel, **not** the Prosecutor **not** the gallery, and most assuredly – **not** the "expert" Juror Selection Consultant. Because **if** you <u>can't</u> *predict* verdicts you <u>can't</u> *predict* Juror propensities

The interested Parties can read their astrological charts or throw darts, or rely upon the advice of a *courtroom soothsayer*, but the result will be the same. When the Jury returns to the Courtroom to render its verdict, EVERYONE will be sitting on the edge of their seats *wondering – and sweating*!

It's not that Bob wasn't on police radar after Katherine's disappearance. He **was** – but there are sooooo many possibilities! And they'll <u>all</u> be milked dry by esteemed Counselors for the Defense – in a *flourish* of rhetorical fireworks calculated to demonstrate **reasonable doubt**. They'll zealously leave <u>no</u> phrase unturned. When there are <u>no</u> bodies a *plethora* of arguments will roll off their tongues. We <u>can't</u> count the ways.

When Katherine disappears the possibilities are **endless**! It's a fact in this veil of tears called mortality, that persons **do** go missing of their *own* accord. And they don't *telegraph* they're going missing. They <u>don't</u> say anything to anybody. They just **go**!

Katherine has disappeared without a trace, but her disappearance alone does not establish Criminal Homicide. **Not** everyone who vanishes is a murder victim. Katherine may be an *accident* victim. Perhaps, she's *amnesic* or *schizophrenic* or *suicidal*. Possibly, she's simply a societal or family *dropout*. Katherine may be infused with a cacophony of *wanderlust*. She may be *depressed*. She may have suffered a nervous *breakdown*. She may have wanted a *new life*. Maybe she wants a new job and new friends and new surroundings. And the *combinations* of these possibilities stretch to infinity.

Human beings <u>are</u> unpredictable. This fact is not debatable. People aren't robotic and they aren't puppets on a string. Mothers <u>don't</u> always *want* to stay mothers. They <u>don't</u> always want to sacrifice big chunks of their time for the sake of their kids. They <u>don't</u> always have the proper temperament for motherhood. Mother's are usually wives too, and they're <u>not</u> *all* eternally happy with the prick they're stuck with. There are wives who just take a powder – without warning.

Further, Las Vegas Realtors <u>don't</u> necessarily stay Las Vegas Realtors all their lives. And San Diego nurses <u>don't</u> necessarily stay that way ad infinitum. Some people decide *on their own* that life is <u>too</u> short to be lived in the same monotonous rut. They seek excitement and glamor and change. So, where's the beef if the Prosecutor doesn't have a body? Where's the proof of crime?

Police and Prosecutors learn to be circumspect, and the *circumspection* may last for years. They must try to take <u>every</u> possible factor into account *before* they proceed. There's a Double Jeopardy Clause in the Constitution. The law allows them only **<u>one</u> bite** out of the apple. *Before* Law Enforcement charges murder without a corpse, they've got to *really* believe they can make it stick.

Yes, Bob is on the radar screen. But the guys with white hats have to be able to **<u>prove</u>** beyond a reasonable doubt that he's *mean*. They have some things. However, they're <u>not</u> sure what they have is enough. A decade +two years passes.

Then – along comes **Laura**. Enchanting, stylish, unsuspecting Laura. She doesn't know his history. **If** – **if** – if –– *if* ONLY Bob <u>had</u> been arrested <u>after</u> Katherine! How *vividly* the view can be framed when we look <u>back</u> at events as they have unfolded. Hindsight is always a scintillating *twenty-twenty*!

Laura has a turbulent six year relationship with Bob. The flies in the ointment being her *promiscuity* and <u>his</u> *possessiveness*. It's a lethal nexus of traits that constantly tugs the partners toward polar extremes. Like mixing oil and water. The union is stunted by an inherent antithesis. It's an affair that seems destined to have a serious tipping point. It <u>isn't</u> easy putting a fence around Laura, but Bob keeps trying.

Friends and business associates describe Laura as "a glamorous, very beautiful woman." She exudes a sensuous sophistication. Her attire is stylish and alluring and revealing. A fact that is bittersweet to Bob. He enjoys it but he's simultaneously repulsed by it. Her clothing and her manner make her seem illusive, and – hard to *corral*. She is. That's a serious dilemma for one who is a *controller* by nature.

A co-worker explains that Bob <u>often</u> came into the Realty Office and just sat there for hours. Not saying anything. Simply staring. She sees Laura change from a happy-go-lucky personality to an unhappy, stressed-out person. She'd be "wringing her hands" and saying, "Why is he out there? I can't get my work done with him out there." She said she'd "probably lose her fingers before she got *rid* of Bob!"

Another realtor said Laura spoke of an impending breakup, "I'm going to <u>break up</u> with Bob because he's become too jealous and possessive." She reiterated her intention to a daughter. "*Four days* prior to her disappearance, Mother said she intended to <u>break up</u> with Bob. He was incredibly jealous."

Hey, this guy has a penchant for violence. Katherine's history and Laura's lucky. Six years into a tumultuous relationship and she's still around? It's fortuitous Laura has lived this long. Don't mess with Mister Bob, Madam. You'll get dragged into deep water. He's a rip tide. The man's got a thing about rejection. He's got a <u>dark</u> side to his moon.

Laura's best friend calls it "a <u>strange</u> relationship. Laura slept with *other* men and <u>didn't</u> hide those affairs from her jealous boyfriend...I often said, Aren't you **scared**? <u>How</u> can you *flaunt* something like that in someone's face...On October 5, 1980 some<u>thing</u> was bothering her, but she wouldn't tell me what it was."

Uh –– maybe it was a premonition. Hideous promptings of imminent retribution."Let's talk of graves, of worms, and epitaphs." (ibid.)

She's gone within hours, and after that, <u>nobody</u> *sees* her again – ever!

What about Bob's ladies? He gives a recorded statement to Police after Laura's disappearance. It's typed by Metro, but <u>never</u> signed by him. On November 1, 1980 Bob is walking on the sidewalk along Bel Aire Drive. He's confronted by the Metro Detective working the case. The language of the Cop is coercive and accusatory <u>by</u> design. It's a ploy to rattle the *primary* person of interest in regards to Laura's disappearance. It's a stand-off at OK BEL AIRE. The Detective is <u>thinking</u> about Laura – but he's also *remembering* Katherine. Bob is <u>thinking</u> about Laura too. He's *remembering* Katherine also, and he's thinking it's getting *too* hot for comfort in Las Vegas, Nevada. And he's not concerned about **hot** weather – it's early November. He's concerned about putting some *space* – some big-time real estate – between himself and a pit-bull Detective. The guy's in Bob's face! He's doing some serious finger-pointing.

The Detective says, "I think you're *good* for it." Bob queries, "Good for what? What are you talking about?" The vehemence of the stern reply <u>verbally</u> accosts Bob: "Good for **Laura's** disappearance!! I can't prove it *yet*, but I'm gonna be all over you until I do. Mark my words well, Mister, I *don't care* what I have to do. I'm going to *lock* you up for the murder of this lady. I'm going to see you *die* in the slammer."

Bob gets the message. It's like he's been cold-cocked in the jaw. He acts punch drunk. He sways and steps back a bit. Then, he blanches and begins to shake. The color <u>visibly</u> drains from his face. If the Detective had been holding a bucket under Bob's chin his color would have *dripped* into the bucket. A face isn't going to get any more transparent than Bob's face became.

He just stood there for a few moments, not saying anything. Finally, he stammered, "Well, if that's how you feel Mr. Know-it-all, I'll see you around." And he immediately walked away. Off into the sunset, so to speak.

Excuse me, I'm getting ahead of myself. Bob <u>first</u> goes to the residence of relatives. Two days after his close encounter with the cop on Bel Aire, he makes a clandestine night-time visit to the home of his sister and his brother in law. Bob asks to *borrow* their pickup truck. He's been storing some things at their house. He retrieves his brief case, personal effects, and cash. Tells them he's pleased he has a passport, and *asks* them <u>not</u> to tell **anyone** he's borrowed the truck. Then –– he rides off into the sunset – not. Actually, Bob drives into the darkness and <u>obscurity</u>.

He'd promised to return the pickup on November 5, 1980. He doesn't. Eventually, it's recovered from the parking lot of a southern California airport. There's not a peep from Bob until his sister gets a post card in early February 1981. The mailing address is Central Post Office, Plaza Jose F. Veragara, **Vina Del Mar**, **Chile**.

Wanting a change in scenery? A trip to the southern hemisphere as winter approaches? Seeking to get the color back in your cheeks, Bob? Or needing quiet- time away from Vegas Cops?

Bob has succeeded in putting a lot of *space* between himself and the long arm of Nevada Law Enforcement. The length of time he stays in Chile is unknown, but he is <u>on the lam</u> for six and a half years. He's here. He's there. He's known by this or that. He's making himself *scarce*. Hard to find.

What about Bob? Bob is in a defensive mode. **Bob is in flight!** What about Bob's *two* ladies? **They're sleeping** and *they* <u>won't</u> be waking up!

Prosecutor's have an evidentiary <u>label</u> for suspects who *turn rabbit* when the heat gets turned up and run to the border to hide – or wherever they go to find a hole to crawl inside. We call it **consciousness of guilt!**

Let's face it. Bob had *no* intention of seeing the Detective again when he said on Bel Aire, "I'll see you around." His focus is high-tailing it out of Vegas. How do we know? A month later, or less, he's in Chile. He sends a post card to his Las Vegas relatives. Was the timing of Bob's sudden urge for travel to foreign soil just a *coincidence*? Yeah, the same way it's a coincidence that Canadian Geese head south in the winter. It's a *flight* the honkers consider a matter of survival.

Bob believes it's a matter of his survival as a free man when he tries to drop off the map. The *uptight* man in flight wants to be out of sight. He flees to Chile because a Homicide Dick puts the *fear of justice* in him. Frankly, he doesn't care to spend the <u>rest</u> of his mortal existence in the slammer. But in that case, he'd have been better advised to *sit tight* and act more forth right. When a suspect flees to **avoid arrest**, he's *manifesting* a consciousness of guilt. Innocent people aren't afraid of police scrutiny. An innocent man may *not* welcome prosecution, but he's <u>not</u> *afraid* of prosecution.

We know Bob's back in the States on April 5, 1986. Hey guys it's me, I'm b-a-c-k! See Bob run. See Bob date. See Bob get malicious. <u>See</u> Bob before it's too late! How do we know he's back?

Well – at first, we didn't know. We <u>didn't</u> **see** Bob in time. We *wish* we'd known the moment his boots hit the ground in San Diego. And the fiancé and family of the **third** disappearing woman passionately *wish* we'd known!

Lovely **Latisha** is a San Diego nurse. She's been dating a fellow she knows as **Bob Smith** for approximately six months. However, her enthusiasm for Mister Smith has waned. He's not taking her to Washington, and she's not feeling like she's on cloud nine. The only place he's headed is to hell in a hat basket, or whatever.

She's met a Medical Doctor and is smitten by him. The Doctor lives in Colorado. So, it's been a long distance courtship for the most part. Nevertheless, he proposes marriage in a letter and she gladly accepts. She tells friends she has a dinner date with Bob Smith on Saturday night – **April 5, 1986**. She'll *charm* him with the good news during dinner. Latisha needs someone to watch her back. The change-in-partner-thing may give Bob indigestion and prompt a devious plan for interdiction. She <u>never</u> returns from the date with Bob.

She's <u>gone</u> with the southern California Santa Ana winds. All that remains is her 1984 Pontiac Fiero, conspicuously left in a parking lot on Hotel Circle. There is **no** warning. **No** explanation. **No** cancel-the-wedding-plans-I've-had-a-change-of-heart message to the good Doctor. There is only <u>ominous</u> silence and heartbreak! It's inconceivable to Latisha's betrothed, her family, her friends, and her colleagues in the nursing profession that she would <u>go</u> of her own free will!

San Diego Police diligently investigate the missing person report, but it's a *dead end* to them. They learn of the disappearances of Katherine and Laura in Las Vegas also. The slight evidence of modus operandi that exists is *similar*, but San Diego is hundreds of miles from Vegas. The possibility of **three** *instead* of one <u>isn't</u> a thought that's compelling.

California authorities *see* little likelihood that a nexus exists in their sister jurisdiction.

That's the key isn't it. Possessing the experience and the commitment and the <u>innate</u> good judgment to *see* a connection where a connection exists! The San Diego Prosecutor's Office isn't impressed neither. To this day they have <u>never</u> charged *anyone*. **No one** has been held *accountable* by the State of California for the disappearance of dear Latisha.

She *was* a <u>nurse</u> of impeccable capabilities. A gentle <u>nature</u> without dis-function. A <u>heart</u> abundant with love for all mankind – and for her special doctor. She *was* a genuinely decent human being, but the Criminal Justice System has <u>not</u> given her justice in California. She has <u>no</u> **vindication** in California.

San Diego authorities say in essence: Where's the body? It's extremely difficult to prosecute someone for murder <u>without</u> a body. They say in substance: Assuming for the sake of argument the woman was murdered, <u>where</u> was she murdered? Where is the nexus to us? We can't prove the requisite jurisdiction to conduct a murder prosecution in San Diego County without the corpse, nor will we pursue any other charges. San Diego Prosecutors decide the paucity of evidence in the case DOES NOT justify expenditure of the funds required for prosecution, since the prospect of a successful result is exceedingly slim. And I <u>suppose</u> that view still holds sway to this day.

<u>**BUT**</u> –– authorities in southern Nevada are fascinated by the possibility that San Diego's **Latisha** is linked to **Katherine** and **Laura** of Las Vegas. Especially, when their investigation <u>establishes</u> that *Bob Smith* <u>is</u> their *Bob*! He's been using an alias and working as a salesman at International Consultant Exchange. Curiously, the business is located at 950 <u>Hotel</u> <u>Circle</u> North in San Diego. Tying it all together <u>won't</u> be easy though. There is a definite problem. Bob is no longer employed at ICE. He takes two "sick days" on Sunday and Monday April **6-7**, 1986, and never comes back to work. Therefore, Vegas <u>hasn't</u> got *bodies* and they still have <u>NO</u> BOB! Where, oh where, has ole Bob gone?

Only <u>his</u> shadow knows, because he's on the move. *Bob* <u>is</u> radioactive. He *contaminates* the ladies he courts. They become terminal – although the malignancy lies in him not them.

"There is a Reaper whose name is Death, And,
with his sickle keen, He reaps the bearded grain
at a breath, And the flowers that grow between."
(Henry Wadsworth Longfellow, *The Reaper and
The Flowers*, Stanza I, 1839)

He's a lightning rod to the Las Vegas Metro dicks now. Yet, they're still empty handed!

What about Bob? Where is ole Bob? *Four hundred sixteen days* <u>after</u> Latisha he's found. He's in Tucson, Arizona – and still radioactive. He's dating **Rosie**. Is she terminal now? Is Rosie the next lovely flower about to be cut down by the Reaper's sickle keen? The next episode in the mystery of Bob will disclose <u>her</u> fate. Is she victim or hero? Odds-makers familiar with the unfolding scenario would probably have chosen the former – **until** the show! The show turns everything around. It totally changes the investigatory landscape.

Las Vegas authorities are feeling a fierce urgency to locate Bob. He's had an active Arrest Warrant for years, and they're <u>willing</u> to extradite from any spot on the globe. Two weeks after his <u>borrowed</u> pickup truck was found in a California airport, he'd been charged with felony *Embezzlement of a Motor Vehicle*. The <u>Warrant</u> is more pretext than substantive. Bob's relatives, who own the truck, aren't really interested in prosecution. The truck is back in their hands, and they're thinking – no harm no foul. But the coppers are very anxious to lay <u>their</u> hands on Bob.

Yet, the National Crime Information Center (NCIC) hasn't produced the information necessary to get a lariat around Bob. He's truly become a classic will-o'-the-wisp. The Las Vegas Metropolitan Police Department decides to employ more unconventional means. As the saying goes, beggars can't be choosey.

Vegas Police seek assistance in lassoing Bob from the nationally syndicated NBC television series, *Unsolved Mysteries*. Paradoxically, the <u>profile</u> of Bob's suspected criminal activity appears on the <u>very</u> **first** segment of the show. And guess what? Ole Bob <u>IS</u> **arrested** within *twenty four hours*! Now is that a block- buster start for a TV series or what. A network can't buy that kind of publicity. It's a perfect jump-start to their program. Absolute proof of how much Americans love the Tube? Or is it simply the fickle finger of luck?

Be that as it is, **Bob** is finally corralled. *Ole* Bob is arrested in beautiful Tucson on May 26, 1987 for the embezzlement of an *ole* pickup. The case does have its ironies.

Of course, the focus isn't the truck. The Police have their sight set on a much bigger bone they wish to pick with this guy. The Police focus is *the ladies*. They believe Bob has put them somewhere. And oh, how beautiful is the terrain to Law Enforcement that yields up a *thrice* **murderous fugitive** more than six and a half years after his **flight**.

What about Bob's ladies? Well, he's had a series of ladies. However, the last one ends up being more than he can handle. **Rosie** unravels Bob. She is the trap door that ends his philandering piracy upon the female population. How does she do it? Actually, very easily. She likes television and she's got gumption!

Rosie wants romance in her life and she has a new prospect. She doesn't know he should have come packaged with a **Beware of Bad Dog** warning label. She knows nothing of his past, nor his prior ladies. She only knows what he lets her know. What she sees. He's suave, self assured, and handsome in a mature sort of way. She's impressed by his sophistication and by the attention he gives her. She's experiencing a strong attraction to the guy. To use the popular vernacular, she's blown away by Bob – though she doesn't know he's Bob.

Rosie knows her new romantic interest as *Charles Stolzenberg*. He's got a triumvirate of missing ladies in his past. He figures he's worn out the name *Bob*.

Bob has become Charlie in Tucson. That's his little secret. Let bygones be bygones. Let sleeping ladies lie. Ignorance can be bliss or it can be an invitation to tragedy.

Rosie's ignorance might have been tragic *except* for the show. Rosie watches a lot of television, and she's staring at the Tube on Monday night May 25, 1987. Further, as fate has it, she's watching the NBC network. She sees the premier of *Unsolved Mysteries*. What she sees rocks her world. It's totally off the chart to her. Unfathomable! Rosie immediately gets very sick to her stomach, and it isn't food poisoning and it isn't a virus. It's an ugly glimpse into Charlie's past. Ugh! Damn it! A lonely woman just can't catch a break with her love-life sometimes. Yeah really, but in the larger context Rosie may have been catching the break of her life. What she <u>sees</u> on TV *saves* her. She <u>sees</u> that *Charlie is Bob* – and that Bob <u>is</u> radioactive. The fact is: Rosie isn't simply sick to her stomach, she's shaking like a leaf and she's feeling extremely grateful.

She watches a whole lot of TV and she's got gumption. Here's the gumption part. She could have just shit-canned the revelatory news flash about Bob. Kept a tight lip, gutted it out in silence, and told Bob to hit the road. "Bye– Bye, Chump. Don't let the door hit your rump as you depart my life – for whatever awaits you."

Rosie doesn't let it pass. She's a resourceful, enterprising spirit blessed with that most <u>uncommon</u> commodity known as *common sense.* She's shrewd enough to realize her safety is enhanced by giving the Police their big chance! She also has a sense of responsibility for the <u>other</u> ladies – past and future. And there's something else that factors into the equation. It's a small matter she didn't share with Bob. Rosie has a little *secret* too. She <u>used</u> to be married to a HOMICIDE DETECTIVE, and he's still employed by the Tucson PD.

Oh Bobby, what are the odds that you'd get hooked up with a chick whose the ex-wife of a homicide dick? With due <u>dis</u>respect Tiger, it does seem like poetic justice.

She calls her EX. He promptly relays the information to the Vegas PD. And —— within the next twenty four hours BOB IS IN CUSTODY *at last!* It's not a good percentage, but investigating homicides that lack bodies is a daunting task. Salvaging **one out of four** *ladies* is better than being empty handed.

What about Bob? His Trial <u>begins</u> on April 4, 1988. The *first* day of his Trial is pivotal. It <u>is</u> definitive. The die <u>is</u> cast on the *first* day. It's D Day on the *first* day. It's a precursor for Victory on the *first* day. There aren't ever any guarantees in a Jury Trial. However, the gods of justice are smiling on the Prosecution that *first* day! The odds are stacked against the Defense after the *first* day. An astute Trial Judge, a <u>man</u> of justice, makes it happen on the *first* day!

The Judge has scheduled a hearing for Pretrial Motions on the *first* day. The linchpins in the Defense strategy are encompassed in <u>two</u> motions. Bob is charged with <u>two</u> counts of Open Murder. Court One alleges the <u>MURDER</u> of **Katherine**. Count Two alleges the <u>MURDER</u> of **Laura**. They are the two Nevada residents. Since this case has <u>no</u> bodies, <u>no</u> one knows where the actual crimes were perpetrated – except for Bob. It's a definite handicap to be sure. However, Law Enforcement *presumes* that the Nevada *ladies* die in Nevada. **Latisha** lives in California. Therefore, she <u>isn't</u> a charged victim in Nevada. There is a presumption by Law Enforcement, right or wrong, that Latisha dies in southern California.

Accordingly, the Defense motions are: (First) A <u>Motion</u> for Severance. The Defense does NOT want **Katherine** <u>and</u> **Laura** linked in the same pleading. (Second) A <u>Motion</u> to Strike. The Defense most assuredly does NOT want evidence of **Latisha** to come before the Nevada Trial Jury.

But this is NOT the Defense's day. They AREN'T going to be winners today. They're NOT going to catch lightning in a jug today. Bob's Trial Judge is NOT going to transform his Judicial Robe into the cloak of a magician today. He WON'T be a legal wizard plundering relevant evidence. There will be NO *judicial sleight of hand* that makes evidence disappear today. Bob has already touched that base on <u>three</u> separate occasions over the past two decades.

It WON'T be a matter of *cabbages* and *kings* today. There WON'T be a subversion of *procedural justice* today! **TODAY** begins the process of exacting PERSONAL ACCOUNTABILITY from a methodical <u>predator</u> who preys upon beautiful women!

There is a slight incongruity in the Courtroom. The Judge is named Bob too. Bob will be judging Bob, but Judge Bob <u>isn't</u> going to be giving Defendant Bob any brownie points because they share a name. Judge Bob looks askance upon licentious conduct towards ladies. He has reviewed the case evidence. He's pondered the circumstances. He's <u>not</u> in Bob's corner on this one.

Therefore, the Defendant's *linchpin* motions <u>are</u> denied. Slam dunked into the judicial trash bin by the mental acumen of an agile Judge. He carefully makes his record. Astutely explaining the rationale behind his decisions. **Katherine** <u>and</u> **Laura** <u>will</u> be LINKED together in the same pleading. The Trial Jury <u>will</u> receive the full batch of evidence regarding <u>both</u> absentee *Nevada ladies*. Also, evidence of the disappearance of **Latisha** will <u>not</u> be stricken from the record. The Trial Jury will learn of the LINKAGE of Latisha to the *other ladies*. The rulings are <u>**huge**</u> to the Prosecution and *stinging* <u>**setbacks**</u> to the Defense. Thus, the *first* day ends.

Why is the *first* day so pivotal? So decisive? Well, stated succinctly, **it's the <u>numbers</u>**. Most folks understand that people do disappear on occasion – for a wide variety of reasons. A man's wife or girl friend may suddenly vanish and the event may have nothing to do with her husband or boyfriend. Most folks <u>can</u> buy into a disappearance that <u>is</u> *singular*. However, if it happens *twice* to the same man, that <u>raises</u> eyebrows. A bolt from the blue <u>doesn't</u> often strike twice in *successive* relationships. **BUT**, if it happens *three times*, THAT'S A PATTERN! That's a beef multiplied to the third power that's hard to chew. It's a **series** of deplorable circumstances that seem almost inconceivable. It's compelling evidence of <u>**criminal**</u> complicity. It's a scenario that gives a Prosecutor's supple *tongue* plenty to *sweat* over.

"COMMON DENOMINATOR – The Dictionary, in pertinent part, defines *common denominator* as 'a common <u>feature</u> of members of a group.' The *group* at issue in this instance consists of **Katherine**, **Laura**, **Latisha**. <u>and</u> BOB. <u>Three</u> lovely women who had the star-crossed misfortune, over time, of knowing the <u>same</u> mindless, spineless, contemptible man. The **Defendant** is the *common denominator* of this group. HE'S the conniving, unforgiving, <u>murderous</u> *common denominator*.

"The *group* is a bizarre linkage for *three* of its four members. The women are a <u>diverse</u> group. Katherine and Laura both lived in Las Vegas, but in different neighborhoods on opposite sides of the city. Latisha lived in San Diego. Katherine is a homemaker. Laura is a realtor. Latisha is a registered nurse. They <u>didn't</u> hang out together. They <u>didn't</u> shop together. They <u>didn't</u> have their nails done together. They <u>weren't</u> soccer moms together. They <u>didn't</u> go to Church together. They <u>didn't</u> go to Continuing Nursing Education courses together. They <u>didn't</u> go to movies or on vacations together They <u>didn't</u> go to the same dentist or the same shrink. They <u>didn't</u> car pool. They <u>didn't</u> double date nor triple date. They <u>didn't</u> do any of these things together, because they

DIDN'T KNOW EACH OTHER! All these women had in common is gender and beauty and BOB. They did *each* date Bob. They did *each* make love to Bob.

"But sharing the same bed doesn't always mean a man and a woman share the same lifetime. There's a thin line separating love and hatred and malicious intent. Love is often full of torment and jealousy and lament.

"WHAT ABOUT BOB'S LAIDIES? They aren't *connected* to each other, but they are each *connected* to Bob. He laid his *ladies*. Now, he's laid them to rest. Most men aren't connected to a *single woman* who disappears without a trace – who simply drops off the face of the earth. But the Defendant effortlessly, his history suggests, manages to acquire relationships with *three women* who just fly away over a nineteen year time span! **Serial disappearance**, it seems. Balderdash!

"What About Bob's Ladies? Ole Bob must have something contagious. Maybe some resourceful publicist for the pharmaceutical companies can give his syndrome an acronym. Something like BD, i.e., *Bob's Disease*. When you catch it you just disappear. His *ladies* **all** seem to get *itchy* feet after they've been around Bob for awhile. Or does Bob get *bitchy*?

"What's so incredible about *Bob's Disease* is that **his ladies** sudden *itchy* feet disorder includes their children, their extended families, their friends, their jobs, their interests –– their lives as they were. These women don't just abandon Bob, they leave EVERYTHING behind. Cold turkey!

"The Defense wants us to believe that ALL THREE of these women just closed the book on their previous lives – their loving ties – all they formerly idolize – to do what? Chase butterflies. No way. No Sir. Not in a million years. These women aren't transients. These three women are intelligent, mature, stable, responsible individuals. Their roots were buried deep in the resilient sod where they lived. There's nothing to analyze here. The Defense premise defies the reality of these three *LADIES*!

"Well, let me tell you something. I *don't* believe in coincidence. Man-makes- the-circumstance! An **evil** man made these circumstances. The odds AGAINST such an inexplicable phenomenon *naturally* occurring to the *SAME* man on *THREE* separate occasions with

THESE <u>types</u> of women is a *billion to one*. The Defense contention is unreal – totally beyond the pale – **inconceivable!** The disappearances of **Katherine** <u>and</u> **Laura** <u>and</u> **Latisha** were NOT <u>coincidental</u>. They were NOT <u>voluntary</u>. They AREN'T random, unrelated, lightning bolt events. These disappearances were malicious, deliberately designed, premeditated events perpetrated by the SAME MAN. He is the *single* **dark thread** that <u>ties</u> these women together. HE <u>IS</u> THE COMMON DENOMINATOR!"

I will highlight a number of additional factors. They also serve as *identifiable* <u>track</u> <u>marks</u> of Bob's ancient crimes. <u>Each</u> *track mark* leads to him!

"THREATS – The Court's Instructions define **threat as, 'A** *Declaration* of an <u>*intention*</u> *to inflict death* or bodily harm or injury upon another person.' Have the elements of this Instruction been satisfied? Legally, **threat** is a word of art. The Defendant <u>has</u> made threatening statements against **Katherine**. That, I submit, is indisputable. But do the comments <u>manifest</u> an *intention to inflict death*? That is the issue. The State has been the moving party in bringing evidence of threatening declarations before you. Obviously, the Prosecution believes the declarations have relevance. I made the proffers.

"However, I desire to be objective in my arguments. I <u>never</u> want to indulge in *legal hyperbole* when addressing you. Passing judgment upon another human being is an awesome responsibility. Ultimately, you decide <u>what</u> evidence is persuasive. The Ladies and Gentlemen of the Jury are the Triers Of Fact. You are to give <u>whatever</u> weight you deem is appropriate to the **<u>threat</u> evidence**. The Jury decides what evidence *truly* connects the accused to the commission of the charged crimes. Not the Prosecutor, not the Judge – THE JURY is charged with the duty of determining what weight the evidence will be given. It is your decision, and yours alone, to determine the guilt or innocence of the accused. And I urge you to be thoughtful and objective and just in your task!

"That said, I must also point out, in the spirit of fairness, that *threatening* remarks have to be put into context. Often words that seem threatening by their nature are not threatening in their context. It <u>is</u> the *intention* behind a declaration that makes the difference.

"Words are cheap. Every Court Reporter who has graced a Courtroom knows, from a constant bombardment of rambling Lawyer rhetoric, with what *ease* words tumble from the mouths of barristers. It's the way they ply their trade. Their *sweating* tongues <u>define</u> them. And the same may be said of <u>many</u> of the human species. When people are resentful or angry, it's not uncommon for their mouths to race down fast tracks far ahead of their minds. Their tongues are in overdrive, but their brains are in neutral. The so called phenomenon of 'foot-in-mouth disease' is hardly a rare occurrence. The crudely crafted limerick, 'He has diarrhea of the mouth and a constipation of thought,' satirically emphasizes the difficulty humans have in *coordinating* their brains with their mouths.

"Which is precisely why *threatening* words have to be put into their proper context. Why are they uttered? What is the circumstance? What is the frame of mind? What is the <u>intention</u> that really drives the remark?

"A *threatening comment* can simply be a thoughtless, ill-advised statement generated in the heat of passion-driven personal pique or anger. It may be dip-stick stupid, but <u>unpersuasive</u> in a Courtroom. Symptomatic of the human malaise that is constipation of thought. Representing a need to vent and unrepresentative of an <u>actual</u> intent to carry out the threatening language. <u>Not</u> a statement to be taken seriously.

"It is an irrefutable fact that people often *say* things they <u>don't</u> mean. And even *if* folks <u>do</u> mean them when they *say* them, after a cooling off period, they **don't** do them! When a **declarant** *speaks* about something he would *like to do*, that does <u>not</u> mean he *will* do it. The *threatening* remark is merely an <u>indication</u> that he *will* do it.

"A *threatening* statement is a **crime indicator**. It isn't proof of the commission of crime. Let's face it, if *threatening* words aimed at a spouse were always carried out an awful lot of marriages would be *missing* spouses! What torments lie within the small circle of a wedding band? Sadly, *threatening* rhetoric is common within the institution of marriage. And deplorably, it is rampant within a multitude of circumstances related to human relationships in general.

"Such inane phrases as, 'I'm gonna hurt you,' or 'Sometimes I'd just like to kill you,' or 'I wish you were dead,' or 'Why don't you die,' or the curious oxymoron, 'I love you to death' are repugnant expressions. But at the end of the day, they're *usually* only acerbic banter, and those who indiscriminately use them don't end up in Criminal Court. That doesn't happen unless the acerbic banter *happens* to **target** someone who *dies* or *disappears*.

"THAT'S THE PROBLEM HERE!! Bob HAS threatened to make **Katherine** go away – and she HAS gone away. She's *gone missing* for a few days short of twenty years. TWENTY YEARS **is** the problem here! Katherine has been gone for *twenty years*. It's **the numbers** again! BOB'S **vitriolic** ranting strikes me as being considerably more substantive than acerbic banter.

"**Katherine** is *terrified* of Bob. A daughter testifies she knows that for a fact. A friend of the victim testifies, '...[Katherine] was *deathly* afraid of the Defendant.'

"Sandy says Bob telephones her around Easter 1968. His comment is cryptically incriminating. He declares, 'I'm *afraid* I said I would LIKE TO KILL... [KATHERINE] in front of some of my friends.'

"So, what about Bob's ladies? Why does he pick up the phone, make a call, talk to Sandy, and impart this bizarre message ? He's **afraid** he said it? What does that mean? Is he **afraid** he's said it because it's true? He does want her DEAD?

" He doesn't know if he's said it, but he thinks he's said it? Is he sleep walking? Is he in a fugue state? High on coke? Smokin weed? He doesn't know what he's SAID? What's up with this? **Or** is it that he knows exactly what he's SAID? Because what he's SAID is specifically WHAT he's GOING to do to Katherine. And in a moment of candor he spills his guts about what he's GOING to do? He lets all his pent-up spleen spill out to some confidantes, and he's **afraid** they *won't* keep his confidence? He thinks they're going to spill the beans, and he's trying to take the *sting* out of the block buster revelation by *preempting* their disclosure to the Police?

"LOOK, **if** Bob doesn't mean what he's said why is he *worried* about what he's said? This declaration of intent is BEFORE Katherine disappears. Simply saying you'd *like to kill* a woman isn't a crime. The words Bob's uttered aren't criminal. Bob hasn't committed an indictable offense <u>YET</u>.

"Aaaah – there's the rub. Bob <u>hasn't</u> *killed Katherine* <u>YET</u>, but he <u>does</u> *still* INTEND to **kill Katherine**. That's the *only* thing that makes sense out of this bizarre telephone message to Sandy. He <u>wasn't</u> kidding when he said, '...I WOULD LIKE TO KILL...[KATHERINE]...' He **really –– really** MEANS IT. When Bob *inexplicably* tells some friends, <u>**He–wants–to–kill–Katherine**</u>, he speaks of *an act* that is **high** on his WILL DO <u>LIST</u>. That's the bottom line to this weird scenario. Both the DECLARATION <u>and</u> the TELEPHONE MESSAGE <u>are</u> **a–forecast–of–murder**! You <u>can</u> take that to the bank. IT'S A FACT, and facts are extraordinarily stubborn.

"Bob calls Sandy because he's telegraphed his <u>INTENTION</u> TO KILL and now he wants to **scramble** *the message*! He's made a public DECLARATION of an **intention to inflict <u>death</u>** – and he wants to **sanitize** *the message*. Clean it up. Defuse it. Make it seem innocuous – UN–sinister?

"Damn! This is sooooooo clumsy Bob. And sooooooo *enlightening*! Thanks much, Fella. Have a pleasant life in the Slammer.

"And by the way, for the sake of **context**, Easter Sunday <u>is</u> APRIL 14,1968. ONE DOZEN DAYS before ground zero for **Katherine**."

"*Eleven days* later, Joe and Judy are at **Katherine's** house. It is **April 25, 1968**. They are friends of Katherine. Joe is also her attorney. Katherine gets a telephone call between 6-7 p.m. She speaks for 3-4 minutes. It's Bob. He's continuing to use a land-wire to *talk nasty*. You got a problem with civility, Bob?

"Joe testifies, '<u>When</u> **she** hung up she got really *pale* and *white* and started *shaking*. Katherine immediately exclaimed, It was **Bob**! He THREATENED TO KILL ME <u>AGAIN</u>!'

"Hmmmm, Bob continues to stir the pot. On the eve of **Katherine's** demise, between 1800 and 1900 hours he's still spouting <u>**his intention**</u> *to inflict death*. His ploy is to make her <u>suffer</u> *twice*. Terrorize then victimize! Scare her to death before he chokes her to death. It's a rising **crescendo** of *threats* that contemplate a <u>savage</u> **climax**. Bob is engaging in a <u>deliberate</u> campaign of terrorism. It is a **prelude** to THE FINAL ACT!

"Bob <u>calls</u> again around midnight. How do we know? We know because **Katherine** <u>calls</u> Joe around midnight and reports that Bob says, **'He's going to kill me!'** Joe testifies, 'There is TERROR in her voice.'

"Oh where, oh where has **Katherine** gone? Where has Bob put her? And where has he put the others? All we know is that **Katherine** is missing on APRIL 26, 1968 and Bob is <u>so</u> overwrought he goes fishing on *April 27ᵗʰ*.

"None of this is predestined. <u>IF</u> only Bob had been put on the shelf sooner. But in deference to the Police investigators – there were *no bodies*."

"DIARY ENTRIES – They <u>weren't</u> words of *endearment*, to be sure. **The Diary** is intriguing. Compelling in its evidentiary value. It's a glimpse inside the mind of the scribe. Which makes the saga of the Diary truly odd – an evidentiary anomaly. What's mind-boggling is there really <u>isn't</u> a diary anymore. During the investigation of vanishing **Laura**, A DIARY is recovered from BOB'S Regency Towers apartment by the Detective assigned to the case. A handwriting examiner confirms that the entries are written by the Defendant. The <u>object</u> of his *profound* **disaffection** is the buxom, ill-fated Ms. Laura.

"However, this matter moves through the system with the speed of an arctic glacier. It's an *open* investigation, but movement is virtually non-existent. **The Diary** is <u>booked</u> into the Metro Evidence Vault on October 9, 1980. After that it gets <u>very</u> *dusty*. BOB FLEES. Years pass. No action is taken. Progress is indiscernible to the Custodian of the Evidence Vault in the matter of the <u>disappearances</u> of **Laura** and **Bob**, but crime statistics soar in the jurisdiction. The Vault is crowded. More space is needed. An inventory is taken with an eye toward culling out any unnecessary evidence still being stored. Of course, the matter of <u>Laura</u> and <u>Bob</u> remains an *open* case. Notwithstanding it's *official* status, a clerical error occurs. A Supervisor concludes that the matter of **The Diary** is closed. Therefore, he signs off on an <u>order</u> to *destroy* **The Diary**. It is booked out of the Vault and *eliminated*. Pitiful. **The Diary** needed a longer *shelf life*.

"What the hell, sometimes the good guys can't catch a break. The mistake isn't discovered until we're preparing for trial. Aarrgh! The esteemed Counselor for the Defense <u>doesn't</u> need a Court Order *suppressing evidence* this time around. His dirty work is accomplished **in-house**. Metro *suppresses* its <u>own</u> evidence. Hey, nobody's perfect. But that's of little solace to the Missing Persons Detective <u>and</u> the Prosecutor on the <u>dreary</u> day the GOOF-UP is made public.

"Let's see, we've got NO *bodies*, we've got NO *crime scenes*, we've got NO *autopsies,* NO *dying declarations*, NO *confession* –– and now we've got NO *DIARY*! Great roaring rockets. What will happen next?

"Praise the Lord, there's A COPY of the <u>pertinent</u> pages, that's what. However, what does pertinent mean? Pertinent to whom? The impounding Detective? He's made photocopies of THREE PAGES. The original Diary consists of seventeen pages. FOURTEEN of those pages are <u>un-copied</u> and **all** the original SEVENTEEN are unavailable. What's pertinent to Bob? Naturally, the esteemed Counselor for the Defense argues that **all** seventeen pages are <u>pertinent</u> to Bob. He strenuously argues that the Prosecution should <u>not</u> be allowed to *cherry pick* the pages they want. He says it's *impossible* for the Jury to establish context and determine relevancy without the **entire** document. If the Jury is to be forced into the role of mind reading, it <u>must</u> be able to read all that the mind has written!"

Nice presentation. But on this occasion, <u>not</u> nice enough. The Judge is the ultimate arbiter of what the Jury receives, and Judge Bob still isn't cutting Defendant Bob any slack. He'd rather have seventeen pages of **the Diary** entries, but he'll settle for three! The disposal is a *disconnect* between the Vault Keeper and the Case Investigator. It's a *mistake*, but it's <u>not</u> deliberate. It's <u>not</u> done in bad faith. This is highly relevant evidence. If the best the Prosecution can do is THREE PAGES then the Jury will have to settle for three pages. Judge Bob thinks Bob is good for this, the case equities militate <u>against</u> an exclusion of the exhibit.

The Court denies the motion to exclude the Diary entries. He says the objection goes to the weight to be given the evidence, not to its admissibility. Judge Bob says esteemed Counsel for the Defense may <u>argue</u> the issue of weight during his summation.

"**The Diary** entries read in substance,'**Laura is dead for sure. Laura's a lying, two-timing bitch. She's a f––ing cunt. Laura's dead for sure. It's <u>death</u> for the prevaricating whore!**'

"Really, it's bad enough that he's a killer. This Dude has to exacerbate his malicious intent by maligning his *victim* with bad poetry. It doesn't matter whether the cursive malignment occurs *before* <u>or</u> *after* the foul deed. **The Diary** is *defining* evidence in this trial. Through the insightful <u>lense</u> of **The Diary** we're able to look into the *mind* of a killer. **The Diary** provides us with 20/20 *vision* of the <u>fact</u> of MURDER, and an astonishing *acuity* into the irascible aberrance of ole Bob. He's made his record. We *witness* his irrepressible <u>record</u> of murdering! **The Diary** shreds the *nice guy veneer* that Bob displays in the Courtroom. What he <u>tells</u> HIS DIARY portrays the *real Bob*. He's a man of vindictiveness and stone-cold violence."

The Vault Keeper comes within *three* pages of absolving Bob of a frightful lapse of memory in his crime cover-up. Yup, he got <u>rid</u> of Laura's BODY. But he neglected to get <u>rid</u> of **The Diary**. He leaves for the southern hemisphere on 11/3/80 with such haste that he leaves his *pernicious* RECORD behind. It's a captivating tidbit just waiting to be discovered inside his Regency Towers apartment. An unintended gratuity from stingy ole Bobby. When he fled Vegas to *avoid prosecution* he needed to have **his record** under his arm.

There's that banal entertainment expression, "Break a leg." Actually, it's the arm that Bob's writing hand is appended to that needed to be broken in this instance. "Break an arm, Bob." No diary entries– **much** less of a problem dealing with the *issue* of **Laura**!

"SINISTER LIES – Ladies and Gentlemen of the Jury, a lot can be learned about a man <u>from</u> the things he *lies* about. What about Bob's *ladies*? When Bob *lies* about his *ladies*, what does that tell us about Bob? What is the <u>necessary</u> inference regarding the *ladies'* **fate**?

"1.Bob fraudulently <u>buys</u> REAL ESTATE a court has awarded to **Katherine** – approximately <u>NINE</u> years after her disappearance. He <u>procures</u> an unidentified woman, presents her to title companies as Katherine, and has her *forge* Katherine's name on DEEDS conveying *two* houses and the parcels upon which they sit to HIMSELF. *Brazen Bob.* These transactions are <u>both</u> *bald-faced LIES*! **ONLY KATHERINE'S KILLER**, ONLY THE PERSON WHO SAW HER <u>DIE</u> would know he could *forge* her name, *misrepresent* her identity, and *collect* thousands of dollars for the sale of HER property – WITHOUT **fear** of **consequence**! Lets talk about *graves* and *worms* and *epitaphs*.

"2. Bob has curious comments about **Katherine** going missing. He tells one of her daughters, 'She probably *worried* about getting work and money, and her <u>mind</u> <u>snapped</u>.'

"He tells an investigating Officer, 'She was *going* through <u>menopause</u> and taking <u>tranquilizers</u> **the night** she disappeared.' WHOA, that sounds like a *Freudian slip*! HOW does he <u>know</u> about her condition and about the pills she's taking for her condition –– **UNLESS** HE'S *with her*?

"A friend of **Katherine** calls Bob several days after the disappearance. She states, 'I was angry. I <u>knew</u> he'd done something with her. I asked him right out, Bob, you did something to her didn't you? And he said, Well, she's *either* had a nervous breakdown *or* SHE'S <u>DEAD</u>!' In April 1986 an associate asks him about **Katherine**, Bob says, ' SHE <u>DIED</u>.' Now, it's an *unequivocal* statement. He's sure <u>now</u>. But Bob would <u>know</u>, wouldn't he?

"There's a DINNER DATE with **Laura** the Sunday night she disappears. Bob asks her out, but he wants her to furnish the transportation. Laura's friend Susie listens to the answering machine recording after the fact. Bob slyly implores, 'Laura, I want you to have dinner with me at my place. I have <u>something</u> SPECIAL *planned*! Come by and pick me up at 8:00 p.m.'

"Here's a **stupid** *question*, what <u>so</u> SPECIAL about getting **murdered**? Bob sets the hook and reels her in. He's had his fill with **Laura's** promiscuity. He's decided she won't *chippy* on him anymore. He's <u>not</u> remotely interested in dinner with her *really*. He has <u>nothing</u> SPECIAL *planned*. It's A LIE to <u>entice</u> her to join him. He only *wants* to say, 'Bye-Bye.'

"He's calculating and amoral. Carnal to the marrow of his bones. Perhaps, they eat dinner. Perhaps, they sip vintage wine. Then he uses some ruse to get her <u>out</u> of his apartment and <u>into</u> his clutches. Maybe she's in to star gazing – or maybe he's <u>got</u> **a <u>weapon</u>** and she doesn't have a choice. However he pulls it off, Bob gets her one-to-one in a *private* place of his preference. Overpowers her – and drops her in a deep, dark hole. Probably an abandoned MINE SHAFT.

"Bob's done some prospecting. He's familiar with many of the abandoned shafts in the arid land around Las Vegas. Bob says, '**Laura's** <u>not</u> a woman a man can put a fence around.' It's true. *Don't fence me* *in* is the axiom that charming, stylish, <u>unsuspecting</u> Ms. Laura likes to live by. However, a woman must not take chances. There aren't any guarantees. Evidently, Bob <u>does</u> find a way to put A FENCE around her! A predator impatiently awaits his opportunity to pounce. If only she'd known of his predisposition and of the danger implicit in being who she is – with him being who he is." Let's talk about *graves* and *worms* and *epitaphs*.

"BOB has a Saturday evening DINNER DATE <u>WITH</u> LATISHA the night she vanishes into thin air. She's to meet him at HIS APARTMENT in San Diego.

"**Latisha** tells <u>Sheila</u> about it on Thursday and Friday, April 3ʳᵈ and 4ᵗʰ. <u>Sheila</u> *never* sees her again. She tells <u>Edie</u> after work at 5:30 p.m. on Friday the 4ᵗʰ. <u>Edie</u> *doesn't* see her again. **Latisha's** a no-show at work on Monday. She tells <u>John</u> she's having a dinner date with Bob in a few hours. Their conversation happens on SATURDAY, April 5, 1986. The TIME is <u>1:00 p.m.</u> The sands of time are sliding swiftly through the hourglass. The clock is ticking. She's reluctant but resolved. She says, 'I suppose I've GOT to do it.' <u>John</u>–*never*–sees– **Latisha**–again!

"Bob's friend <u>Ben</u> says **Bob** and **Latisha** normally date on Saturday night. This has been the pattern for months. 'To my <u>knowledge</u> Bob went out with... [**Latisha**] on 4/5/86.'

"THE DINNER DATE WITH BOB is an event that, undoubtedly, is the foremost thing on her mind this particular weekend. **Latisha's** going to tell Bob she's made a choice between him and Kelvin – and <u>it's</u> KELVIN. 'I'm going to marry Kelvin. Sorry, Guy. You'll just have to live with **rejection**. Have a great life.'

"What about Bob? **Latisha's** about to become one of Bob's absentee *ladies*. Too bad for her. She <u>doesn't</u> know about BOB'S HISTORY. She's <u>unaware</u> of the *risk* inherent in being one-to-one with Bob as the shoe <u>is</u> dropped on a relationship. She's ignorant about Bob's prior relationships. She's ignorant concerning Bob's disdain for rejection, and ignorance <u>isn't</u> always bliss. Ignorance can be hell! IF only **Latisha** <u>had</u> known. She'd have been more gentle in breaking the news. Better still, she'd have taken the first available flight out of San Diego to Colorado – and into Kelvin's PROTECTIVE arms! She'd have sent Bob a *Dear John* letter with <u>no</u> return address.

"News of **Latisha's** disappearance prompts <u>John</u> to make a telephone call to Bob at **6:00 a.m.** on Monday, April 7th. <u>John</u> wants to know about the dinner date. He wants to know WHAT happened to **Latisha**. Well, Bob is the *wrong* person to ask. He's got very tight lips about **Latisha**. Bob's got a personal agenda to cover-up WHAT'S happened to **Latisha**. She's in a dark mine shaft. He wants WHAT'S happened to **Latisha** to remain buried in his deep hole. He's NOT tellin' nobody what happened to **Latisha**.

"Bob says, 'No, I was supposed to have dinner with her SATURDAY NIGHT, but she called in the afternoon and *cancelled*.' **Liar–liar–pants–on–fire!**

"John testifies, 'That Bob sounded very calm, but <u>seemed</u> TO WANT to get off the phone quickly!' I'll bet he did. When **a man <u>lies</u>** about having A DATE in HIS DIGS with a woman who *DISAPPEARS* the night of THEIR DATE, Ladies and Gentlemen, that is straight-out, no holds barred, flashing neon light ADVERTISEMENT of his **<u>consciousness</u> of guilt**! And it's a LEAD PIPE CINCH this *Turkey* is going to start to TROT – somewhere.

"**4/7/86** at **7:00 a.m.** – Bob knocks on <u>Ben's</u> door in San Diego. He states, 'See you <u>later</u>. I'll be gone for a few days on a business trip. *I'll be back* at the <u>end</u> of the week.' The <u>end</u> of WHICH WEEK Bob? A month of Sundays from now? Until the twelfth day of <u>never</u>? Actually, **Bob <u>never</u> comes back!** *He's an inveterate liar*. He's arrested as a fugitive from justice in Arizona on **5/26/87**.

"**4/9/86** in Chula Vista, California he tells a <u>daughter</u> he's going out of town for *six weeks or longer*. He mentions Houston, Texas. She asks about **Latisha**. He replies, 'She's going back to Colorado to school so she can get a better job.' That's ridiculous! It's a **craven, despicable** *lie*. Neither her fiancé, nor her family, nor friends, nor the Health Institute, where she's been <u>happily</u> employed for years, nor any school on the face of the globe —— ever sees the classy nurse again!

"Bob asks his <u>daughter</u> to take him to a San Diego motel. He picks up a few belongings, then wants to be dropped off at the Bus Depot. Prior to parting, he uses a pink slip to <u>sign</u> over the title to a red Buick Skylark convertible to his <u>daughter</u> – just in case 'I fall off the end of the earth.' It's the <u>last</u> time she *sees* him until she *sees* him in Court <u>over</u> **two years** later. The **Turkey** <u>is</u> on the *trot*.

"Let's talk of *graves* and *worms* and *epitaphs*."

"ADMISSIONS – **May 1987** – Bob's in Tucson. He's reinvented himself. Well, almost. He's got another AKA. Bobby's become Charley – that is *Charles Stolzenberg*. His arrest stops the Turkey *trot*. He'd seen the NBC show, but he tells **Rosie** in the Pima County Jail, after the bust, that he didn't think anybody would recognize him except for her. And he didn't think she'd *rat* on him. Of course, he didn't think her ex-husband was a Homicide Dick neither. **Rosie** has an unforeseen connection to the guys in blue.

"Bob is concerned about masking his true identity. Shortly before his arrest, he'd driven Richard's car. He tells <u>Richard</u> he wouldn't object if he *detailed* the interior of the vehicle as a favor. He says his <u>prints</u> will be on the car, since he's driven it to the store to pick up steaks.

"Bob says he *dislikes* women. He tells <u>Richard</u>, 'My downfall has been booze and women!' He uses profanities in describing his *ladies*. He calls them 'F–– ing Cunts.'

"Bob tells **Rosie** he feels like he's been used by <u>all</u> the females in his life. She asks him why he didn't run. His quick retort is peppered with resignation: 'I didn't have the money, and they'd probably have spotted my car anyway.' The *trotting–Turkey–*<u>is</u>–out–of–breath. She tells police, "He NEVER said he was *innocent*."

"Pima County's incarcerated fugitive *is* pensive in conversation with <u>John</u>. He says, 'I'd *wanted* to walk across the border to Canada from the State of Washington.' He's upset when he returns from Court one day. He tells <u>John</u> he is going to be EXTRADITED to Nevada. Bob asks if <u>John</u> knows 'ANYBODY **who**

can take care of <u>some</u> **heavy business**. *Certain* PEOPLE, WITNESSES, and THOSE who FILED CHARGES *against* me.' He asks <u>John</u> to be a witness *for* him – to <u>make</u> his case stronger. Let's talk about *graves* and *worms* and *epitaphs*.

"ACCOUNTABILITY – With unexcelled moral eloquence, philosopher John Donne proclaims:

'**No** <u>man</u> is an island, entire of itself; **every** <u>man</u> **is** a *piece* of the continent, a *part* of the main; if a *clod* be washed away by the sea, Europe is the less, as well as if a promontory were, as well as if a manor of *thy* friends or of *thine* own were; **any** <u>man's</u> *death* diminishes me, because I **am** involved in <u>mankind</u>; and therefore **<u>never</u>** send to know *for whom the bell tolls*; IT TOLLS FOR THEE.' (*Devotions* [1624]. XVII)

"A <u>truer</u> *moral* principle was never uttered. Bob's *ladies* are gone, but they are not forgotten. The State of Nevada has <u>full</u> REMEMBRANCE of **Katherine** and **Laura** and **Latisha**. Their *worth* is great in the State of Nevada. NO <u>woman</u> is an island, entire of herself. EVERY <u>woman</u> **is** a *piece* of the continent, a *part* of the main, a *portion* of **each** of us – as well as if **they** were a manor of *our* friends or of *our* own. ANY <u>woman's</u> *death* diminishes you and me, because we **are** involved in <u>humanity</u>.

"Ladies and Gentlemen of the Jury, **<u>never</u>** send to know *for whom the bell tolls* –– for when THE BELL TOLLED for **Katherine** on *April 26, 1968* and for **Laura** on *October 5, 1980* and for **Latisha** on *April 5, 1986* –– **IT** TOLLED FOR THEE AND ME!

"Mr. Defendant, on this Thursday, April 21, 1988, almost TWENTY YEARS after your first murder –– the BELL *STILL* TOLLS. **It tolls** in REMEMBRANCE of these three ladies, and **IT** TOLLS FOR **<u>JUSTICE</u>**.

"Ladies and Gentlemen, at long last – finally – thoughtfully – objectively – appropriately, based upon **proof beyond a reasonable doubt** that the Defendant has committed THREE **heinous crimes,** you have the power to bring JUSTICE into this Courtroom. I implore you, <u>based</u> upon the evidence to TOLL THE BELL OF <u>PERSONAL ACCOUNTABILITY</u> for the Defendant. He has **maliciously** and **methodically**, over a span of two decades, set himself up as **Judge** – **Jury** – and **Executioner**. That's three **<u>too</u>** many hats Bob. **<u>None</u>** of them *fits* you. BYE-BYE, Bob!"

The Jury heeds the plea of the Prosecutor. **Bob's** *Journey to Justice* hasn't been a straight line. The path is a hodgepodge mosaic painted by decades of police investigation that often seemed futile. The canvas is a

<u>stuttering</u> caricature of justice for the most part. Tragically, **one** <u>missing</u> *lady* becomes **two** then **three**. The lack of bodies, the Defendant's flight, the aliases, the incongruities, the spacing between crimes, the jumbled witness portfolio, the timidity in charging Bob, the double jeopardy clause, all combine to fuel practically interminable delay. But the END of the process is **<u>not</u>** a mocking imitation of *personal accountability*. It's a validation of the Criminal Justice System. It's PERSON-SPECIFIC. It's a culmination that carries a set of real consequences. It's **tough justice** that <u>imposes</u> stiff penalties. Do the crime serve the time. It's vindication for **Katherine** and **Laura**. As for **Latisha**, she gets the vindication in Nevada she's been denied in her domiciliary state.

The Jury deliberates for about six hours. They return to the Courtroom with **Verdicts** on April 22, 1988. BOB <u>IS</u> CONVICTED ON BOTH COUNTS! He is convicted of **Murder in the First Degree** in the *disappearance* of **Laura** and <u>four</u> days <u>shy</u> of TWENTY YEARS after her *disappearance*, Bob is convicted of the **First Degree Murder** of HIS WIFE – **Katherine**!

That right, **Bob's** <u>not</u> the butler, the baker, or the candlestick maker – nor a feisty deviant physically abused as a child – or a highly eccentric recluse. **He's the ex-husband!** It all starts with *connubial* discord. Bob's the fellow whose just had the plug pulled. A card carrying member of the *disunion* of obstinacy and hate that a failed marriage *can* become. The guy whose divorce, initiated by his wife, has been finalized for only *fifteen days*. The guy who <u>began</u> to make *monthly* Court Ordered $200.00 alimony and $200.00 child support payments on April 15, 1968. The <u>same</u> guy the Court has **divested** of substantial property pursuant to the **Divorce Decree** *settlement*. The Court having **awarded** *two* houses and *extensive* furniture in a <u>third</u> house to his former wife, the <u>late</u> **Katherine X**.

The **Decree** begins the *process* of re-inventing Bob. Making him a *reluctant* dating-eligible single man again. His umbilical cord nuptials severed after fourteen years of marriage. Teetering on the brink of estrangement from his children, cold cash, and valuable property.

Yeah, that guy. The head of the family whose <u>lost</u> control of his family with *one* swipe of a Judicial Pen. The fellow who feels emasculated, robbed of his dignity, his self esteem, and cast adrift. Deprived of the anchor of his family. The **Decree** changes Bob – and not for the better.

The relationship which is a living hell to the partner filing for divorce, may to the other partner be the *only* living heaven he knows. Wedded disharmony is often shared by divergent bedfellows with vastly differing views.

Oh marriage, thy torment is extreme, but **thy** *failure* may be the **trip-wire** to disaster. When Bob becomes an ex, un-yoked, bereft of conjugal condiments with his spouse and familial ties with his children – a dark side seizes him. Once the lock in wedlock is broken *for Bob* – shock, heartbreak, and disillusionment follow – in that order. It's a volatile sequence. A tinderbox wired to explode. An episode infecting the *out-ed* **one** with a lingering malignancy: a jaundiced view of the system and of those women who have the temerity to reject him.

Rendition of Sentence is scheduled for <u>one</u> month following the verdicts. The delay facilitates preparation of a Pre-sentence Report by the Nevada Department of Parole and Probation. The Report usually contains *recommended sentences*.

This is <u>not</u> a Capital Case. The Prosecution believes the **burden** imposed upon the Jury of convicting **Bob** for two counts of **murder** in the <u>absence</u> of *bodies* of the murdered victims, should not be exacerbated by adding the <u>monumental</u> **burden** of grappling with a <u>death sentence</u> . *Incarceration* is one thing, but voting *execution* is a quantum leap beyond. It goes without saying that **Juries** impose <u>death</u> <u>penalties</u> only when there is NO DOUBT of guilt. The standard in Criminal Cases **<u>is</u>** Proof Beyond A <u>Reasonable</u> Doubt, yet without bodies a lingering doubt may *always* exist – though it does <u>not</u> meet the test of *reasonable doubt*.

The punishment affixed is **two** *life sentences <u>without</u> the possibility of parole* –– **running wild**. That is, they are to be served consecutively <u>not</u> concurrently. The State of Nevada does <u>not</u> give Bob a *pass* on either murder!

The final act occurs in the Nevada State Penitentiary approximately *five years* after rendition of sentence. Bob's **denouement** is abrupt. He <u>dies</u> in the slammer.

So in reality, the State of Nevada gets a *death sentence* without seeking one. Nevada imposes life, but it gets death. A *belated* **execution** being imposed inside the Big House. As the world turns, the Metro Detective's coercive and accusatory remarks during the November 1, 1980 stand-off on BEL AIRE DRIVE —— **are prophetic!**

"Mark my words well, Mister, I *don't care* what I have to do. I'm going to lock you up for the murder of this lady, [**Laura**] I'm <u>going</u> to *see* you DIE in the slammer." The Declarant <u>does</u> continue to be among the living when Bob is laid to rest.

Is Bob plucked away by an *act of God* – an <u>interdiction</u> by a high authority seeking *spiritual* jurisdiction? Did an *extra-terrestrial* <u>extradition</u> shift Bob from his asylum cell in Nevada to a different venue? Has the Highest Court of the Realm decided to fast-track its review of Bob's Case?

Let's talk about *graves* and *worms* and *epitaphs* —— and <u>contemplate</u> those **judgments that are to come.**

How Great the Grief a Little Fire Kindles

"From ghoulies, and ghosties and long-leggety beasties
And *things* that go <u>bump</u> in the night,
Good Lord, deliver us!"
(Old Scottish Prayer)

CHAPTER 8

The **Gonzalez** family is an embodiment of the American vision.

"Give me your tired, your poor,
Your huddled masses yearning to breathe free,
The wretched refuse of your teeming shore,
Send these, the homeless, tempest-tossed, to me:
I lift my lamp beside the golden door."
(Emma Lazarus, *The New Colossus: Inscription
for the Statue of Liberty, New York Harbor*)

THE DEMOGRAPHIC FABRIC OF AMERICA IS A patch-work quilt. Diversity is the hallmark of this land. America is a map consisting of people from every climate, every latitude, and every land under the sun. America is an alloy of every race or color or ethnicity, every religion or philosophy under the heavens. We are a nation of immigrants. Every American is an immigrant <u>or</u> a descendant of an immigrant. We aspire to be one, and the fulfillment of the aspiration in <u>each</u> generation will *always* be oneness that is the derivative of many. We are E pluribus unum. (Out of many, one.)

America is a land of liberty. It's Declaration of Independence is premised upon a venerable concept: "We hold these truths to be self-evident, that *all* men are created equal, that they <u>are</u> *endowed* by their Creator with certain unalienable rights, that among these are life, liberty, and the pursuit of happiness."

America is a *great* country with great traditions and fabulous opportunities. America is a *good* country – most of the time. It's probably greatest when it's most good. But it <u>isn't</u> always good, nor hospitable.

It <u>isn't</u> good and it <u>isn't</u> hospitable on Hurricane Way in Las Vegas, Nevada, on Saturday night, March 3, 1990. America **is** a *hellish* NIGHTMARE to a choice Clark County family on this solemn weekend night! What despair can be unleashed by a single act of stupidity involving a *small* **bag of dope**

<u>Seven</u> members of the **Gonzalez** family and <u>a</u> family friend are sleeping in the house. Their tranquil dreams are about to be demolished. It's 4:30 a.m. There is no warning to alert the occupants of impending disaster. Only the ominous sound of shattering glass as a Molotov Cocktail crashes through the living room window in the seamless darkness. The conflagration comes as a *deadly* **bump in the night**

The motivation for the *volatile* **act** on Hurricane Way is *pathetic*. The ignited inferno is *detestable*. Mindless tom-foolery sets the stage <u>three</u> days earlier. Joe and Tim and two friends go to a Terrible Herbst Lube on West Flamingo. It is February 28, 1990 at about 3:00 p.m. The vehicle is a blue, 1986, 4-door Chevrolet. Joe is the registered owner and, presumably, he is the driver. Curiously, the car misses the tire guides on its approach, damages the undercarriage of the vehicle, and bends some of the metal supports over the lube pit. Other acquaintances are hanging out at the business. Police are summoned by management.

Alas, there are three items of contraband inside the Chevy. A rifle, a .22 caliber starter pistol, and a zip-lock, <u>snack</u> baggie of marijuana. It's about **one ounce** of "skunk weed." Joe runs off with the rifle. Tim gives the pistol to Derek and Joe's baggie to Billy for *safekeeping*. **If** only Billy had given it <u>back</u>. **If** only Billy had understood he didn't get the weed on consignment. But – my bad. I speak from the clear, unimpeded view of hindsight.

Police arrive. They conclude the accident is alcohol related. Joe has slipped through the dragnet, but they find the pistol. Derek has thrown it under a bush. Tim remains at the scene. He's arrested. The blue Chevy is impounded. It all seems rather trivial and soooooo very silly. Yet, the chain of events triggered at *Terribles* is TERRIBLE in its **consequence**. BUT FOR the four-finger lid of pot given to Billy, **tragedy** could have been averted.

"...[H]ow great a matter a little fire kindleth!" (*Holy Bible*, James 3:5) When characters who don't think straight get hot under the collar, things can get *white* hot for **those** who've offended them – and for **persons** *outside* the loop who are caught in the ensuing firestorm.

Tim is released Thursday, March 1st at about 1:30 p.m. from Juvenile. His mother posts bail. She should have left him in the pokey, but she didn't realize the implications. She doesn't have a crystal ball.

Tim showers and begins to drink again – Old English and Budweiser. He and Joe live in the same apartment complex. Tim goes to Joe's place. They're worried about Joe's POT. Tim calls Taylor to determine if he's had his ear to the ground. Taylor says the word on the street is that Billy's trying to sell it.

Tim and Joe and Taylor make a *three way call* to Billy on Friday March 2nd between 3-4 p.m. Tim asks about the marijuana. He wants to know why the police find the *pistol* but not the *pot*. Billy says, "I don't got it." Tim replies, "Well, discuss it with Joe. It's his pot."

Joe emphatically tells Billy, "I want my weed back or I want the money!!" Billy continues to say he doesn't have it. Not surprisingly, Tim and Joe don't believe him. They think Billy is lying, and his *lies* make them angry.

Both Tim and Joe have been partying almost non-stop since Tim's release. A sad truth that only exacerbates their chagrin over losing the baggie of pot. The fact is they're making a mountain out of a mole hill. Still, young tough guys require transportation to fulfill their fantasies. It's *horses* in the old days of the wild west, it's *wheels* in west Las Vegas on the first Friday in March 1990.

There's a glitch in the unfolding scenario, however. Joe's set of wheels has been in lock-down since the afternoon of the lube pit fiasco. The gendarmes continue to baby-sit his Chevy. Not a problem! Joe and

Tim secure the release of the vehicle from police impound at 5:17 p.m. on March 2nd. How *timely* for the young toughs, as events evolve, how *untimely* for their targets. The irony is bitter.

They go to **Matt's** apartment on West Charleston. He's dropped off at his grandmother's place a little later. He's picked up again around 7:00 p.m. by **Tim** and **Joe**. Tim's driving at this point. The <u>three</u> of them pick up Dick and Taylor about an hour later. They drive to Little Caesars at Westcliff and Rainbow.

Ferrel remembers seeing Joe and Tim and Matt outside Little Caesars between 9-10 p.m. And he remembers Joe saying, "<u>**We're**</u> going to *take care* of Billy <u>tonight</u>!" Ferrel testifies, "That's the exact words, '<u>**We're**</u> gonna go to Billy's house and *take care* of him <u>tonight</u>.'" Question: "Who was Joe talking to?" Answer: "To Matt and Tim."

Ryan recalls a reference to Billy outside the pizza joint as well. There <u>are</u> *three* individuals connected to the conversation. *One* of the three says, "We <u>**know**</u> Billie has <u>our</u> marijuana. <u>**We're**</u> going over to Billy's to *take care* of him <u>tonight</u>."

They leave and continue to drive around with Taylor and Dick. Taylor says additional conversation occurs inside the car between 10-11:30 p.m. Joe and Tim and Matt discuss **the marijuana** <u>and</u> getting **even**. Joe says, "He shouldn't have taken my marijuana. Why did Billy gank my ounce?"

They speak of **Molotov Cocktails**. Tim explains how they're made and how they work. The device is simple to create and inexpensive. Only five ingredients are necessary: a bottle, a sock, a match, a decent arm, and <u>**gasoline**</u>. The incendiary capability is considerable. The bottle is filled with gas. A wick is fashioned from a sock or a rag and inserted into the neck of the bottle. The wick is lit and hurled hard toward the target. The bottle breaks upon impact. Allowing the gasoline fumes to mix with the air – forming a flammable vapor. This vapor is ignited by the burning wick of the device.

There is consensus. Joe and Tim and Matt <u>**all**</u> mention that a Molotov Cocktail "does a lot of damage." Significantly, several empty alcoholic beverage bottles are strewn on the floorboard. Further, Joe is upset because he hasn't been able to get any Wild Irish Rose wine yet. He says he's going to buy some."...[H]ow great a matter a little fire kindleth!" (James, ibid)

Taylor and Dick are dropped off sometime before 12:00 a.m. **Joe** is driving now. He's going to find some Wild Irish.

IT HAPPENS. What would be unthinkable to most persons –– happens! It is **evil** and brazen and reckless and senseless –– BUT IT HAPPENS! And it happens at **4:15 a.m.** There are **eight** human beings **ASLEEP** inside the Gonzales residence that somber morning, but that *isn't* a deterrent. It STILL HAPPENS.

<u>Why</u>? Because <u>three</u> moronic clowns are concerned about a *little* **baggie of pot** – probably valued at less than $200.00. It's a sickening caper carried out by boneheads high on booze and dope and phony machismo. Their brains have shut down. Their judgment has been high-jacked by irrational rage. Their sense of rectitude, at this hour on this morning, is AWOL. A six year old knows you don't *play* with **FIRE** while people are sleeping!

The three bombardiers assemble *two* Molotovs. That's right – **two**. TWO'S the number. Double trouble for the night-time skulker's prey. Joe's the <u>wheel</u> <u>man</u>. His car. His ride. It's part of their pact. One car – one driver. Two Molotovs – two bombers. Joe steers his blue Chevrolet around to the side of Billy's house in the 7100 block of Hurricane Way. He stays behind the wheel with the motor idling. Poised for a quick getaway.

Three sets of hands are pointed toward the other two sets in this case, it's hand-pointing unanimity. It's <u>not</u> Joe or Tim or Matt. **NOT ME** did it! However, based upon the totality of the evidence harvested, police conclude that Matt picks up <u>one</u> of the incendiary devices and exits the car. Furtively, he strides up to the dark living room window, lights the wick, and braces himself to heave the explosive.

Did the Gonzalez family say their prayers before they retired? Do they pray for deliverance from *long-leggety* **beasties** and things that go **bump** in the night? If ever a night calls for fervent praying for safekeeping, this one does! Right <u>now</u> – at this <u>precise</u> moment, the Gonzalez family *needs* an act of divine intervention. They need to have these three characters experience an <u>immediate</u> memory lapse. Young Billy needs to have Joe and Tim and Matt spend some time thinking about the hereafter. Like, WHAT <u>are</u> we *here after*? WHAT is the axe we have to grind with the people in this house, REALLY?

They need to have Matt's arm *drop* off <u>or</u> have him *trip* and fall on the shoulder of his throwing arm completely *tearing* the rotator cuff <u>or</u> have all ten fingers suddenly develop *atrophy* to the extent he's unable to *grip* the bomb <u>or</u> have him *get* religion in the blink of an eye and *change* his mind about this evil folly ––– **or** something.

But there is <u>no</u> act of divine intervention and <u>no</u> change of heart by the perpetrators. The <u>moral</u> **agency** of the <u>three</u> conspirators is *allowed* to be **exercised** <u>immorally</u> – without heavenly interdiction. Sh–t happens in this life. **Matt** *throws* the Molotov Cocktail through the window into the living room. Then runs to the car, and the **three** zoom into the predawn darkness. Inside, the bottle breaks and a fiery explosion engulfs the room. The flames spread rapidly. Deadly smoke sweeps throughout the house. The debacle is irreversible!

A 911 call is made from the neighborhood. Police, Firemen, and Emergency Technicians respond. Evidence of <u>extremely</u> dire circumstances threatening the well-being of an entire family and presenting the potential for a chaotic toll on human life and property is immediately apparent. The human crisis is addressed FIRST.

Evidence of arson is <u>later</u> detected and items are impounded by investigators. The *base* of a bottle and *four* other pieces of charred broken glass are found on the floor. Chunks of concrete, carpet, and carpet padding samples are recovered. They are examined by the Crime Lab. The concrete chunks are subjected to chemical testing. Each is <u>positive</u> for *gasoline*. The samples of carpet and padding <u>all</u> contain residues of *gasoline*. The **origin** of the fire is in the living room close to the fireplace. The **cause** is human hands. It's incendiary in nature – ARSON. "Evil is easy, and has infinite forms." (Pascal, ibid.)

The parents, Denny and Jenny, had retired for the evening at 9:00 p.m. Billy Gonzalez goes to bed about 11:00 p.m. – after his friend Derek has left. Clark and Donny watched the Miss America Pageant before going to sleep. Jade and Merrill returned from a trip to 29 Palms, California about 11:30 p.m. He is a marine, and he is her fiance. Freddie has come back from a date about 2:00 a.m. The doors are locked. He's had to rap on a window for Clark to let him inside the house.

It's a quiet, serene night on Hurricane Way – at <u>two</u> in the morning. There's nothing suspicious. Nothing threatening that is perceptible to those inside. No broken living room window. No gasoline residue on the concrete or carpet or padding. No burnt pieces of glass on the floor. No fire! No smoke! No death nor injuries nor soot nor devastation. It is the calm before the fire-bomb! All this changes in <u>two</u> hours. And once it starts it only takes *seconds* to turn the lives of a close-knit family inside out. The Crime Scene is a <u>grim</u> testament to the breadth of the tragedy.

DENNY – D0A. A loving husband. A caring, involved, loving father of seven is lifeless at forty six. **Dead** at the time firemen *arrive* where he lies. This is despicable. He's discovered in a corner of the NE bedroom – face up. He's there <u>trying</u> to save his children. His wife testifies she tried to go down the hallway but couldn't. **She** <u>tells</u> her husband to go <u>get</u> the *kids*. Denny sacrifices himself for the sake of his children.

Denny is pronounced dead at the scene on March 3rd at 5:52 a.m. He's a stiff corpse on a cold, sanitized table at the Clark County Morgue at 11:35 a.m. An autopsy examination is being performed. Where is justice for Denny?

There are 2nd degree **burns** on the tip of his nose, his upper lip, the right side of his chin, his right arm, and right flank. **Soot** covers his head and nose, his mouth and his lower airways, his arms and the trunk of his body. His blood <u>and</u> organs are **cherry** red. His carbon monoxide **saturation** is 63%. He is <u>dead</u> of **asphyxia** due to smoke inhalation!

Up in smoke for a bag of dope! Where is the promise of Denny's years? The head of the Gonzalez family is victimized by a SINGLE thoughtless, over-the-top act of *mindless* self interest – as though the only things that matter are the imbecilic machinations slip-sliding within the stupor of three skulls. The explicit danger in their incendiary device probably never dawns on these young hoodlums. It probably never penetrates the cognition of these half-wits, that people can die in house fires. Otherwise, why do we have fire alarm systems. Duh!

All they're thinking about is <u>pay</u>-back for **ONE** *OUNCE* of weed. They're not thinking about Denny. He's a great guy. A maintenance painter at the Golden Nugget Hotel and Casino. A dependable craftsman who takes pride in his work and toils without complaint to provide for his family. Why? Because his family means everything to him. He loves sports. The fact is he's coached his kids in wrestling, basketball, baseball, and football – for the camaraderie and so they'll share his love of sports, and learn the basic values taught by athletics.

Denny's a patriotic American, a responsible citizen, and a wonderful husband and father. What a waste, <u>all</u> for a measly **four finger lid of pot**! It's an absurdity!

BILLY – A loving son who occasionally runs with the wrong crowd – but basically a good kid. He's just past fifteen – a Bonanza High School student with many friends and a well-spring of audacious hope. He's bright and athletic. He **isn't** DOA. Nevertheless, young Billy <u>requires</u> an *obituary* too. He's just getting a good start and it's **over**. Shameful! "...[H]ow great a matter a little fire kindleth!" (James, ibid.)

Billy's found in the dining room wrapped in a blanket. He's unconscious. He has **soot** in his nose, mouth, and throat. The *time* interval estimate from incendiary <u>impact</u> to his <u>discovery</u> is *ten minutes* at most. However, intense heat and heavy smoke are pervasive inside the entire residential structure. <u>No</u> vital signs are initially detected.

Paramedics work frantically to resuscitate Billy. They get a heartbeat. He's transported by ambulance to the University Medical Center Burn Unit. He has **severe** smoke inhalation, *singed* nasal hair, extensive facial *burns*, and respiratory failure with cardiopulmonary *arrest*. Young Billy is placed on a respirator.

But there is <u>no</u> neurological function, and blood gas tests reveal he has <u>no</u> blood flowing to his brain. HE'S BRAIN DEAD. Billy is DAA. He's *officially* **dead** the *second* day <u>after</u> his admission to the Burn Unit. The cause of death is SMOKE INHALATION! The <u>pronouncement</u> is **3/5/90 at 11:25 p.m.**

What of his friends? His family? What of his tender years? What of the well-spring of audacious hope? "Where is the promise of...[Billy's] years, Once written on...[his] brow?...Where sleeps that promise now?" (Adah Isaacs Menken, ibid.)

And What of Joe and Tim and Matt? What of their *ounce* of skunk bud? What of their audacious hope? Where *lies* the snack baggie now? Did this **act of absurdity** bring it back? Was there ever any likelihood of a positive result? A tick for a tack. Brilliant! ONE of **you** called him your friend. But you **made** Billy brain dead that fateful morning. Well, the neurons weren't functioning in **the three** of you neither. You **made** yourselves BRAIN DEAD too. And YOU-have-to-live-with-it!! Where sleeps the promise of **your** years?

JENNY – A loving mother of seven and a loving wife of one. She's a forty two year old **one man** woman. *Emotionally* knit to her family. They <u>are</u> her life, and she is a major player in their lives. She's discovered by the *first* Fireman inside the inferno. Jenny is lying near the sliding glass door leading to the patio. She's in extremis. She has a pulse, but she's unconscious. There is <u>no</u> visible evidence of breathing.

She's hastily removed from the house. Once outside there's an agonal breath, and her rescuer thinks she's dying. He's heard the sound on other occasions under similar circumstances. Jenny is rushed to the Burn Unit suffering severe smoke inhalation with respiratory failure. Her mouth is full of soot. She has 1st and 2nd degree burns of her face and right hand. She's uncooperative, disoriented, and has to be connected to a respirator.

But she is responsive to oxygenated therapy and, miraculously, she survives. Jenny Gonzalez is discharged from the Hospital on March 11, 1990 – **eight** days later. She cheats the grim reaper, and testifies against those who brought a plague upon her house. She says she tried to crawl down the hallway to her children but she couldn't. She tells her husband to get the kids. Then murmurs, "**This is <u>evil</u>,** I give up," and passes out.

Where is the *promise* of Jenny's years? What of the *expectation* of living her golden years with her husband? How does a mother cope with the *loss* of a child? How does she deal with the emotional and physical scars inflicted upon the rest of her family by this fiery trauma?

CLARK – Another loving child of the union of Denny and Jenny. He's fourteen. The fireman who discovered his mother finds him in the NE bedroom. Clark is totally limp, unconscious, and <u>not</u> breathing. His pulse is weak. He's still comatose when he arrives at University Medical Center.

He has blisters over parts of his body, 2nd degree burns, and severe smoke inhalation The early teen is covered with soot from his head to his toes. There is soot in his airway and he has singed nasal hairs. His eyes are deviated upwards and to the right. There are considerable carbon deposits on his tongue.

An attending Doctor testifies, "The child had a very stormy few days at first and was given IV fluids, antibiotics, and respiratory ventilation – with gradual improvement. He was in a *coma* for weeks."

Clark is discharged from the Hospital on April 4, 1990 – after **thirty two** days of confinement. At the time of his discharge, he opens and closes his eyes on request, but makes <u>no</u> other voluntary movements. The Pediatric Neurologist states, "He requires *long term* <u>rehabilitation</u>. The prognosis is guarded."

Clark testifies at trial with great difficulty. Confined to a wheel chair, young Clark has difficulty speaking, a problem using his hands, and BRAIN IMPAIRMENT!

Formerly, athletic and vivacious – now, unable to go to the bathroom without assistance. Where is the promise of his years? What of this child's *hope* for a normal life? How <u>great</u> is the **grief** a little fire kindles!

DONNY – He's the baby of the family. The first fireman into the NE bedroom finds the eight year old. He lifts Donny into his arms, and rushes him outside. The boy <u>is</u> unconscious, and covered with soot. He suffers from 2nd degree burns and severe smoke inhalation. Initially, Donny has <u>full</u> cardiac pulmonary arrest.

When admitted to the Hospital, he still has poor color and only slight blood pressure. But the child is placed on a respirator and progresses nicely. He is discharged on March 17, 1990 – **fourteen** days after admission.

FREDDY – He's twenty. The last one to retire for the night. He hears the hysterical screaming of family members. Jumps up and has to *dive* through a window to get out of the house. Once he's outside he panics. His despair is incalculable. Freddy makes an abortive attempt to go back through the window to rescue his mother, but is repelled by intense heat, smoke being emitted from the house, and jagged edges in the damaged window. He receives numerous cuts, severe lacerations, and 2nd degree burns to his feet. But does <u>not</u> incur life threatening injury. He's treated at University Medical Center and released.

JADE and **Merrill** – They're both eighteen. They escape out the same window Freddy *dived* through. Both suffer mild smoke inhalation. They are treated and released at the Hospital.

It is a tragedy of epic proportion for the **Gonzalez family**. The **father** and a **son** are DEAD. <u>**Five** members of the family</u> are carried out of the house <u>**unconscious**</u>. <u>**One**</u> of those is a child of *eight*. <u>**Neither**</u> he nor his mother is breathing when they're removed from their home – that place which is supposedly a sanctuary of safety. A <u>**child**</u> of *fourteen* requires over a **month** of hospitalization. Still confined to a <u>**wheelchair**</u> at the time of Trial, he <u>may</u> suffer from permanent **brain** <u>**impairment**</u>. Imagine the plight – the emotional anguish – the *confusion* of this good family in the aftermath! Why – why? What did we do? Why us?

How great the GRIEF a little fire kindles! Good Lord, deliver us from *things* that go **bump** in the night.

Incredibly, the *malicious mischief* of the <u>**three**</u> pothead beatniks of the 90s doesn't end on Hurricane Way. They've constructed a <u>second</u> incendiary device. It <u>hasn't</u> been an empty ritual. They have another beef. A second score to settle. They aren't finished raising *hell*. The <u>**three**</u> bombardiers proceed from ground *zero-first* to ground *zero-second*. It's in the 6500 block of Hillview Avenue – about a <u>mile</u> away.

Matt gives directions. He's the only <u>**one**</u> of the three who <u>knows</u> WHERE Rory lives. **Joe** drives. **Tim** <u>does</u> the *dishonor* of heaving the *burning* missile this time. It smashes through the bedroom window of a <u>second</u> **home**. Arching over the bed where Sherry lies sleeping. It's **4:53 a.m.** – *twenty three* minutes after the first **arson**. Sherry's *two* sons, Rory and Dicky are also in the house.

The ignited Molotov smacks into a bedroom wall, instantly erupting into a blazing fire. Flames extend to the ceiling. Sherry awakens, *screaming* in disbelief. Her sons rush to the bedroom and are able to guide their mother to safety. The fire is extinguished. Arson Investigators respond to the scene. The room reeks with the smell of gasoline, and pieces of a broken wine bottle are recovered. The brand name is "**Richards Wild Irish Rose**." It would seem Joe <u>got</u> the wine he craved.

Hell fires, this is hard to fathom! What's wrong with these lunkheads? Just what is the axe they're *grinding* at HILLVIEW AVE? It must be <u>really</u> important for them to be chucking a fire bomb into another house in the darkness of night.

Yeah, sure. It's big-time bull sh––t. It's over a **black eye** this time.

Four days prior, <u>Rory's</u> friend <u>Chunk</u> Ashwell **smacks** <u>their</u> friend <u>Taylor</u> in the **face** outside Garside Junior High. The <u>tattletale</u> network kicks into gear. Taylor reports the "mouse" under his eye to Matt and Matt tells Tim. He calls Taylor for confirmation. Then Tim tells Joe. Thus, the beef is born. It's a gang thing. A matter of honor to these punks.

It seems like such an incongruity. These so-called tough guys have **<u>such</u>** thin skin. They need to be chillin not **<u>causing</u>** more killin! It's crazy!

The **<u>three</u>** pothead beatniks of the 90s go to Trial. **Do the crime, do the <u>time</u>**? *Well, we'll see.* A TRIAL is a <u>series</u> of unexpected events. And there are going to be some <u>major</u> procedural ANOMALIES in this one.

The **<u>three</u>** Defendants are <u>each</u> charged with **two** counts of **open murder**, **<u>eight</u>** counts of **Attempted murder**, and **two** counts of **Arson**. The charges are severe. *Will* the *punishments* be severe as well? <u>Or</u> *will* it be a mixed bag?

The CASE <u>purports</u> to involve **<u>one</u>** *wheel man* and **<u>one</u>** *bomber* at <u>each</u> crime scene. So, why are the **<u>three</u>** charged with IDENTICAL crimes? The answer lies in **two** longstanding <u>legal</u> <u>principles</u>.

THE FELONY MURDER RULE – Within the State of Nevada, charges of **<u>open</u> murder** encompass the crimes of <u>first</u> degree murder, <u>second</u> degree murder, <u>voluntary</u> manslaughter, and <u>involuntary</u> manslaughter. I have listed the four offenses in their descending degrees of culpability. **<u>If</u>** the Trial Jury believes a Defendants **has** been proven guilty beyond a reasonable doubt, they have the *discretion* to choose the offense applicable to the evidence before them.

Naturally, the four offenses <u>all</u> have elements that must be established. For example, **Murder in the <u>First</u> Degree** requires the element of PREMEDITATION. First Degree Murder is a <u>premeditated</u> killing, that is to say, an **intent** or **design** to *kill* must be formed at some point prior the murderous act. However, the Law does <u>not</u> impose a specific *time* frame during which the <u>premeditation</u> must occur. The <u>design</u> <u>to kill</u> may be formed for a week or an hour or at the **very moment** preceding the fatal act. It may be as *instantaneous* as successive thoughts of the mind. All the Law requires is a <u>clear</u> <u>intent</u> <u>to</u> <u>kill</u> formed *sometime* PRIOR to inflicting the fatal wound.

So, where is the <u>premeditation</u> in the **case at bar**? When did Joe or Tim or Matt, collectively or individually, form **a clear intent** to kill? The truthful answer is *probably* <u>never</u>! As **absurd** and **reckless** and **tragic** as these FIRE BOMBINGS were, it is highly *improbable* that these pinheads acted with a **design** to kill. Their intention was **malicious mischief** <u>not</u> **malicious murder**.

This being the logical inference to be drawn from circumstances related to the deaths of **Denny** and **Billy**, WHY does the Prosecution present the Trial Jury with an OPTION of **First Degree Murder**? The answer is: THE FELONY MURDER RULE!

Society recognizes that certain FELONY CRIMES are by their nature **inherently <u>dangerous</u>**. It is a <u>fact</u> that crimes such as **Robbery**, **Rape**, **Kidnaping**,

Residential Burglary, and **Arson** are so intrinsically <u>perilous</u> to human life that society has a <u>vested</u> interest in deterring them. Deterrence is best accomplished when the CONSEQUENCE for commission is grave. Therefore, the State Legislature has made it a matter of PUBLIC POLICY to ascribe <u>STRICT</u> <u>LIABILITY</u> to those individuals who **kill** human beings, *without* any intent to do so, during the commission of dangerous felonies <u>enumerated</u> in the Penal Code.

The Arson of a family home is <u>one</u> of the listed felonies. Accordingly, by **statutory** *definition*, those who are <u>participants</u> in the perpetration of a night-time <u>FIRE</u> BOMBING are <u>guilty</u> of **Murder in the <u>First</u> Degree** – <u>IF</u> persons DIE as a result of **the Arson**. The <u>element</u> of PREMEDITATION is <u>satisfied</u> by the INTENT to <u>commit</u> an inherently dangerous felony. The <u>element</u> of **premeditation** is IMPUTED to the **perpetration** of such an offense!

THE RULE CONCERNING AIDING AND ABETTING – The second principle that **<u>enables</u>** the STATE to prosecute Joe and Tim and Matt for IDENTICAL crimes, <u>including</u> the offense of **Murder in the <u>First</u> Degree**, is the **Law of <u>aiding</u> <u>and</u> <u>abetting</u>**. The *linchpin of culpability* <u>is</u> PARTICIPATION. The issue is: are <u>all</u> **three** of these Potheads ACCOMPLICES? Did <u>all</u> **three** carry out <u>specific</u> roles that *substantively* AIDED AND ABETTED the commission of the crimes?

IF <u>SO</u>, **each** is guilty of the charged offenses! Those who *substantively assist* in the perpetration of an offense <u>ARE</u> PRINCIPALS and may be **prosecuted** <u>and</u> **convicted** as <u>principals</u>.

Therefore, **IF** THE CASE TRUTH <u>presented</u> by the **Police** <u>and</u> the **Prosecution** <u>is</u> FACT, Joe and Tim and Matt are <u>all</u> PRINCIPALS —— and <u>may</u> *each* be *charged* with the IDENTICAL crimes of **Open Murder, Attempted Murder,** and **Arson**.

For instance, does THE WHEEL MAN *substantively* **aid and abet** in the commission of the crimes in the case at bar? OF COURSE!! **BUT FOR** *a driver*, the *others* may <u>never</u> have arrived at the **crime scenes!** If they're <u>not</u> present, NO ONE gets **fire-bombed**, right? Does THE BOMB TUTOR *substantively* **aid and abet** in the commission of the crimes? OF COURSE!! **BUT FOR** *the know how,* the Molotovs could <u>never</u> have been **constructed**. Do THE PURCHASING AGENTS of the component parts *substantively* **aid and abet?** OF COURSE!! **BUT FOR** *the parts,* <u>nothing</u> can be **built?** Do THE BOMB BUILDERS *substantively* **aid and abet?** OF COURSE!! **BUT FOR** *the builders* there are <u>no</u> **bombs?** DO THE BOMBERS *substantively* **aid and abet** in the commission of the crimes in the case at bar? OF COURSE!! **BUT FOR** *the bombers,* the Molotov Cocktails may <u>never</u> have been **thrown,** and given that scenario, there is absolutely <u>no</u> **injury** or <u>**loss**</u> of life or property. Does THE TOUR GUIDE *substantively* **aid and abet** in the commission of the **second** bombing? OF COURSE!! **BUT FOR** *an address and directions,* there is <u>no</u> *second* **crime scene**.

Right? Actually, I'm forced to hedge a smidgen. The evidence <u>isn't</u> going to be manifested with such clarity. So many *variables* pop up during the course of a Trial. Expect the unexpected! The thing of it is, THE TRIAL turns out to be **THREE** TRIALS IN ONE. Several pages back, I spoke of some <u>major</u> procedural ANOMALIES occurring in this matter. This one is huge. We had **three** trials *running wild* – in the <u>same</u> Courtroom with the <u>same</u> Judge at the <u>same</u> time. Sounds confusing, doesn't it? **It <u>was</u> confusing** – with all due respect to the Court. <u>Who</u> had the best of intentions. However, a procedural anomaly **won't** always fill everyone with glee. **Three** in this circumstance is a decision about which many will disagree! That's what I'm saying.

This is the scoop. There are <u>THREE</u> DEFENDANTS. The State of Nevada believes **Joe** and **Tim** and **Matt** are co-conspirators. Each person being involved in the <u>same</u> *common scheme and plan*. The Police and Prosecution pencil in all **three** as princip*als*. But can they make it stick? **The Three** <u>don't</u> concur with Law Enforcement's assessment. Why am I not surprised? This caper is about like every other <u>joint</u> criminal venture that goes to Trial. **NO ONE** wants to take any responsibility. **Joe** says he <u>didn't</u> do it. **Tim** says he <u>didn't</u> do it. **Matt** says he <u>didn't</u> do it.

Let me clarify. They **<u>don't</u>** say they <u>weren't</u> THERE. They concede they were THERE. Together in **Joe's** blue, **four** door Chevrolet in the 7100 block of Hurricane Way and the 6500 block of Hillview Avenue the morning of the firebombings. **<u>BUT</u>** they didn't do it! NOT NEITHER TIME, no sireee!

Joe's driving. However according to him, he's too *drunk* <u>and</u> too *dumb* to be accountable for what's happening, but the Molotovs were tossed by Tim <u>and</u> Matt. Joe's defense is <u>diminished</u> <u>capacity</u>. **Tim's** there. However according to him, he's *asleep*. A sleeping boy doesn't know what's happening, but Joe's driving – so the Molotovs must have been tossed by Matt. Tim's defense is <u>diminished</u> <u>cognition</u>. **Matt's** there. However according to him, he's *asleep* TOO. A second sleeping youngster wouldn't know what's happening, but Joe's driving – so the Molotovs must have been tossed by Tim. Matt's defense is <u>diminished</u> <u>cognition</u> TOO – and <u>age</u>. He's only *fifteen* when it comes down.

Therefore, the only thing we can be sure of <u>according</u> to **Joe** and **Tim** and **Matt** is that NOT ME did it. Nobody is fessing up. Nobody's stepping to the plate. The sly culprit has to be NOT ME.

This is <u>dilemma</u> <u>one</u>. It is the Defendant's *quandary*. The honorable, inestimable Counselors for **the Three** young hoodlums have EACH filed a **Motion for Severance**. The legal basis being, that an IRRECONCILABLE *conflict of interest* exists between the <u>three</u> Defendants. Essentially, for the reasons recited above. They argue that **Joe** and **Tim** and **Matt** <u>can't</u> possibly receive a *fair Trial* unless they're tried <u>separately</u>. Hmmmm, that would be THREE TRIALS.

This is <u>dilemma</u> <u>two</u>. It is the Judge's *quandary*. THREE TRIALS is not a happy prospect for His Honor. He's got a very crowded

Court Docket. He doesn't have time to conduct <u>three</u> SEPARATE Murder/Attempt Murder/Arson Trials. Yet, he must be sensitive to the fundamental RIGHT of <u>each</u> Defendant to have a *fair Trial.* And HOW can EACH *receive* a fair Trial in a JOINT TRIAL, where <u>each</u> Defendant is pointing his finger at the OTHER two.

This is <u>dilemma</u> <u>three</u>. It is the Prosecutor's *quandary.* He's busy too. He's got a *lengthy* list of pending Trials. But that issue can be dwelt with in due course. The over-riding concern of the Advocate with the white hat is that the PEOPLE <u>aren't</u> going to get a *fair Trial* –– **IF** it <u>isn't</u> a JOINT TRIAL! SEPARATE <u>Trials unreasonably</u> **empower** the Defendants under the specific circumstances of their criminal enterprise in this case. These **three** firebombing conspirators will **<u>all</u>** be able to *cherry-pick* the <u>partial </u>evidence *favorable* to them in <u>separate</u> Trials to the EXCLUSION of the <u>totality</u> of evidence that is <u>unfavorable</u> to <u>all</u> **three**! Separate Trials will lift **the three** Defendants out of the NATURAL CONTEXT of their criminal *modus operandi.* Such a path is T–R–O–U–B–L–E for the Prosecutor!

It's an imperfect world. <u>Every</u> Defendant receives an <u>imperfect</u> Trial – regardless. If it please the Court, don't <u>tie</u> the Prosecutor's *sweating tongue* by INSULATING **the Three** from their feckless finger pointing. Do **<u>not</u>** order SEPARATE <u>Trials</u>. Where <u>EACH</u> FINGER is pointing at the <u>OTHER</u> TWO, that would seem to be convincing evidence of CONSCIOUSNESS OF GUILT – X – **THREE**!

His Honor **RULES**. Bless his heart, it's a rather novel approach. A sort-of attempt to please everyone. The procedural ANOMALY is: there will be <u>ONE</u> *hybrid Trial*, but it will feature <u>THREE</u> JURIES. Now is this accommodating, or what? **Joe** and **Tim** and **Matt** are <u>each</u> to be the proud recipients of their very own Jury. What's more, the EVIDENCE the respective Juries receive will be *tailor-made* to fit the <u>special</u> needs of **each** Defendant. The Juries will be shuttled in and out of the Courtroom in a manner His Honor deems appropriate – <u>each</u> hearing only a *sanitized* version of the total Trial evidence. **The Three** will be plucked away from the *natural context* of their **criminal modus operandi** and tried as <u>lone</u> wolf pups.

Thus, a single Judicial Edict completely changes the Trial landscape. Theoretically, the objectionable, *irreconcilable* <u>conflict</u> of interest between the Defendants will be neutered – and FAIRNESS will abound. EQUAL justice will be achieved. EACH Jury will be <u>insulated</u> from the bad stuff. They won't *receive* the slightest evidentiary *hint* concerning the feckless finger pointing going on between **the Three**. The Juries won't have a clue that **Joe** points the finger of culpability at **Tim** and **Matt** – while **Tim** points to **Joe** and **Matt** – and **Matt** blithely blames **Joe** and **Tim**. Therefore, the Juries will know <u>nothing</u> about CONSCIOUSNESS OF GUILT – X – **THREE**. Actually, they <u>won't</u> know sh––t from shinola.

I've got to say, what is *theoretically* the best is often <u>not</u> *realistically* the best decision. The Judge is a good man. He's a legal scholar, and a credit to the bench. But he's <u>not</u> infallible. When the Court neuters the <u>alleged</u>, irreconcilable conflict between the Defendants, he emasculates the Prosecution. His *hybrid Trial* that features **three Juries** becomes a <u>three</u>-<u>headed</u> MONSTER to me. Metaphorically the equivalent of **Cerberus** of Greek and Roman mythology, a three-headed **dog** guarding the gates of Hades. Only the Judicially created **Cerberus** of the Twentieth Century <u>didn't</u> guard the gates very well. The disparate and incongruous results of the *hybrid Trial* were, through the lens of the Prosecution, really rather **<u>hellish</u>!**

I don't want to be <u>too</u> negative. So, I'm going to try to *lighten* the mood. I **<u>loved</u>** being a Trial Lawyer, and I think a Trial advocate has to keep his cool and maintain a strong <u>sense</u> of CIVILITY even in the toughest of times.

I have a *special* friend who is a cop to the core and a **<u>good</u> one**. Surprisingly, and thankfully – he does possess a certain level of grudging tolerance for Lawyers. Accordingly, he graced my Christmas season, four consecutive years beginning in 1992, with *gifts* of LAWYER JOKE BOOKS. He figured I'd enjoy laughing at myself and at my profession from time to time. He's right. I appreciate the thoughtfulness, Dan. I'll <u>never</u> forget your kindness, nor your friendship! This **Joke** is one of my favorites. It seems quite relevant right here – right now.

Once upon a time in the Caribbean, a cruise ship founders on a reef during a severe tropical storm. The ferocity of the tempest has ripped gaping holes in the belly of the vessel, and the communication system is totally disrupted. Treacherous waves continue to pound the hull. The

Captain, a **Pastor**, and a **Lawyer** meet on deck. Simultaneously, the remaining lifeboats are smashed into pieces on the jagged coral ridges below. The First Mate isn't going to be any help, he's seen cowering in a far corner of the deck, commiserating with passengers.

The ship is marooned about a mile from a seashore village.

The **Captain** declares, "The situation is desperate. <u>Someone</u> will have to jump overboard and swim to the pier for help." The **Captain** and the **Pastor** and the **Lawyer** hurry to the rail and stare intently into the churning surf. What they see makes their blood curdle. A school of sharks swims menacingly below – biding their time, it seems.

The <u>**Captain**</u> speaks again. There's a noticeable tremor in his voice, "It's out of character for the Captain to abandon his ship, but I see no alternative. Desperate times call for desperate measures. I'm a man of the sea. I've been part of the cruise industry all my life. I have experience sailing the waters of the world. I'm familiar with the ocean currents. The safety of the ship and passengers is my responsibility. I'm a strong swimmer and unafraid. I will jump into the roily brink and swim for help. Goodbye good ship, I do this for those on board and for thou."

Then, the **Captain** resolutely climbs over the railing and jumps. The other two peer anxiously over the edge, horrified by what they see. A hungry shark swims over as soon as the valiant Skipper touches down – opens its mouth wide and swallows the poor fellow. He's gone, but not forgotten.

The two on deck are shocked. The smooth-tongued Counselor at Law is <u>completely</u> discombobulated and speechless. His rhetorical skills are in recess – his *sweating tongue* frozen. All he's able to do is whimper and shake like a leaf. Each man averts the gaze of the other.

Finally, the **Pastor** clears his throat and says: "I'm a man of the cloth. A man of faith. I preach the message of salvation. I'm perfectly cast for the role of saving my brothers and sisters on board this ship. What the Captain has been unable to do, I will do. I <u>will</u> go for help. I'm not a good swimmer, but the Lord will protect me."

He glances heavenward as he proclaims: " I take this small step for mankind. Goodbye good ship, for now." That said, he jumps. However, his fate is exactly the same as the Captain. When the Pastor lands in the water, a voracious Great White scoops him up before his hair is even wet. He's gone, but not forgotten – though his decision to swim is certainly ill-gotten.

The **Lawyer** sees it happen. He's traumatized in a way his cringing *tongue* <u>can't</u> possibly describe despite his rather sizable vocabulary – and he's not a hero. But he <u>is</u> a pragmatist! It's a matter of choosing one's poison. The prospects don't look particularly promising on board neither. Who knows? It may be different strokes for different folks –– in the water.

The glib gladiator of the Courtroom Arena shrugs his shoulders, exudes a lingering sigh of resignation, clambers over the railing, reaches into his wallet, removes his <u>current</u> Nevada State Bar card, pins it to his lapel, stares into the dorsal-finned milieu below, holds his nose, – and JUMPS.

It's a near perfect entry. There's barely the hint of a splash as the water embraces the victim-to-be –– or <u>not</u> to be. The chief shark glides over for a look-see. He spies the State Bar Seal. He signals the others. Immediately, the SCHOOL of sharks PARTS. Sort of a reprise of Moses raising his arm on an ancient bank of the Red Sea to part the waters. Only we're parting sharks not waters. The sharks recognize a colleague – THEY PART! And it's clear swimming for this denizen of sharkdom – all the way to the dock.

Sure, his arms are weary, he's out of breath, he swallows buckets of water – or so it seems, and the sea continues its turbulence. But he's a man with a mission who has the permission of a squadron of marine escorts.

The **Lawyer** strokes to the shore and climbs to safety. The unfolding drama has been witnessed by a crowd of people assembled on the shore. They rush up to congratulate the callow fellow. He's <u>somehow</u> survived an epic swim with ravenous sharks. "It's a *miracle*," they exclaim.

Spitting water and sea weed, the **Lawyer** gasps a terse retort: "*Miracle*, <u>**hell**</u>! It's a matter of PROFESSIONAL COURTESY."

Please **indulge me** now. I believe the swimming with sharks joke conveys an important moral point that goes well beyond a few teasing chuckles. We live in an environment that contains far <u>too</u> much antagonism and disrespect and meanness. Human beings <u>NEED</u> to get along with each other. It <u>can</u> begin in the Courtroom.

I've previously spoken of **case attitude**. I want to mention **courtroom attitude** also. We call it an *adversary system*, but being <u>adversarial</u> in Court doesn't mean we have to be *personally* <u>adversarial</u> outside the Courtroom. A Prosecutor's <u>enemy</u> in the Courtroom is NOT *Defense Counsel*. They're <u>crucial</u> cogs in our great system of jurisprudence. True, they have a different job description and it's a dirty business. But **somebody** has to do it!

The <u>enemy</u> *is* **INJUSTICE!** And it would be an <u>injustice</u> to convict persons <u>accused</u> of murder without the *benefit of Counsel*. We **want** GUILTY bastards **convicted**, but we want it done within the parameters of **Due Process of Law**. Counselors for the Defense most assuredly are part of Due Process.

I urge my fellow Prosecutors to take their cases **personally**, but NOT to take the *antics* of Defense Counsel **personally**. They'll *push* the envelope as <u>far</u> as the Court permits. That's the nature of their practice. If things jump the track, <u>where</u> does blame lie? It *reposes* with the **source** of Courtroom <u>power</u>, of course. If the Prosecutor has a beef, he should <u>focus</u> on the **Judge**. When the law becomes an "**ass**," <u>the</u> <u>Court</u> makes it so! His Most Honorable dishes up the regimen of donkey-power.

Cultivate *good* <u>relationships</u> with Defense Counsel. Legal eagles should be **courtly** – *well* **mannered** – *subtly* **urbane**. The legal world needs <u>more</u> **courtesy**, <u>more</u> **civility**, <u>more</u> **chivalry**, <u>more</u> **diplomacy**, <u>more</u> **tact**, <u>more</u> **gentle<u>men</u>** and **gentle<u>women</u>** and **esprit de corps**. Individual Practitioners need a <u>greater</u> **appreciation** for the *roles* performed by <u>other</u> members of the Bar and a <u>greater</u> **deference** for the professional *stature* of <u>others</u> within the Criminal Justice System.

At the end of the day, the **true spirit** of the *Criminal Law Profession* IS a <u>spirit</u> <u>of</u> <u>camaraderie</u> and FRIENDSHIP! This is the <u>time</u> honored traditional of our **legal fraternity** – even in Shakespeare's era.

He counsels his peers, "And **do** as *adversaries* **do** in law, *Strive* <u>*mightily*</u>, but *eat* and *drink* <u>as</u> **friends**." (*The Taming of the Shrew*, Act I, Sc.2, Line 281) To which I'll add, **the Trial** WASN'T *easy*, but I felt lifted by the amicable counsel.

184

Further, a Prosecutor's <u>enemy</u> in the Courtroom, ultimately, **<u>isn't</u>** the *Judge*. The *Judge* has an amazing <u>task</u> to perform, and for the most part, that responsibility is skillfully discharged – with dignity and objectivity. On those days when **a Prosecutor** <u>is</u> feeling particularly positive about his world, he needs to try being *nice* to the **<u>Judges</u>**. They're people too. I'll say it again, the Prosecutor's *only* **<u>enemy</u>**, his *sworn* **<u>enemy</u>** *is* **INJUSTICE!**

MR. PROSECUTOR: let the *sweating* begin – **big time!** The Judge has put me between a rock and a hard place on this one. What I'm saying is: **<u>three</u>** JURIES IN ONE, <u>one</u> Trial that is. Consider the effect upon **SUMMATION**. Consider the toll upon **STAMINA!**

The Prosecutor needs to stand <u>tall</u> on a *triangular* case. He needs to be able to *see* the big picture, and that's hard to do for a <u>short</u> guy like me. This is how it played out. I succeeded in sanitizing my OPENING STATEMENT sufficiently to facilitate the presence of all <u>three</u> Juries for a <u>single</u> presentation. However, the Judicial FINDING of irreconcilable conflict of interest between **the Three** <u>mandates</u> **three** separate SUMMATION presentations. Such a scenario places a heavy *rhetorical load* upon the People's Man.

A short refresher course on procedure *might* help establish the point. The Guy with the white hat has the BURDEN OF PROOF. The guys in the black hats DON'T have to prove anything. **The Three** Defendant's are <u>each</u> cloaked in a legal PRESUMPTION OF INNOCENCE that follows them through the Trial <u>until</u> the submission of Trial Evidence is complete. The anomaly of a *triangular* Trial is that nearly every *step* comes in **<u>threes</u>**, especially at the end. That is, **<u>three</u>** sets of Jury Instructions, **<u>three</u>** SEPARATE summation hearings, **<u>three</u>** SEPARATE Jury Deliberations, and **<u>three</u>** SEPARATE sets of VERDICTS. **Three** Trial Juries will **<u>each</u>** decide if the <u>presumption</u> has been overcome as to *their* Defendant, and whether their <u>specific</u> Defendant has been proven guilty beyond a reasonable doubt. Verdicts reached regarding the **other <u>two</u>** are NOT pertinent to verdicts entered with respect to a <u>specific</u> Defendant.

Furthermore, **The Law** awards a REBUTTAL ARGUMENT to the Party having the Burden of Proof. Hence, the Prosecutor is entitled to **Open** and **Close** FINAL ARGUMENTS. The extra argument is intended to be an equalizer. It gives the Prosecutor a leg up in his effort to convince the Jury his evidence has overcome the presumption of innocence and proven guilt beyond a reasonable doubt. The net effect being: the little ole Prosecutor flying SOLO on this case has <u>**SIX**</u> final arguments, while esteemed Defense Counselors have <u>**THREE**</u> final arguments divided by <u>**three**</u>. Each Defense Team argues ONCE before their respective Jury.

Frankly, my tongue <u>never</u> *sweat* more during FINAL ARGUMENTS in my career than on this case. Making <u>**SIX**</u> arguments, and they weren't short, over a span of TWO DAYS is exhausting. The *tongue sweat* eventually morphs into a bad case of cotton mouth hems un haws and emotional fatigue. All I could do is hope the <u>three</u> Juries would pick up the slack. But it's damn hard getting a *leash* around a **three**-headed dog. Especially, when <u>none</u> of the three heads knows what the others are thinking. These circumstances aren't conducive to a Prosecutorial **hat-trick**! Too many variables – too much isolation – too myopic. How could <u>anyone</u> reasonably have expected the <u>**three**</u> Triers of Fact to be in sync? Actually, the Judicial formatting <u>made</u> that IMPOSSIBLE!

The incongruous results are predictably <u>arbitrary</u> and <u>capricious</u>. THE DRIVER (**Joe**) is *convicted* by his Jury of <u>**two**</u> <u>**counts**</u> of MURDER IN THE <u>FIRST</u> DEGREE, <u>**eight**</u> <u>**counts**</u> of ATTEMPT MURDER, and <u>**two**</u> <u>**counts**</u> of FIRST DEGREE ARSON. Yet, according to the Prosecution's theory of the case he <u>DIDN'T</u> throw either Molotov Cocktail. THE RIDE-A-LONG COCKTAIL CHUCKER on Hillview Avenue (**Tim**) is *convicted* by his Jury of <u>**two**</u> <u>**counts**</u> of MURDER IN THE <u>SECOND</u> DEGREE, <u>**eight**</u> <u>**counts**</u> of ATTEMPT MURDER, and <u>**two**</u> <u>**counts**</u> of FIRST DEGREE ARSON. Yet, according to the Prosecution's theory of the case he <u>DIDN'T</u> throw the Molotov Cocktail on Hurricane Way. THE RIDE-A-LONG COCKTAIL CHUCKER on Hurricane Way (**Matt**) is found *not guilty* of ALL COUNTS by his Jury. Yet, according to the Prosecution's theory of the case **he** <u>DID</u> throw the Molotov Cocktail on Hurricane Way <u>and</u>

he is the only ONE of **the three** who knew where Hillview Avenue was located.

Now is that result about as *clear* as mud? As *logical* as a mud **pie**? It's **very**, **very** hard to get *a leash* around a three-headed dog! The Trial devolves into **three Juries** *running wild*. The Prosecutor's Courtroom **enemy** is INJUSTICE. Sadly, his **nemesis** can be an unwitting accomplice sitting on the bench. His Honor writes the script for this travesty!

"...[H]ow great a matter a little fire kindleth!" (James, ibid.)

ADMISSIONS – The **Three** drive to Taylor's house an hour or so after the fire bombings. It's between 6:00 and 7:00 a.m. on this grim Saturday. Matt goes to Taylor's window. He exits the house and comes out to the car.

Tim says, "Billy's house burned last night." **Matt** adds, "I'm sorry. I didn't mean to do it. I was drunk and it was an accident." Taylor inquires, "DO WHAT?" **Matt** replies, "I said I was drunk and I–didn't–mean–to–do–it, but–I–**did–throw–** it. I got out of the car and walked up by the bushes next to the house. I lit it on fire and THREW it. The bottle sounded like it HIT the bricks in front by the window. It hit the bricks." **Tim** said, "I didn't want to be around the house when it happened so **Joe** drove over to the side of the house a little.

Matt tells Taylor, "After I threw the bottle I ran to the car and got inside. Then we left, and went to Rory's place." He's excited as he says it. " Rory's house got one thrown through it too. I didn't do that one. I–ONLY–**SHOWED**–THEM– HOW–TO–GET–THERE." **Tim** acknowledges, "Yeah, I threw it and I heard a SCREAM when it went through the window."

Taylor refers to **Joe's** attitude that morning. "He was sitting behind the steering wheel. He just sat there with a big old grin on his face, and commented, 'Well, Billy shouldn't have stolen my pot.'"

The Constitution isn't offended when guilty young men stub their toes by shooting off their mouths too much.

Matt speaks to his friend Derrick. He says **he** and **Tim** and **Joe** were at a party by Valley High School. "They went to a 7-11 and got gas and some other things. He said **he knew** they were gonna fire bomb somebody...**he knew** they were gonna get somebody." Question: "Did he say who <u>they</u> were?" Answer: "He said **Joe** and **Tim**...He said he was sitting in the backseat behind the passenger and **Joe** was driving. **Tim** got out, lit it, threw it, and got back into the car. He said **they** went and <u>firebombed</u> Rory's house too." He said, "Then WE <u>went</u> and did Rory's house!"

Tim telephones his girlfriend about 4:00 p.m. on March 3rd. She testifies, "He sounded down and kinda sad. I asked what was wrong, and he said he was just tired. So I asked, 'Well, did you go see Billy?' And he said, 'Yes.' And I said, 'Do you know what happened?' And he goes, 'Yeah –– CAN I TRUST YOU?' I said, 'Yes.' And he goes, 'Me, Matt, Joe, and Taylor were out partying and we *took Taylor* home.' Then he said, '<u>THEY</u> FIREBOMBED BILLY'S HOUSE.' **Tim** said, "<u>They</u> threw a Molotov Cocktail into Billy's house.'"

Tim's girlfriend says, "I asked him what a Molotov Cocktail was. And he said, 'It's a bottle FULL OF GASOLINE with a rag on top of it. You light the rag and you throw it and IT EXPLODES!'"

Three weeks later **Tim** travels to New York State. His girlfriend is interviewed by Las Vegas Police several months after the firebombings. She calls **Tim** with news about her conversation with the Police. She explains, "The Police were asking about you?" **Tim** responds, "Why me? I <u>didn't</u> do it. MATT DID IT...MATT THREW IT!"

Tim tells his friend Roy "there were <u>two</u> fires, and it was my idea to use cocktails."

PRESENCE – **Joe** and **Tim** and **Matt** are <u>all</u> there. They admit they're there. The argument is: **The Three** are suspiciously cruising about in the late morning hours of **3/3/90**, ergo, **the Three** are <u>each</u> perpetrators. It's a <u>joint</u> venture. The adrenalin is flowing. **None** of these **three characters** <u>is</u> asleep. NOT ME <u>didn't</u> do it. ALL **THREE** me's did it. The ONLY logical deduction when **three young hoodlums** are partying and plotting inside a moving car is: (a) When there's conversation – **three** converse; (b) When there's a scheme hatched to **firebomb** two houses – the automobile is an incubator carrying **three** conspirators; (c) When there's a description of how to make Molotov Cocktails – <u>one</u> is instructing and the other <u>two</u> have their EARS on; (d) When there's a collection of firebomb <u>parts</u> – <u>all</u>

three are collectors; (e) When the bombs are assembled – <u>all</u> **three** build them or condone the assembly; and (f) When FIRES <u>are</u> being made – <u>all</u> **three** are firemen by some form of aiding and abetting complicity! Absolutely, **<u>none</u>** of this is done in a vacuum! This is NOT blindman's bluff. These characters <u>aren't</u> individually on a *frolic* of their own. Each of these pot-heads is intent on delivering the stuff – the Molotov Cocktails. They're PARTNERS!

THE KEY WORDS --- PARTNERS – TWO – ACCOUNTABILITY. Okay, the number TWO <u>should</u> have changed everything. The Defense of *avoidance* <u>loses</u> its credibility when a SECOND **crime** comes on the heels of the FIRST. This happens **TWO TIMES**! The first time these young hoodlums do this it's morally reprehensible. The second time it's despicable. These <u>aren't</u> school boy pranks. **TWO TIMES** is over the edge. It's inexcusable, unconscionable, and <u>highly</u> **inculpatory** of <u>each</u> PARTNER. It manifests a **reckless indifference** to the sanctity of human life and basic rights of property. If the Criminal Justice System stands for anything, IT <u>MUST</u> STAND FOR <u>PERSONAL</u> <u>ACCOUNTABILITY</u>!

The Defendant's NOT ME boogeyman <u>doesn't</u> EVER do anything! Atrocious crimes are committed by SPECIFIC, tangible, breathing, calculating, maliciously **stupid** and incredibly **immature** human beings. The CAR <u>didn't</u> **drive** itself. The FIRE BOMBS <u>didn't</u> **make** themselves. The FIERY COCKTAILS <u>didn't</u> **propel** themselves through the <u>night</u> into the HOMES of two families as they lay sleeping. DENNY and BILLY <u>didn't</u> **die** of naturally induced cardiac arrest. The other INJURED MEMBERS OF THE GONZALEZ FAMILY <u>weren't</u> simultaneously **stricken** by some virulent respiratory disease. These are SPECIFIC ACTS of **premeditated vengeance** that call for SPECIFIC ACTS of **premeditated punishment**. Do the crime do the time ACCOUNTABILITY!

Unfortunately, what the PROCEDURAL ANOMALY of the Judicially created **three-headed dog** JURY ALIGNMENT accomplishes <u>is</u> a PROCEDURAL MISCARRIAGE OF JUSTICE. The so-called Criminal Justice System ends up <u>being</u> organized **chaos** <u>rather</u> than a **system**, a <u>dispenser</u> of disparate, contradictory verdicts <u>rather</u> than verdicts <u>rooted</u> in consistency and **justice**. However, it may on occasion be tempting to say that the so-called Criminal Justice System <u>does</u> live up to one of its labels. The Gonzalez family undoubtedly thinks what the Criminal Justice System <u>did</u> in this case <u>is</u> **CRIMINAL!**

"From ghoulies, and ghosties and long-leggety beasties
And *things* that go BUMP in the night,
Good Lord, deliver us!" (ibid.)

Finding Humor in the Courtroom

(Lawyers can be <u>funny</u> people too)

"I never saw a Purple Cow, I never hope to see one;
But I can tell you, anyhow, I'd rather see than be one."
(Gelett Burgess, *The Purple Cow*, published in *The Lark* magazine, 1895.)

CHAPTER 9

WHO DAT MAN? – MY CAREER IN the Courtroom didn't get off to a very propitious start. My very first assignment was a Preliminary Hearing in Justice Court. The offense involved a convenience store *robbery*. <u>Convenient</u> to whom, a punster might ask. Back in the days when convenience stores didn't have a security guard posted on the premises as part of their marketing motif and carried a bit more green in the cash drawers than the paltry sum that is presently maintained, robbers seemed to believe such businesses were an implicit invitation to **stop and rob**.

A **gun** is used in the commission of this **one-on-one** crime. It occurs about 7:00 a.m. A single female clerk is on duty. A man walks inside the store, pretends to shop for a few moments, walks to the counter with a candy bar, hands the clerk a dollar bill, she takes it, and opens the cash register. The man immediately pulls a hand gun and points it at the clerk. His words are ominous, "This is a robbery. Pass me all the money in the drawer, or I'll shoot." Naturally, the clerk is frightened. She heeds the admonition of the miscreant standing before her, and hands him the seventy one dollars she has in the register. He takes the money, puts the gun away, and exits the business without further incident. The robber is <u>not</u> wearing a mask and makes no attempt to conceal his face.

Police are summoned to the scene. They conduct a cursory investigation, there really isn't much to investigate. Photographs are taken of the store and the empty till. The victim is escorted to the Station House where she makes a statement and views several books of mug photos. She **identifies** the robber after about five minutes, telling the Detective she's <u>positive</u> of her identification. However, the state of mind of a victim does fluctuate over time. Uh, maybe she is positive then! But time clouds memory and threats can occur and a victim may lose her resolve – or she may have merely offered an educated guess in the first place. Lots of factors come into play.

Six months have passed. Only the convenience store clerk is subpoenaed. Robbery is a crime against the person. No property crime is involved in the allegation before the Court. The clerk <u>is</u> the victim not the business. She has <u>two</u> responsibilities on the witness stand, i.e., provide the elements of the crime and connect the accused to the crime. The Honorable **J. Herman** is presiding. A Public Defender, whose name escapes me, is there to keep the rookie Prosecutor on his toes. The Public Defender Rep <u>doesn't</u> have to work much during this outing. Which is probably why I don't remember who it is.

It isn't that I didn't prepare well. I diligently read the police reports and witness statements. I studied the applicable Criminal Procedure Code for Preliminary Hearings, and I *canned* the questions I would ask my witness on Direct Examination . The witness appears pursuant to the service of process, and I speak briefly with her in the hallway prior to the beginning of the Hearing.

The Judge does his job. Things go fine at first. I sail through the initial phase of my canned Direct Exam. The **victim** identifies herself. Her employment at the store is established. Venue becomes a matter of record. The witness dutifully testifies that the robbery happens within Las Vegas, Clark County, State of Nevada. She relates that Seventy One Dollars is removed from the cash register and handed to the robber as she looks down the barrel of a hand gun. She explains that the transfer of monies from her to him is <u>not</u> consensual. She does it out of fear. She's not going to argue with a gunman. She doesn't want to get shot. Come on now!

The questions are building, building, building to the grand climax — **identification** of the robber. I supposed it was going to be a lot like shooting a fish in a rain barrel. You're certainly going to nail the chubby gilled guy, it's only a matter of time. And I'd <u>given</u> the **witness** the time. The Defendant isn't swimming in a rain barrel, and I don't have a piece of scratch paper with the word ROBBER, printed in large letters, pinned to the front pocket of his jump suit. But really, this guy's decked out in his Clark County Jail ensemble. There's no mystery in the Courtroom about who the **bad** guy is <u>supposed</u> to be.

The exclusionary rule has been invoked by the Deputy Public Defender. He's not taking any chances, but he could have saved his breath. There's just a <u>single</u> witness subpoenaed. The others present in the room are Court personnel <u>or</u> Lawyers. There's J. Herman and his Bailiff. The Judge is wearing a black robe and he's on the Bench, of course. The Bailiff isn't to be confused with the robber. He's a different color and he's wearing a Law Enforcement uniform. He's hardly a prime candidate for early morning convenience store robberies. Then, there's a lovely blonde Court Reporter, a cute little Court Clerk, the Defendant's smug P.D., — **me** – and the guy in the mug photo my victim has positively ID'd shortly after the crime. Not another person graces the Courtroom with his presence. Nobody!

So, the stage is set. The foundation is laid. The case is about to be made, or so I thought. I say, "Ms. Victim, do you see the person in the Courtroom who took money from you at gunpoint on the date in question?"

And she calmly looks directly at the sullen man in the Jailhouse jump suit, who so obviously is **the guy** he just as well have been saying, "Pick me, pick me. I'm the man who robbed you, pick me! Just get it over with, Please. I want to get the hell out of this Courtroom and go back to my cell;" — and she quips, "**Who dat man**?" Three extremely portentous words for the occasion. A largely rhetorical question that says, "You're outta here, Buddy. That's *strike three*." Ms. Victim is talking to him <u>and</u> to me. He's hitting the streets again, and I'll soon be back at my office hitting the books about how to prevail at a Preliminary Hearing again.

You could have picked my chin up off the floor with a pooper-scooper. I hear two voices after that. Oddly, they seem quite far away.

The first voice is the smug Deputy Public Defender. He says flippantly, "Move to dismiss." The second voice is His Honor. He is chuckling softly into the microphone. The voice says, "Granted. Case dismissed." Aaarg! There's no calvary waiting in the wings when the crime is **one on one**.

I'm going to say it again for **the record**, there aren't any guarantees in a Courtroom! I'm in another zone. Swept away in a purple haze. The rapidity of the case demise leaves me stunned. Oh, thoughts of owls and purple cows.

"I never saw a Purple Cow, I never hope to see one; But I can tell you, anyhow, I'd rather see than be one." (Gelett Burgess, ibid.) And **if** I'd had my druthers in Court, at this moment anyhow, I'd rather have seen a Prosecutor than been one.

This afternoon the smug Deputy Public Defender will be regaling his cohorts at the Defender's Office about this one. Their raucous *laughter* will ricochet from wall to wall at my expense. Over there they don't get many victories, and they really like to milk the ones that do come along.

MIGHTY SMALL STAKES! – **Baruk** is a former Pakistani Airman. He's small of stature, but wiry and strong. I'd say the strength of the grip in his hands is particularly impressive. He has also immigrated to the United States, and married an American woman.

Actually, she's a whole lot of American woman. She's a big-boned, buxom redhead who probably towers over her spouse by at least five inches. Furthermore, she has a shrew-like assertiveness, that is surely galling to a sensitive Pakistani man, once the thrill of fresh romance has gone into deep chill. He isn't accustomed to a strong-willed woman. A wife is supposed to be an ornament for sexual pleasure and procreation. She speaks when spoken to. The first law of marriage in Baruk's world is obedience.

The union of this pair is akin to mixing a jalapeno pepper and a grapefruit. Burn and pucker are a daily occurrence. Sparks fly regularly in their volatile relationship, and sometimes the conflicts become physical. Perhaps, the difference in size lulls **Cassie** into a false sense of security – and aggression. Possibly, she thinks her larger physical stature gives her the right and the power to intimidate her husband. It's been said that during physical altercations, Cassie <u>picks</u> Baruk up like he's a little *Teddy Bear* and shakes him until he conforms to her point of view.

Impressive! Yet not without risk. Baruk is a proud man steeped in Islamic culture and the traditions of his fathers. He can be physically shaken, but can the American wife shake the Pakistani mind-set out of her husband? The answer is –– negatory!

Eventually, Baruk has his fill of Cassie's rough-housing technique. He's humiliated by his wife's unfeminine, controlling approach to their relationship. He feels emasculated and estranged. He believes his wife is having affairs. Their opposing religious values are profoundly exacerbated by his perception of marital indiscretion. Over time, Baruk forms the opinion that his American wife is a shameless, godless infidel. It's an intractable clash of cultures, values, and personalities. Love, it seems, has departed the marriage for a more hospitable environment.

So, **he kills her**. He says it's *self defense*. However, one wonders how a woman is manually strangled to death – **in self defense**.

The case becomes my <u>first</u> **murder** Preliminary Hearing. I'm flying alone against Gentleman Jim, **thee** Public Defender of Clark County. He's the main man for the Defenders. The crime antagonists present sharply conflicting gender and cultural issues. The attorney protagonists present a sharp contrast in experience and style. Gentleman Jim is loose and confident and articulate. I"m tight and tentative and inarticulate.

The irrepressible Justice of the Peace is **Judge Roy**. He is a former Deputy District Attorney. I started my tenure with the Office of the District Attorney as a law clerk on the <u>fourth</u> floor of the Courthouse. My digs were in the library, and that just happened to be next to Roy's office. I've always liked Roy. He's friendly and charming. During those early days his manner on the telephone made a strong impression on me. He talked loud and that could be distracting. It was impossible not to hear him converse as I did my legal research. But I liked his confidence and the bold sound of his voice when he took calls. A Deputy District Attorney gets phone calls from all sorts of characters.

We never had a telephone when I was growing up on the farm. That fact may explain, in part, why phones have always slightly intimidated me – and fascinated me. Obviously, Roy is perfectly at ease doing business by land wire. His incoming calls invariably got the same greeting. I'd hear the telephone ring. Roy would adroitly lift it off the cradle and bark into the receiver, "**Roy here**!" Then speak to the caller with "The calm confidence of a Christian with four aces." (Attributed to Mark Twain) I thought that was really cool! Actually, I think Roy is cool. I have a lot of respect for *confident* people who <u>speak</u> their minds.

I'll put the brakes on these initial underpinnings of my work on the fourth floor of the Courthouse for now. It's the day of State vs. Baruk and we're doing business on the <u>second</u> floor in Justice Court.

A guy's first murder prelim is going to be stressful. A whole lot is riding on the outcome when a human life has been taken. Of course, the issue at this stage of the proceedings is not guilt or innocence. The Magistrate has the sole responsibility of deciding if the Defendant should be *bound over* to District Court <u>for</u> Trial. The Prosecution's burden of proof at a Preliminary Hearing is <u>probable</u> <u>cause</u>. That's a relatively low burden. <u>Slight</u> evidence connecting Baruk to the homicide will be sufficient. Once an unlawful killing has been established, the evidence doesn't have to show that the Defendant did much more than sneeze into the victim's face to get him *bound over*. Still, it's my first time out of the chute on an open murder charge, and I don't want to get bucked off. I <u>am</u> uptight.

My preparation has been meticulous. The necessary witnesses are under subpoena, and I've canned **each** question I intend to ask them on the witness stand. The Hearing proceeds smoothly until the State rests. Then in a matter of speaking, the wheels *almost* come off.

Following quickly on the heels of the Prosecution ending it's case, suave Gentleman Jim moves to *dismiss* the charge. His grounds are succinct, he claims the Deputy District Attorney has **failed** to establish jurisdiction. The ever-so-fluent Mister Public Defender says the Prosecution has **not** presented a single scintilla of evidence that the crime happened in Las Vegas, Clark County, State of Nevada.

Now, that is a serious allegation if the Court goes by the book. Technically, the Magistrate has no authority to bind Baruk's case over to District Court for Trial, irrespective of the evidence offered against him, **if** the *crime venue* is <u>not</u> a matter of record.

I'm not a procedural aficionado at this phase of my fledgling career, but I am savvy enough to recognize a legal basis for the Defense gambit, and its impact upon my murder case **if** Judge Roy *grants* the Defender Motion. I quickly peruse my CANNED questions, my pulse quickens, and the sweat begins to form under my armpits. Heck, suits aren't all that cool in the heat of battle in the Justice Court arena. A Prosecutor pushes more moisture through his pores than *tongue sweat* under such circumstances.

Other persons have entered the cracker box Courtroom. The Magistrate has additional matters to consider on his Court Calendar this day. Those who have joined us consist of several attorneys and a few Courthouse junkies. One of the attorneys who now sits several rows behind me is already a *familiar* adversary to readers of my Courtroom chronicles. It is none other than Mr. High Powered, the inestimable Counselor who choreographs the acquittal of Ms. Sarah Cool in Chapter 2.Though that debacle, actually, comes about a year AFTER the case at bar.

Be that as it is, I want to get back to Courtroom *sweat*. Somehow, Roy isn't looking so cool at this moment neither. However, he's going to speak his mind in due time. He noticeably sighs. I'm sure his displeasure stems from a perception that the rookie has committed a grave faux pas of omission. Judge Roy's head shifts from left to right. His gaze comes to rest on me as he queries, "Counsel, what is your response?"

I defend my case proffer. I say, "Your Honor, I did establish venue. I asked the first responding Officer if the crime happened in Las Vegas, Clark County, State of Nevada, and he replied that it did."

But Mister Public Defender has a different recollection. His Fluency fires back, "It's **not** in the record Judge. The State has **failed** to establish jurisdiction. Not one question has been asked concerning the address of the alleged offense, and no witness has volunteered any evidence regarding venue. The record is totally deficient. The Case must be dismissed. The Court doesn't have jurisdiction to hold my client to answer on the charge."

Then there's a brief exchange of verbal forays. It goes back and forth for a few moments. I'm standing firm that it's in the record. Gentleman Jim is equally adamant that it isn't in the record. Each of us attempting to sway His Honor by drowning out the comments of the other.

The Court reigns in the standoff between the Protagonists. Judge Roy looks disgruntled. Evidently, he believes he's been victimized by the *sloppy* work of the greenie from the D.A.'s Office. He's stuck on the horns of a dilemma that is <u>not</u> of his making. Sure, he can dump the case due to this little Chump's mistake. However, it doesn't look good on a Magistrate's resume to be dismissing a **murder** charge on a legal technicality.

Frustrated Judges sometimes get a little whine-a-cious. His Honor's face is etched in displeasure. However, he's made a command decision. He's decided to be the knight on a white horse in this instance. It'll read better in the morning paper than a dismissal. He'll rescue the poor little Deputy from his sorry plight. His judicial face flushes and contorts. The exasperation is palpable in Roy's voice.

"Well, I'm **not** going to dismiss a MURDER case simply because evidence of *Clark County* **isn't** in the record. I CAN take <u>judicial</u> <u>notice</u> that the killing occurred in Clark County. But for *crying* out loud, Mel, in the future **don't forget** to <u>establish</u> JURISDICTION before you *rest* your case."

Stick with me on this one. The comment from the Bench goes all over me. The chagrin and condescension of the Court is infuriating. Roy just as well have poured a pint of distilled vinegar on the crown of my head. I took personal offense at the Court's umbrage – convinced I was being <u>unjustly</u> accused of misfeasance.

I know I'm a rookie. This is my <u>first</u> murder Preliminary Hearing. But I'm <u>not</u> an idiot, and I can read! I'd prepared thoroughly. I'd meticulously set out all the elements of the crime, **including** JURISDICTION in my notebook. I've previously mentioned that I canned **each** question. I'll be even more specific now in an attempt to make my point. I had **personally** CANNED, that is, written out verbatim <u>every</u> word of <u>every</u> question for <u>every</u> witness. Then as the Hearing progressed, I'd personally READ verbatim <u>every</u> word of <u>every</u> question for <u>every</u> witness I called. The first witness I put on the stand was the initial responding Officer, and my CANNED questions to him **included** a question concerning jurisdiction. My notes **specifically** spelled out Las Vegas, Clark County, State of Nevada. Sooooo — I **KNEW** I'D ASKED THE FIRST OFFICER ABOUT **VENUE**! It isn't my fault the Judge and Gentleman Jim aren't paying attention when the pertinent fact is offered.

I jump to my feet and loudly proclaim, "Your Honor, I **know** evidence of JURISDICTION **is** in the record. I CANNED all my questions to the witnesses. I DID NOT **FORGET** to establish **jurisdiction**! I stand on the record. I **know** I put it in the record. The record speaks for itself! [Pausing for full effect.] I'LL STAKE **MY REPUTATION** ON THE FACT that **jurisdiction** is in the record!!"

Then I sat down in a Prosecutorial huff. And immediately a cavalier, highly recognizable voice, two rows behind me, and slightly to my right **crows** ——— "MIGHTY SMALL STAKES!"

It is the folksy twang of the inestimable, Mr. High Powered putting a GREENIE in his place. Vegas is not a venue where a young Deputy D.A. should be laying a STAKE before the Court that is **unsupported** by any NOTEWORTHY RECORD of accomplishment in the legal community. It's an ill-advised, hollow boast by a character whose *tongue* **is** in such a *lather* that it's flapping out of control. CHECKMATE and a SOUNDTRACK of **laughter**.

Those gathered inside the Courtroom, from the Bench to the Bailiff to the back door, *spontaneously* **erupt** into a huge GUFFAW at my expense. And I'm not laughing. So they're laughing at me **not** with me! My ears get beet red. It's a moment that lives in infamy in my memory. It was awful! Had I heeded my initial impulse, I'd have climbed under the table and covered my ears.

Following the interlude of comedic relief, the almost forgotten Baruk – who laughs at me only because everyone else is laughing, AND who alleges he has *manually strangled* his wife to death in SELF DEFENSE – has to temporarily swallow his laughter. He's **bound over for Trial**. Judge Roy takes judicial notice that the offense has occurred in Clark County.

In defense of my rhetorical courtroom peccadillo, I feel compelled to humbly assert that this incident is merely a misunderstanding. When I spoke of STAKING **my reputation** I'm not speaking of my LEGAL REPUTATION. I'd only been a member of the Nevada State Bar for a few months. I had NO legal reputation – good or bad. However, I learned a valuable lesson from the experience. Thank you, Mr. High

Powered. I learned that an Attorney who is going to be successful has to be **precise**. He <u>has</u> to SAY what he means and MEAN what he says.

I stood lamely before the Court on that occasion decades past and spoke **imprecisely**. I did <u>not</u> SAY what I meant. I had **no** legal reputation, but I **did** have a reputation of *trustworthiness* among those who really knew me. I'm speaking that day in Judge Roy's Courtroom about, what *I perceived* to be, a REPUTATION OF PERSONAL INTEGRITY among my peers – my Family and my Friends and my Professors and my Religious Advisors. I'm trying to say, "I **am** a truthful person. **If** I say, 'IT'S IN THE RECORD,' then you <u>can</u> *damn well be sure*, you can make book on THE FACT, that it **IS** in the record!"

I'm giving the word REPUTATION a narrowly construed definition. In the true spirit of *Through the Looking Glass* I'm saying, "When I use a word it means just what I choose it to mean – neither more nor less." (Lewis Carroll, ibid.)

Having been assigned the case, I follow it to District Court. But things don't get measurably better for me there. It seems Baruk and Cassie were star-crossed lovers, and the criminal charge may not have been blessed with proper astrological alignment neither. It turns out that Judge Roy has only given the Case a provisional reprieve. <u>After</u> Roy there is the Jury. Hands down, the Jury is the greatest variable in the Criminal Justice System. The Prosecutor who **fails** to pick the *proper* Jury **fails** to get the *proper* verdict!

I made **two** errors of judgment in the matter of Baruk and Cassie. At the Preliminary hearing I wasn't PRECISE and at the Trial I wasn't PERCEPTIVE. I selected the wrong Jury and, I believe the **case truth** suggests, the Jury selected the wrong verdict.

REALLY, how does a man **manually** strangle a woman to death IN SELF DEFENSE? I need to have that explained to me.

Is **Baruk's** alleged *"Teddy Bear"* indignity a basis for acquittal? An autopsy examination is performed upon the deceased. The <u>Chief</u> County Medical Examiner details his *findings* on the witness stand during Trial. He's performed over five hundred autopsies. The CAUSE of death is **manual strangulation**. The MANNER of death is **criminal agency**. The opinions of the Medical Examiner are that death has <u>not</u> been caused by <u>disease</u> or <u>natural</u> process, nor <u>accident</u>. Death is <u>not self</u>

inflicted. This killing **IS UNLAWFUL**! The deceased is a VICTIM of a **crime**. An individual has *cruelly violated* Cassie in reckless disregard of consequence and social duty. He has *placed* his hands around her neck and *squeezed* until she's **dead**! Further, this isn't a **who-done-it** mystery. Baruk CONFESSES he did it. Ka-ching? Guilty? Next case?

Hardly, it doesn't work out that way. Expect the illogical. Verdicts come in every form and nuance. The mystery *isn't* the identity of the perpetrator. Everyone in the Courtroom knows WHO–that–is. The **HUSBAND** did it! THE MYSTERY is how this Jury could decide what this husband did to this wife *isn't* **a crime**!

With all due respect to the venerable Jury System, a **verdict** of SELF DEFENSE in this case is as extraordinary as *seeing* a PURPLE COW – and I'm an expert on cows. I grew up on a **dairy farm**. I've probably milked a thousand of them. I've seen tons of them. I've seen Holsteins, Jerseys, Guernseys, Herefords, Brahmans, Charolais, Black Angus, Brindle, and others. But I've NEVER *seen* a PURPLE one, and I've NEVER *seen* a verdict quite like this one.

Look, the Medical Examiner testifies that Baruk *grasps* his wife from BEHIND. He has formed this **opinion** to a degree of medical certainty due to the essentially horizontal, red pressure point impressions he sees on both sides of the victim's neck. They are consistent with outstretched fingers extending from BACK TO FRONT. The tips of these strangulating digits clearly **end** just below the chin. Bruised spots over the windpipe are consistent with fingernails digging into the tissue. Also, pinpoint hemorrhaging known as petechiae is observed around Cassie's eyes. Tiny burst blood vessels are present under the eyelids.

Thus, the juxtaposition of the killer and his victim is an atypical **reversal** of *most* justifiable cases of self defense. Ordinarily, lethal force may be employed **only** if a killer **IS** FACING an aggressor who threatens him with imminent bodily harm. Instead, it is highly probable in this case that Baruk sneaks up behind an unsuspecting wife and grabs her around the neck. HE **initiates** the physical assault.

He chooses a moment when she's most vulnerable. The disparity in the size of these two and the essentially horizontal pressure points on both sides of her neck suggest she may very well have been SEATED at the time of the attack. If so, is she reading? Watching television? Speaking on the telephone? Is she asleep? Sick? Inebriated? Crying?

He has to catch her off-guard. Otherwise, what he does is impossible. It's **not** going to be *easy* for a wiry little guy like Baruk to *subdue* a big boned buxom, aggressive woman like Cassie. IMAGINE **his** state of mind: the resolve, the determination, the effort, the **tenacious** pressure he exerts with his hands and fingers to accomplish this grisly task!

We're talking MANUAL STRANGULATION here. Such an **event** isn't over in a split second. Manually strangling another human being TO DEATH takes time. Strangulation by digital **compression** of the neck involves *blockage* of blood flow and *interference* with respiratory function. The primary lethal effect arises from pressure applied to jugular veins in the neck. This prevents blood from flowing out of the brain and the head, where it stagnates and oxygen content is quickly used up.

In addition, compression of the wind pipe restricts breathing and impairs oxygenation of the blood. A victim's face becomes congested with blood and takes on a livid purple-blue coloration. She <u>loses</u> CONSCIOUSNESS and, **some minutes later**, BRAIN DAMAGE and DEATH occur from lack of oxygen!

HOW is this ENTIRE **process** accomplished in *self defense*? Please tell me. I'm trying to make sense out of this. JUSTIFIABLE *self defense* ENDS when imminent threat of bodily harm to the killer ends!

When she's *subdued* it ends! The killer can get the hell out of there. He has NO NEED to kill. When she *stops resisting* there's NO NEED to kill! When she's *UNCONSCIOUS* he has NO NEED! When she *STOPS BREATHING* **WHY** is this f—-ker still applying a vise-like grip to her neck???

Didn't this numb skull ever contemplate DIVORCE? Is there **no** limit to indulgence in SELF WORSHIP?

Enough said. The issue can <u>only</u> be resolved by a Higher Authority!

TIME IS MONEY or whatever – <u>Some</u> Judges like to throw their weight around. They derive a certain sense of gratification from putting Lawyers in their place. They enjoy playing a beguiling game of <u>power</u> ball in the Courtroom arena. Lawyers are their playthings. The assertion of Judicial Power is evidently a big-time egotrip. Most of these guys are rather pleasant fellows in *real* life. However, a **metamorphosis** occurs when they slip into the Judicial <u>Robe</u> and *ascend* the <u>Bench</u>. It's a truly awesome transformation, a breath-taking change that is inflicted upon the humble practitioners who appear before them. It's like they become a <u>different</u> human **species**.

The Dictionary calls *metamorphosis*, in the Zoological sense, the transition between an immature form and an adult form., e.g., from pupa to an insect, or from a tadpole to a frog. Well, the Dictionary comes through again. That's it! **Judges** <u>aren't</u> immature any more. **Judges** are people who have *grown up*. They've <u>morphed</u> from tadpole to frog — to **prince**. Judges are royalty. Courthouse Princes. And the catalysts for this wondrous transmutation seem to be the <u>Robe</u> and the <u>Bench</u> — and the Judicial <u>Appointment</u>.

The **Appointee** enters a *surreal* existence. He puts on the **Cloak of Authority**, climbs Olympian heights to the **Bench**, and is suddenly endowed with **Deity-like** maturity and judgment.

"For now we see through a glass darkly;
but then face to face: now I know in part;
but then shall I know even as...I am known."
(Apostle Paul, *Holy Bible*, 1 Corinthians 13:12)

Judges are a bit like the great Apostle Paul. Before their Judgeship they see through a glass darkly. Yet, after their transformation to the *Judicial Species*, they *see* through a glass *clearly*. <u>Knowing</u> even as they are known. At least, that's what they seem to think.

The Investiture Ceremony of **Judge Harry** is illustrative of the change. Those present <u>**see**</u> the transfiguration happen before their eyes. We're in a Federal Courtroom. We see Harry as a <u>mere</u> mortal before the proceedings begin. He takes the *oath* of his revered position, the **Robe** is respectfully placed around his shoulders, he climbs the lofty mountain to the **Bench,** sits down, and surveys the congregation gathered below.

A few minutes later, Judge Harry is invited to offer his acceptance remarks. He stands and strides confidently to the splendid podium. Stares intently at those present for several moments. Then clears his throat and quips: " I'd never realized how SMALL the rest of you are — <u>until</u> I got up here."Evidently it's a question of altitude. We look LITTLE from up there, and our trifling size bestows a sense of enlargement upon the Honorable Judges. Of course, for the record, Judge Harry always was a <u>smidgen</u> uppity.

We <u>see</u> **Judge Paul** before he assumes the Bench. During his life before life OTB, Judge Paul labors as a Deputy District Attorney and as an Assistant United States Attorney. His amiable manner, his keen intellect, and his sharp wit make him an extremely charming man. Five or six of us prosecutive types regularly enjoy lunch together at the Horseshoe. Judge Paul is an engaging companion as we break bread.

I remember vividly that day several decades past when <u>one</u> of our group tried to choke to death on a chicken dumpling at lunchtime. We're chattering away at a circular table in the coffee shop. Regaling one another with tales from the Courtroom, when someone says, "What's wrong with Stan?" We all look at Stan, perhaps in the nick of time. His face is beet red, he's sweating profusely, mucous is running from his nose, and he's spasmodically coughing.

The guys seated next to Stan begin to slap him between his shoulder blades. The situation is touchy for a few seconds, but then the obstruction is dislodged. Stan wipes his face and sighs deeply. Then smiles sheepishly. There's a spontaneous exclamation from the rest of us, "Stan, you had us worried. Are you okay?"

Thankfully, he was okay. And what's left of our lunch hour proceeds uneventfully. As we rise from our chairs to leave, Judge Paul wryly remarks with a twinkle in his eyes: "Well fellows, it's been a *slice of heaven!*" Oh Paul, I love ya man – and I miss you.

But I'm thinking now of that occasion after the *metamorphosis*. Paul's <u>become</u> Judge Paul. He's not quite so prone to humor now. He's quit <u>seeing</u> through a glass darkly. He's part of the *Judicial Species* now, and <u>sees</u> through a glass clearly. He <u>sees</u> things in stark black and white from the Bench.

I've forgotten the particulars, though it's apparent I'm having a Trial in Judge Paul's Department. I've been a tad tardy getting back to the Courtroom during a series of recesses. The Prosecutor often has a lot tending and mending to do during Murder Trial recesses. There's precious little rest and relaxation. The Trial is on the First Floor and my Office is on the Seventh Floor, so there are logistical challenges.

Sometimes elevators don't cooperate, and on occasion the business at hand doesn't cooperate with rigid time constraints imposed by the Court. But I've been doing the best I can under the circumstances.

I'm somewhat out of breath when I get to Judge Paul's Court. He's got his black Robe on and he's waiting for me at the door into the Courtroom. I'm only guessing, but I don't think Judge Paul is <u>thinking</u> my timing is *"a slice of heaven,"* and he's not <u>looking</u> very *amiable* at this point in our relationship. Actually, Judge Paul is scowling.

He mutters quietly but firmly, "Counsel, glad you could <u>finally</u> join us. We're reluctant to intrude on your personal affairs *just* to conduct a Murder Trial. I said we'd be in recess for fifteen minutes not twenty five minutes. So, you may want to *listen* more closely <u>and</u> *remember* what I'm going to tell you <u>now</u>. Counselor, the next time you're late getting down here, I'm going to hold you in **contempt** <u>**of**</u> **court** and FINE **you** a THOUSAND DOLLARS for <u>**every**</u> MINUTE you're <u>**late**</u>!" WOW!

I didn't need to have him repeat the warning. The *clarity* of his edict is immediately apparent, albeit, <u>slightly</u> on the heavy handed side of the ledger. The fact is I found it tantamount to squashing an **ant** with an anvil. And I'm thinking, "Hey Paul it's me. Are you forgetting my middle initial? It's <u>**T**</u>. Some people say that stands for TURTLE. We're friends, right?"

In all candor, at that precise moment, I'm probably not feeling quite as fondly toward Judge Paul as I usually am. I'm a little agitated too. It ain't easy being a Trial Lawyer!

However, he gets my attention. **He said a <u>thousand</u> <u>dollars</u> a minute!** A THOUSAND DOLLARS per minute spread out over –– say, <u>ten</u> minutes would make several county paychecks disappear and create a powerful dent in my checking account. I *listened* closely and I've <u>never</u> *forgotten* the warning he administered. I <u>wasn't</u> tardy any more during the Trial and tried to toe the time-line thereafter. Judges appreciate **<u>punctuality</u>**!

Another intriguing example of Courtroom *power ball* also involves **Judge Paul**. I should have known my work was cut out for me on this one. The victim's nickname is **Crowbar**, and from all accounts the handle is well deserved. This character is a mean dude. But that's present tense. Crowbar is past tense now. He's a dead dude!

The red flag implicit in a *victim* called Crowbar is the flip-side of another Murder case where a name <u>should</u> have given me a case of cold feet. Believe me, a Prosecutor starts with two strikes against him if a *Defendant's* first two names are '**Benjamin Franklin**." It bodes ill for conviction when the accused is named after a founding father who is a signatory of <u>both</u> the Declaration of Independence and the Constitution.

The expiration of **Crowbar** occurs on Christmas Eve. He's killed by a shot from a rifle on a Christmas tree lot. A decidedly unchristian act that would seem to be a contradiction of the Gospel of "peace, good will toward men." (*Holy Bible*, Luke 2:14) And at Christmastime? The attempt to settle petty disputes with a gun barrel is deplorable. There's no closure in violence!

Here we have the booze factor and an allegation of *self defense*. It's a given, **if** the killer's identity is known, the **defense** is going to be either *self defense* or *insanity*. They're related, first cousins actually. On the one hand the killer avers he HAD to do it; on the other hand the killer avers he's deluded and THOUGHT he **had** to do it.

The shooter is charged. He's being tried by a Jury of his peers in the Courtroom of Judge Paul. We're involved in Summation. Mr. Smooth, loquacious Counselor for the shooter, has just completed the Defense Argument. The remarks of the two strong-jawed Lawyers have been lengthy. His Honor believes the Jury has heard all it needs to hear, and he's become impatient. He's anxious to get the cause to the Jury ASAP. However, there's a slight monkey-wrench in the Court's ordained timetable. *Mr. Long-winded* still has his **Rebuttal** Argument to deliver.

Let's put this sketch into context. I believe I've already mentioned how <u>fond</u> I am of Rebuttal Arguments. The words a Prosecutor offers in Rebuttal Argument are incredibly sweet to him. They are the LAST ringing rhetoric the Jury hears before it deliberates. It's verbiage that can be a game changer. The opportunity to CLOSE argument is *cherished* by a Trial Advocate. **No** Prosecutor worth his salt wants to be short-changed by a quick gavel. He wants his *last say* to reap a **big bang** effect in the Jury Room. NO Courtroom *power ball* from the Bench during Rebuttal Argument **please**!

Judge Paul has declared a ten minute recess prior to Rebuttal. The Bailiff informs me the Court wants to see me in Chambers. His Honor meets me at the door. We briefly confer ex parte. **His**–Let's–Get–This–Turkey–To–The–Jury– Quickly asks me how long I'm going to take. Sometimes <u>candor</u> has to be *compressed* a little within the raging realities of the Courtroom. It occurs to me that this is one of those times. I tell Judge Paul I'll take <u>about</u> *forty five* minutes. The operative word is <u>about</u>. Judge, I'm not saying I'll be done in *forty five* minutes on the nose. I'll be needing some elbow room. This is Mel *compressing* candor. Come on now. He visibly winces. Then obligingly says, "Alright, Counsel."

I begin the Rebuttal Argument. Mr. Smooth, loquacious Counselor for the shooter has been scintillating. He's left me with a bunch of loose ends to connect. Such a task takes time. Obviously, <u>too</u> much time –as circumstances unfold.

It's mostly my fault. I have this peculiar knack for saying in *ten* minutes what is typically said in *two* minutes. I love to embellish. I enjoy the use of words, and I don't like to take anything for granted. So, I flail away with the rhetorical hammer in an effort to **nail** things down.

The attribute, of course, is not unknown to Judge Paul. We're not exactly at our first Courtroom dance on this tense afternoon. He knows who he's dealing with. But the *forty five* minute time line has expired, and he's becoming exasperated. He's decides to <u>cut</u> in, to use dance floor parlance. I'm quite sure he believes an acquittal is in order. He doesn't want to give Harmon too much rope. The shooter might get hanged.

Nevertheless, don't **judge** the Prosecutor too severely, Yer Honor, **IF** you're **not** *standing* in his moccasins. A person – any individual, probably has to be <u>at</u> the lectern delivering his Rebuttal in a high profile Murder Trial to fully grasp the gravity of the situation. This is the **quintessential** opportunity for the Prosecutor to make a difference. For three solid weeks, he's invested hour upon hours of toil and strategy searching and sweat to get to this moment. His time before the Jury is precious, and he'll zealously guard it– even from encroachment by the Bench.

An Advocate isn't particularly cognizant of the passage of time while he argues. He's obsessing on what he's saying. The points he's presenting. And so it is, as the world turns, on this afternoon at the Clark County Courthouse.

I've worked up quite a head of steam. *Waxing eloquent*, I'll say. Expressing a view that belies my inherent modesty. I don't realize that the **three quarter** pumpkin hour <u>has</u> expired. The distraction begins unobtrusively. But I notice it after a few seconds. His Paul-ship seems to have a frog in his throat. The Judge starts to give me this – <u>ahem</u> shot, like he's maybe scraping mucous off his airway. It happens once, twice, three time, and more over several minutes. I get this <u>not</u> fully articulated – <u>ahem</u> treatment. Each successive salvo raises the decibel level on the guttural noise he's making.

Aaaaah, *now* I'm conscious of **time**. I get it! It's undoubtedly become obvious to everyone else in the Courtroom ahead of me. His Honor is trying to get my attention. He's projecting his displeasure that I'm taking so long. Yeah Judge, I get it – but I'm undeterred.

"Other sins only speak; **murder** <u>shrieks</u> out." (John Webster, ibid.) A **murder trial** is *raw* and *real*. The crime <u>is</u> a solemn event with *actual* down and dirty **consequences**. There's a **dead** **victim** in the cemetery and a **charged** shooter in the Courtroom. I'm unsure how the *passion of advocacy* finds fulfillment, through <u>conversational</u> <u>tones</u> employed in <u>friendly</u> <u>discussion</u> with SPECIFIC, <u>precisely</u> calibrated TIME LIMITS, within the **context** of a **Christmas Eve** SHOOTING. A **Prosecutor's** <u>highest</u> <u>duty</u> in this setting is **not** to his <u>friend</u> who is a Judge, nor to the physical comfort of the <u>Jury</u> he's addressing. HIS HIGHEST DUTY is the *role* of **dynamic** **champion** **for** **justice**! So ———I plow forward!

However, the Court is also undeterred. I've just managed to find my rhythm again. My voice is rising, the heated dialectic of logical disputation is flowing, and the *tongue sweat* is emoting – when I hear it. Tap––Tap––Tap––Tap–––– and my first impression is: "What the Hell! Is there a *woodpecker* loose in the Courtroom? Where did he come from? This is really annoying."

Actually, it's a flashback to my boyhood. I have some experience with woodpeckers. During my *early* years on the farm, woodpeckers made it an almost daily morning ritual to peck away at the northeast eave of our house. The syncopated patter of their beaks rapping against our roof is poignant in my mind to this day.

But no Picidae bird has entered unannounced, uninvited, and <u>unwanted</u> at a critical juncture in my remarks. The rhythmic Tap–

–Tap––Tap––Tap isn't a bird's *beak* in this instance. It's a Judge's *PENCIL*. The insistent rapping is coming from behind my back. I stop in mid-sentence, so to speak. Swing around and catch him in the act. Gotcha, Your Honor. The Woodpecker in the room is perched on the Bench wearing a black robe. Judge Paul's *pencil* is out and he's deliberately tapping it on the edge of his podium.

It's **humorous** to me now, at least he wasn't throwing chalk or gum balls to get my attention – since *ahem* hadn't worked. For the record though, the humor in the escapade flies completely over my head as it happens. I remember thinking, "This is rude, even for a Judge, and his timing couldn't have been worse." By the way, HE *isn't* smiling neither. There's not a glimmer of the characteristic twinkle in Judge Paul's eyes. His gaze is fixed upon me, and he's positively glowering.

The Court needs information from his perceived Mister Motor Mouth. He inquires, "How much longer are you going to be, Counsel?" His unhappiness with my verbosity oozes from each measured word.

Lots of things immediately flash through my head. Among the fast flying tidbits are these bottom line impressions: "I know I'm going to **need** *at least* thirty minutes more to wrap up my Argument, but I can't say that. He may go ballistic in front of the Jury. So, I'll say something that will *please* him. 'About ten minutes,'" I reply. My modus operandi is to try to get along with folks whenever it's possible.

Not cool. *Ten minutes* doesn't make him happy. He knows my game. The only words that could have caused Judge Paul to look graciously upon me would have been, "RIGHT NOW, Judge. I'm preparing to sit down. Right now."

Without expressly acknowledging my ten-minute proffer, His Honor leans forward and barks into his podium microphone, "We're in RECESS." Then he slams his GAVEL down hard!

An intrepid soul in the second row of the gallery quickly rises and prepares to exit the Courtroom. Judge Paul glares down at the early riser, and shouts: "**SIT DOWN! WE'RE NOT THROUGH YET!**" The man blanches into a significantly paler color, and humbly resumes his seat.

It isn't pretty. Instantly, the Room becomes so quiet a pen could have been detected glancing off the carpet. I don't think a soul dared blink. Every eye is glued upon the Bench. The visceral **consternation** of the

Judge is *palpable* in the Room, but there's <u>another</u> far more telling issue. One that has a major impact on the case, I believe. The OTHER factor is: EVERYONE in the Courtroom **knows** WHY Judge Paul IS **angry**. He's <u>not</u> *really* angry at the poor fellow in the audience who purportedly left his seat too early. NO, the Judicial beef isn't with that guy. All he did is inadvertently offer himself as a *vicarious* verbal whipping boy. He's a *stand in* for the REAL **culprit**. Simply a *sounding board*. Performing the same role the *family dog* plays when his master comes home from work in a <u>foul</u> mood. He gets kicked in the flank, right?

The fact is, had Judge Paul's leg been longer, he'd have dusted **my** posterior with the sole of his shoe. The **identity** of the *object* of His Honor's <u>chagrin</u> is the overly argumentative Prosecutor. HE'S THE ONE! That <u>isn't</u> a mystery. Nor do I believe the Judge's REASON for being angry is a mystery! HE'S **angry** because he thinks this People's Advocate is spending too much time ARGUING a case the Court <u>doesn't</u> think is RIGHTEOUS. He's of the opinion that **Crowbar** got exactly what he had coming to him.

His Honorable takes a deep breath. Admonishes the Jury not to discuss the case among themselves, not to read media accounts of the proceeding, nor to form fixed opinions about guilt or acquittal until they begin their formal deliberation. That said, they are excused for fifteen minutes.

Ha!! The part about **not** forming fixed opinions regarding guilt or acquittal is <u>surely</u> an exercise in empty rhetoric––after the hokey theatrics they've just witnessed. The Court's opinion **is** *implicit* in the awkward Courtroom drama he's staged. The members of the Jury aren't dumbbells. They're plugged in to certain power broker verities in the community. They recognize the potential for serious political fall-out from their verdict in this matter.

They're looking for Judicial *nuance*, subtle guidance, some clever indicators from the Bench. They want to know how Judge Paul feels about the case, but they're sophisticated enough to recognize he can't give an **express** opinion from the Bench.

Jackpot! It's been *sevens* across the reel. Judge Paul has just given them their answer. He's found a way to give the Jury a *nudge* toward acquittal without formally <u>advising</u> them to acquit. Since, given the particular circumstances of this case, a formal instruction to acquit is factually inappropriate.

So, whose feeling the <u>chagrin</u> now. The ole Prosecutor, that's who. It's been a teeter-totter ride. And the winner and still champion of Courtroom *power ball* is the Judge, of course. When we sluff off the veneer of Courtroom pro forma, the repository of *real* power in the Room is His Judgeship. A Trial Lawyer has to <u>live</u> with that reality, but he isn't always happy about it. Frankly, I'm thoroughly piss––d off during the recess.

I'm afraid I've just been caught up in a case <u>tipping point</u>. My first impulse is to barge into Chambers and give the Judge a *large* piece of my mind. However, being prudent is the better part of valor in matters of Courthouse etiquette. The air is charged with tension. There needs to be a cooling off period. Otherwise, I might get myself locked up for Contempt of Court. I still have a chunk of my Rebuttal to serve up to the Jury. Although this one may be slipping away, I still intend to milk my Argument until it's dry. A Prosecutor who has acquired the true spirit of his profession doesn't go easily into the dark night of an acquittal Verdict. Therefore, I put off <u>venting</u> until later. Resisting the temptation to storm into Chambers while we're in recess. What is done is history. The script just enacted by a Judge and an Advocate can't be rewritten. The bell has tolled. There are things a Trial Lawyer simply has to accept. It comes with the territory. Ohhh bother!

The Trial Jury <u>does</u> acquit **Crowbar's** shooter. Biting one's tongue in the white-hot heat of personal pique isn't easy, but it's generally the best course of action. Several days <u>later</u> I go see His Honor to do my venting. However, the emotional tension has mostly been spent. It's a cordial meeting. Our relationship is repaired – even strengthened. There is a mutual respect that refuses to be scuttled. The practice of law is <u>so</u> much about relationships.

Power ball is played by <u>others</u> in the Clark County Courthouse. **Judge Bob** is a prime example. When he is holding sway in Justice Court, he seems to delight in belittling whatever DA rep is in sight. Egan's the man on an occasion that's forever fastened itself to my memory bank, though it's entirely inconsequential. It's strange how certain incidents in mortality are readily recalled while a multitude of others have inexorably taken flight to a realm of incognizance.

The Master Calendar for criminal cases in Justice Court occurs at 1:30 p.m. The Deputy and a file Clerk arrive moments before the cattle call, er, Calendar Call begins. Egan has about thirty files tucked under his arm as he enters. Judge Bob, who looks forward to his time on the Judicial stage, has already taken the Bench. His caustic tongue is primed for action. He projects a sly smile, though his eyes are coldly intense, as the Deputy and his Assistant slouch into their seats.

Lights, camera –– action. Judge Bob begins to **rapid-fire** call the Cases. Often the sequence he employs is out of sync with the printed Calendar, as an accommodation to members of the Defense Bar. These fearless fellows are much more to the liking of His Honor than the greenies the Prosecutor's Office sends him. Where's the respect, man? A man of the self-perceived intellectual stature and professional bearing of Judge Bob deserves better, he's thinking.

His manner of calling Cases is deliberate. A thinly veiled expression of his general contempt for law enforcement, and of struggling rookie Prosecutors in particular. When he <u>fast fowards</u> Cases being called out of order, he **knows** it will likely befuddle the DA reps. But that's the fun in it! Ha ha, show me the squirm.

On this sunny–**outside**–but–rather–dismal–**inside**–the–Justice–Court **Day**, the Judge's disposition is typically dour. Cheered only by the discombobulation his process of summoning Cases has created on the DA side of the table. About five files into the Master Calendar proceeding, the Deputy is taking such an extravagant amount of time collecting the *right* file and the *right* thoughts for the file, His Most Honorable decides to verbalize the disdain. He fills up the Courtroom down time with an emphatic, "Don't just sit there like a BUMP ON A PICKLE, Mr. Egan. Do something." Oh, that's classic Judge. But so un-classy. Where's the love, Sir?

Talk about missing the mark. **I** <u>swear</u>, Mr. Egan doesn't look anything like a pickle, Judge. He's a handsome, cool, thoughtful man who's a bit on the shy side, but he's definitely **not** a <u>pickle</u> <u>bump</u>! He was doing his best, Sir. Don't **call** some one out in a public forum whose doing his best. If you think it's *funny*, please be advised: IT WASN'T!

We talked it over up in Prosecution Central at the end of the day. The Court's unprofessional conduct is so flagrantly reprehensible we decide he's earned the JUDICIAL PICKLE OF THE YEAR **Award**.

Then we *laughed* until the tears rolled down our cheeks at the expense of HIS PICKLESHIP!! Touche, Your Honor.

Irascible **Judge Tommy** is a character. He's a short, squat, bulldog of a man. A hall-of-famer in terms of intimidation *power*. When his face gets red and his volatile temper kicks into high gear, it's time for the Lawyer on the receiving end of his histrionics to take cover. A public servant can't dash from the Courtroom whimpering like a baby, so the options are limited. They are: (1) Shut your mouth, (2) Look down, and (3) Take your tongue-lashin like a man!

The Criminal Master Calendar in District Court was also conducted at 1:30 p.m. in the early days of my career. The Calendar rotates among the six Judges. I'll be honest, whenever Judge Tommy is presiding, I approached the assignment with a good deal of trepidation. The Files were copious. It always seemed to me we had to work our way through a veritable *mountain* of Criminal Files under the ever critical eye of His Irascible.

It has to be the **Robe**, and in the case of Judge Tommy, his Irish **Genes** — but the members of the Judiciary don't tend to be *patient* people. The impatience factor is particularly evident during a lengthy afternoon Criminal Calendar. The Court wants to expeditiously wade through the files. He has other geese to feed. Like nine holes of golf or a little Keno over on Fremont Street or a late afternoon at Lake Mead — etcetera. Consequently, the Judge wants the Deputy Prosecutor and his File Clerk assistant to come to Court prepared, and he won't be shy about venting his unhappiness if things don't go well. The problem is it's not *easy* getting up to speed on so many Files.

My vision of trips to the afternoon Master Calendar in Judge Tommy's Courtroom will never be erased from my mind. It's **not** fun getting yelled at, and I've **never** been crazy about being ridiculed. There's no time to catch your breath. The File Clerk shoves case after case in front of the Deputy, who usually has to be *spoon fed* the answers to WHY the File's on Calendar and WHAT you're supposed to say about it. Occasionally, the Case history notes are quickly perused, though never quickly enough to satisfy Judge Irascible. He clears his throat. I'll glance up. His neck is bulging, and his face is getting redder by the second.

It's now that the Court frequently spits out a stinging *critique* of the Deputy. And it's <u>not</u> simply his Court Clerk, your File Clerk, and you <u>and</u> him. It always appears <u>half</u> of Las Vegas is assembled to witness your legal ineptitude. There are legions of Lawyers, it seems, lots of Defendants – in and out of custody, and large numbers of spectators present to enjoy the *carnival* fun house atmosphere.

Several times each week the **<u>rebuke</u>** will conclude with *catchy* heart warming phrases <u>like</u> these: "Stop wasting my time. I've got better things to do [See third paragraph above for possibilities] than sit through these types of *shenanigans* [Is that word of Irish origin?] by some clown masquerading as a Lawyer. What are they teaching you guys in law school these days?

"Take a message back to your superiors up on the Fourth Floor. **Tell them** if their Deputies don't start coming down here better prepared, I'm going to find the WHOLE **District Attorney's Office** –– from the **District Attorney** and the **Assistant District Attorney** and the **Chief Criminal Deputy** all the way down to the <u>lowliest</u> **Deputy** in the damned Office –– in CONTEMPT OF COURT. We'll see how they like the sound of that!"

Whoa! That's a *grandiose* threat. The so-called movers and shakers of the County will be jolted to the core by such a monumental **contempt citation**. I'm saying, to find the ENTIRE **DA'S Office** *contemptuous* of the Court is something akin to a *declaration of war* against the Chief Prosecutorial Agent in Las Vegas by a brash <u>member</u> of the Eighth Judicial District Court! Surely, such a proclamation will ignite an internecine feud between the <u>major</u> component Departments of the Criminal Justice System.

Wheeee! Hold on tight, it'll be a crazy ride. **Mr. District Attorney**, my hirer and mentor, won't get his funny bone tickled by this reckless gambit. **Pappy** will be mad as hell. Raging and ranting on the Fourth Floor, dictating press releases, and calling news conferences. There will be Petitions to **quash** –– as many as it takes. He'll protect his Deputies, and <u>his</u> political fortunes. He won't sulk on the sidelines. Pappy's <u>not</u> a man who'll ever be at loss for words! He may be lecturing ST. PETER on the flamboyant art of Clark County politicking at this very moment. But impetuous ole Tommy. Grudgingly, I gotta respect him for not keeping things bottled up inside. He doesn't hold anything back. His Most Irascible lays it <u>all</u> on the table. He's like a boiling pot of hand ground coffee. However, I worry each time it happens that he's going to trigger an apoplexy. He puts tremendous stress on his system, though he <u>can</u> be a really jovial man in Chambers. Which seems rather contradictory to his Courtroom demeanor.

PS – **It never happened**. Judge Tommy's blustering went unheeded. Deputy preparation didn't noticeably improve. There is <u>no</u> OFFICE-WIDE contempt order. The Judge's bluff is called. There are simply <u>too</u> many files to get a **good** handle on them all. Plodding through a Criminal Master Calendar is a time-consuming chore, by its nature. That's the way it is. <u>No</u> pompous threat of CONTEMPT will change the unchangeable. The problem is endemic to the process.

The post-lunch episodes in blustery are funny now, just charming memories of another time and place. **But may the record show:** it was **not** entertaining then.

Judge Tommy discovers the Office of the District Attorney is <u>stubborn</u> in another sense. Throughout my tenure with the Clark County DA's Office we utilize a pleading previously referenced by me. It's called OPEN MURDER, and it's simple to prepare and efficient to use. I believe, it also effectively puts a murder case Defendant on <u>notice</u> regarding the *nature* and *range* of his charges.

Proper notification is a Due Process of Law issue. An accused can't marshal a meaningful defense unless he knows the nature and extent of his charges. Stated succinctly, Judge Tommy <u>doesn't</u> believe an **open murder** allegation meets Constitutional Due Process requirements. He probably went to his grave as a **non believer** ––– in this *manner* of pleading a Murder Case.

Whatever he may not have been, the Judge <u>has</u> a firm set of values that mold his decisions in the Courtroom. His *brand* of judgment doesn't always find general acceptance in the legal community, nevertheless he'll adamantly stick to his view. Tommy is a man who likes to do things HIS WAY. Something like, *it's my way or the highway.*

The controversy begins when the Judge starts making noises about the **open murder** pleading. It's just talk at first. More bluster, "Tell your Bosses I'm going to start *dismissing* the Informations that charge **open**

murder sua sponte. The g––d damned language only pleads MURDER IN THE SECOND DEGREE."

Big surprise, the pitch from Judge Irascible falls on deaf ears up in DA central. The Big Boys upstairs aren't the least bit inclined to *trash* their time-honored **open murder** pleadings.

The banter goes back and forth for several months. Neither side budges. Spokesman for the Prosecutor's Office tell His Honor they're confident their pleading is appropriate. The Judge's crusade hits the wall. So, he decides to ratchet up the controversy. He'll raise the stakes. He'll show these bastards he hasn't been making idle threats. The debate isn't merely an academic exercise.

Judge Tommy elects to take a *bite* out of an **actual** case. And as luck has it, the case he chooses happens to be one of mine. We're to select the Jury the first day of Trial. I present a typical case introduction to the panel of prospective Jurors. Explaining the date of the offense, the location of the crime scene, the identity of the deceased, names of prospective witnesses, and other broad parameters of the charge. Then I sit down. Which is good, I needed to be sitting down for what comes next. Get yourself firmly anchored, Pal.

My offering is followed by a Rejoinder from the Court –– to my dismay. What the Judge says is a <u>case</u> blockbuster. It's the steadfast position of the DA's Office that the case at bar is deliberate, *premeditated* **First** Degree Murder. However, the information doe s <u>not</u> specifically allege *premeditation*. It simply alleges *malice aforethought*. His Honor is having none of this. His forbearance with the State's pleading language is exhausted. He <u>informs</u> the prospective Jurors, in his inimitable fashion, that the State's **open murder** pleading <u>only</u> charges **Second** Degree **Murder.** Quote, "This *boiler plate pleading* will <u>not</u> legally sustain a conviction greater than Murder Two!" Furthermore, the Court puts the blame for the anomalous circumstances squarely on the shoulders of the Office of the District Attorney. He argues he's being forced to do this because the DA continues his lame brained intransigence with respect to the filing of **open murder** cases. Which, he contends, is a practice <u>clearly</u> forbidden by the Due Process Clause in crimes of **First** Degree **Murder!** Judge Tommy says he's compelled to intervene in the interests of justice, that additional travesty might be avoided. He intends to stop this short-sighted practice of the District Attorney in it's tracks.

Then, His Most Irascible glares down at me. He doesn't have to verbalize his thoughts. His demeanor says it all. The look declares, "Bring it on Deputy, I don't give a rats-ass what you think. Nothing you say will make a difference to me, but it may get you cited for contempt."

I don't take the bait. It's intimidation city, and the cat's got my tongue. I'm between a rock and a hard place. Deputy Harmon, essentially, does a hasty genuflect before the Court, and we proceed with Jury Selection. The groveling continues for the next hour until the Judge takes his mid morning recess.

The break is my first opportunity to sound the alarm. I don't go to the restroom, nor to the concession stand. I don't stop to socialize with any Courthouse groupies. I don't pass go. I get my fanny upstairs. There's a fire in Judge Tommy's Courtroom that needs to be put out.

My message is a call to action. The public servants upstairs act with remarkable alacrity. A Petition For Stay Of Proceedings is hurriedly fashioned. The Judge is being asked to *cease and desist* from the course he has charted.

I head back to Court, and Jury Selection continues for the rest of the morning. The Petition is delivered to His Honor during the lunch recess. Judge Tommy summarily **rejects** THE STAY, and we continue to pick a Jury until the mid afternoon break.

The Trial is abruptly aborted then. Two titans of the Clark County Criminal Justice process are locked in a trenchant legal tug of war. Each *stubbornly* standing by their respective *principles* for the pleading of Murder Cases, and it's a crucial issue that needs to be resolved. The District Attorney's Office has responded to Judge Tommy's denial of their PETITION, by seeking a STAY of all Trial Proceedings from the NEVADA SUPREME COURT. The **Stay** issues.

Thus, my Trial is interrupted by **action** from ON HIGH. It's not an act of Divine Intervention, it's an act of Supreme Intervention. The HIGHEST Court in the State tells Judge Tommy to shut things down until the issues can be reviewed by The Supremes up in Carson City. A formal Petition for issuance of a WRIT OF MANDAMUS is filed with the State Supreme Court the following day. The Latin meaning for mandamus is *we command*.

The Parties enter into a stipulation to vacate the Trial, and the matter is taken off calendar pending action from the Supreme Court. A week later the Higher Court <u>does</u> issue the WRIT OF MANDAMUS to the Lower Court. Therein, formally **commanding** Judge Tommy to <u>reinstate</u> the original **open murder** pleading, and to proceed to Trial.

But there's a standoff in *stubborn–inity*. Judge Irascible is now making *noises* the WRIT is invalid. He says he's <u>still</u> constitutionally correct on the issue, and he has <u>no</u> intention of changing his procedure until the United States Supreme Court <u>rules</u> on the matter. Hence, OPEN MURDER cases are <u>routed</u> around his Department for a time. And I believe, though it's possible I'm revising history, that practice continued until the ACT of Divine Intervention that took Tommy home.

However, I don't want to let Tommy rest until I've documented *two* more incidents of Courtroom *power ball*. I think both arose in Gary's Case. He's a career criminal – according to his record. And it's doubtful he's simply been a victim of circumstance so <u>many</u> times.

The guilt phase of the proceedings is almost complete. Only instructing the Jury and Argument are left. As the Court is reading his Instructions to the Jury regarding **Felony Murder**, that's a <u>killing</u> committed during the perpetration of a dangerous felony – ROBBERY in this example, he suddenly stops in mid sentence. Pauses. Looks down at me, and exclaims: "The elements of Robbery haven't been established. There is no corpus delicti of Robbery in this Trial Record. Therefore, none of the instructions concerning Felony Murder is applicable. I'm deleting them forthwith."

And before anyone could say, "What the heck!" Or, "Don't do that. Or, "Hold on for a minute." Or, "If it please the Court, let's discuss the issue. I'd like to argue that a Robbery corpus has been proven."

His Most Honorable **clenches** the *five* instructions that pertain to Felony Murder, **rips** them out of the Jury Instruction Packet, and sternly **proclaims**, "That should do it!" – To the Jury's surprise and to the utter consternation of the poor Prosecutor! But there is no gimme in Trial practice, not even for the Defense Counselors. Their client <u>is</u> convicted anyway, despite the antics on the Bench.

This time around, Defendant Gary – hereafter mostly referred to as DG – has the misfortune of being on the receiving end of a Jury Verdict of **Murder One**. [Naturally, DG's Case comes <u>before</u> the matter referenced immediately prior to this discussion, that involves a Lower Court trashing of the **<u>open murder</u>** pleading. Though it's all beginning to fit together in retrospect. In Re Gary may have been the Trial that serves as catalyst for what came later.]

So, we're conducting DG's Penalty Hearing. Correction, I should be saying the Prosecution is *attempting* to make a case for Capital Punishment against Gary. As the Hearing commences, I have at <u>least</u> **ten** OUT-OF-STATE witnesses summoned to Judge Tommy's Courtroom to offer testimony against the recidivist guy being sentenced. <u>Each</u> witness represents a <u>separate</u> event in the checkered past of DG. They are present and ready and willing to provide *actual* details of prior **bad** acts, which for the most part <u>are</u> prior **violent acts**. Nevertheless, His Honor is having none of it.

Judge Tommy rules from the Bench in the absence of any Defense Motion, that is, *sua sponte*, that ONLY certified copies of Judgments of Convictions are admissible at the Penalty Hearing. He <u>refuses</u> to receive any **testimony** from the witnesses describing the exact <u>nature</u> of the prior offences, and the witnesses are sent on their way like a covey of illegal immigrants lacking green cards. Thousands of dollars in expenditure by the County are flushed down the *<u>exclusion</u> toilet* as a result of the decision. And the Prosecutor is thinking, "What about the search for truth? Three cheers for Justice and to hell with Courtroom *power ball*."

Still, I suppose something should be mentioned in Tommy's defense, about the *shifting sand* of Death Penalty litigation. To this point, Judges didn't have a wealth of information concerning the methodology to be employed during Penalty Hearings. The landmark U.S. Supreme Court case of **Furman v. Georgia**, 408 U.S. 238, 92 S. Ct. 2726 (1972) *invalidated* most if not all death penalty statutes. Furman required *consistency* in the application of death penalty procedural standards. The Nevada scheme for imposing Capital Punishment is one of many declared unconstitutional in 1972.

The Nevada State Legislature reacts by enacting Capital Murder criteria which, when satisfied beyond a reasonable doubt, mandate the imposition of the Death Penalty. I handled one case under the mandatory system. The Case is heinous in a way probably not exceeded by any other Murder Trial I prosecuted. For some reason not made apparent by the evidence, **Andy** goes OFF on his live-in girlfriend. His weapon of mayhem is a knife, and he inflicts grievous injury upon every person present. The instrument he uses has a *long* blade and an extremely *sharp* cutting edge. He stabs the girlfriend and her pre-teen daughter to death. He also viciously cuts and stabs a younger daughter who is only five years old. Her injuries are horrendous. There are multiple stabbing and cutting wounds. Her throat is sliced, laying open the tissue and integral parts of the neck – causing extensive bleeding. She has been attacked with such ferocity that the blade has penetrated deep into her Esophagus. The child's Voice box and Epiglottis have also been punctured. **Andy's** crimes are unspeakably vile! "Cruelty has a human heart…" (William Blake, *A Divine Image*, Stanza I)

The Jury performs its legal duty with dispatch. This one is easy. They FIND Defendant Andy guilty of *two* counts of **Murder in the First Degree** with use of a deadly weapon, *one* count of **Attempted Murder** with use of a deadly weapon, and IMPOSE a sentence of DEATH. The mandatory test for Capital Punishment has been met by the **murders** of *two* persons, and the perpetration of a **murderous** scheme and intent that involves a great risk of death to *three* persons.

There is no execution. **Andy** cheats the death chamber grim reaper with some assistance from the Judiciary. He's been on death row for about eighteen months when the United States Supreme Court issues an opinion declaring that any sentencing process, **mandating** imposition of the Death Penalty once a specified factual criteria has been established, is unconstitutional. The Opinion also directs state jurisdictions to commute all mandatory death sentences to *life without possibility of parole*.

Thus, **Andy** gets a lifetime in the Slammer to think about the contemptible action that put him there. Sometimes a man can be his own condemner and his own tormentor.

The Death Sentence terrain changes again in 1977. The State Legislature enacts a bifurcated system in Capital Cases. Trials are segmented into a *guilt phase* and a *penalty phase*. Aggravating and mitigating circumstances are to be considered by the Trial Jury as a basis for fixing punishment.

It's within the context of a *penalty phase* sentencing structure that Judge Tommy imposes his unique brand of Courtroom *power ball*. And there's not much precedent to guide the thinking of an Eighth Judicial District Court Judge as he evaluates the admissibility of evidence. So, I'm willing to temper my posthumous critique of Tommy's behavior in DG's case.

Nevertheless, it still *smarts* that DG <u>probably</u> averts a rendevous with the Execution Chamber as a result of Judge Tommy's decision **excluding testimony** concerning <u>prior</u> aggravating circumstances. This <u>ruling</u> effectively emasculates the Prosecutive presentation at the Penalty Hearing. If the Jury doesn't know <u>details</u> of a Defendant's prior bad acts, how can we expect them to render a JUST punishment? If knowledge is power, which I believe it is, then its converse must also be true. Ignorance is impotence!

It's crazy, but a Mother Goose Rhyme just popped into my head.

"Little Miss Muffet, sat on a tuffet,
Eating her curds and whey,
Along came a spider,
Who sat down beside her
And frightened Miss Muffet away."

Little Deputy Steve stood on a tuffet, making his suave tongue sweat. When along came a Public Defender to make a hasty demur. While on the Bench sat the Spider, who did his best to frighten Little Mr. Deputy Steve away.

I'm <u>not</u> a player in this particular game of Courtroom *power ball*, but I am a percipient witness. My associate in the Major Violator's Unit, and good friend Deputy Steve, is presenting his **Rebuttal** Argument. I'm there to give him moral support. I'm seeing the scenario in my mind now, as though it occurred yesterday. And it didn't! It's just one of those odd things that's sticks in my head.

Steve argues a point esteemed Defenders of the Accused find objectionable. A resounding exception echoes across the Courtroom, "Objection to the remark, Your Honor. It's not supported by the evidence!" From the Bench we hear a terse, "Objection sustained."

Deputy Steve stands at the lectern. He replies calmly, "Thank You, Your Honor," and begins to proceed with other comments. But he's stopped cold by the Court. Judge Mike takes offense at being *thanked* by the Prosecutor for sustaining Defense Counsel's objection. He queries, **"What did you say?"**

Deputy Steve does a nifty pirouette to face His Honor, and repeats his previous expression: "I said, Thank You, Your Honor." Judge Mike noticeably raises his voice several decibels, and in a sullen, accusatory tone asks, **"For what purpose, Sir?"**

His Courtship doesn't jump off the Bench, rush up to Deputy Steve, get right in his face, and slap him silly. However, that seems tantamount to what he wanted to do. Undeniably, the Court takes serious umbrage over Steve's *"THANK YOU, YOUR HONOR"* remark. Judge Mike considers it a derisive comment, offered sarcastically and disrespectfully.

IT WASN'T!! I heard it. I know Steve. Trial Lawyers get conditioned into saying "THANK YOU" to Judges. Just like we're conditioned to stand when they enter the Courtroom, and to stand when we're addressing them. It's considered professional practice. Proper decorum. And that's what Little Mr. Deputy Steve is doing in Judge Mike's Courtroom when the Spider, er, Judge tries to frighten him away. Simply trying to be nice. Merely wanting to be agreeable. This is **much** a do about nothing!

Steve replies, "I was just **thanking** the Court for it's ruling, that's all." Now, what's wrong with that, really? Deputy Steve **has** much to be thankful for. This is the United States of America, and he's employed by the Clark County District Attorney's Office. He's filled with gratitude. Lots of things quickly come to mind. REMEMBER, he's offering his REBUTTAL REMARKS. Prosecutor's love **Rebuttal Argument** as I've already made a matter of record. Steve's thankful he's a Prosecutor. Like me, he thinks it's the world's greatest profession. He's thankful he's making his Rebuttal Argument. He's glad he's got a good case which he expects to win, if the Court will let him finish – and if the

Jury cooperates. He's glad to be alive. He's thankful he can breathe and gesture and speak. There's no place he'd rather be at this precise moment, than in this Courtroom arguing this case to this Jury. And he get's a huge bonus besides, his Trial Judge **IS <u>AWAKE</u>**. That's right, they aren't always awake. Some Trial Judges have been known to nod off a little while the Prosecutor is speaking. But HELLO, Judge Mike **IS <u>AWAKE</u>**!

We know he's awake because he sustained the Defense objection the FIRST time it's made. He <u>didn't</u> have to be roused from an afternoon siesta.

So, Deputy Steve has much to be thankful for – he exudes a spirit of gratitude, and **of course** he'll be profusely thanking the Court for <u>whatever</u> it does. **BUT** –– Judge Mike <u>doesn't</u> SEE the big picture. He only senses his personal pique over the <u>mocking</u> words of *Little* Mr. Deputy Steve from *high* on THE BENCH.

Accordingly, His Courtship is stern in his admonition. He pronounces, "Counsel, don't **EVER** *thank me* in this Courtroom again for **SUSTAINING** an objection by the Defense. If it happens AGAIN, I'll hold you in **CONTEMPT** of Court! Do you understand, Sir?" And the poor little maligned Deputy humbly responds, "Yes, Your Honor."

Now is that turning a Courtroom on its ear, or what? An expression of gratitude to the Court brings a Deputy to the brink of **contempt**? Well, it isn't "The Queen [from Alice in Wonderland] turned crimson with fury,...glaring at...[him] for a moment...[and saying], "OFF WITH...[HIS] HEAD!..." (Lewis Carroll, *Alice in Wonderland*, p.86) –– But it's close.

Though I'm –– thinking. Maybe Courtroom *power ball*, as bruising as it can be to a Prosecutor's ego, isn't as bad as a Courtroom *head count*. No pun <u>actually</u> intended. It all starts with the abuse of a HORSE – *Equus caballus*. A solid-hoofed plant-eating quadruped with flowing mane and tail, to be used for *riding* and *carrying* or *pulling* loads –– but **not** to be used as a *street sweeper*.

The unfortunate equestrian nag under scrutiny has been <u>tied</u> with a rope to the tailgate of a pickup, and then dragged for a block and a half along a paved road in the outskirts of Las Vegas. A good chunk of the distance traveled finds the horse *sliding* along the street on its right flank. It's enough to give the Horse Whisperer a case of the Hives. Witnesses are also appalled by what they see, and report the matter to the Police Department.

The owner contends he's within his rights. The mare has a <u>stubborn streak</u>, he says. It needed to be <u>taught</u> a lesson. Predictably, the PETA folks don't concur with the owner's rationale, nor does Law Enforcement. The horse owner with the unorthodox training regimen is charged with misdemeanor **Abuse of an Animal**. The case instantly becomes a cause celebre. Though the *horse* survives her misfortune, only a little worse for the friction blacktop causes to skin on the right flank. The mare's treated pro bono by a local Veterinarian – and released after two days. Six weeks later she's as good as new. The free advertisement the Vet gets from press coverage being money in the bank for him. It's strange how one *horse's* trauma is such a beneficent drama for the *horse* doctor.

The circumstances trigger a groundswell of righteous indignation in the community, and a **huge** turnout of animal rights supporters in Justice Court. As Courtrooms in Justice go, this room offers a rather large seating gallery for spectators. I will tell you, that for this case **every** hearing date of the proceedings produces a <u>full</u> house. <u>Each</u> seat is occupied and the back of the Courtroom is <u>packed</u> with standing animal rights activists. They're lined up three deep across the room. It's as though a circus has taken up residence in the Courthouse.

In twenty nine years of Clark County service, I've **<u>never</u>** seen more spectators in a Courtroom. And that includes appearances of a certain *Deep Throat* porn star on misdemeanor charges. That was a media frenzy to be sure, but in terms of sheer numbers of the Clark County populace turning out to witness Justice Court justice or injustice, <u>nothing</u> I'm aware of, ever equals the fervor displayed in the *horse dragging* misdemeanor.

I've gone to Justice Court on **murder** cases involving multiple <u>HUMAN</u> victims, torture and mayhem, explosives, Molotov cocktails, guns, knives, ice picks, ligatures, 2x4 boards, tire irons, hammers, rocks, soft drink canisters, frying pans, baseball bats, poison, booby traps, etcetera, and unthinkable blood and gore and murderous intrigue. I've presented cases where small **children** have been fondled, gagged, stabbed, sexually abused, viciously slapped, whipped, and choked. Where innocent young **women** are callously, savagely beaten, raped, and left for dead. Where the **elderly** are accosted in their homes and subjected to despicable abuse and indignities and unnatural death, but NONE of these cases creates the hype or spectator turnout nor circus atmosphere I witnessed in the *horse dragging* proceedings.

Look, I **don't** believe *horses* or any *other* type of living creature should be treated in an abusive way. **This–is–my–problem**, WHY does the public **outrage** manifested in a *horse dragging* case **overshadow** the public's abhorrence, visceral interest in, and vehement Courthouse protest AGAINST **horrendous abuse** inflicted upon HUMAN BEINGS? I **don't** get that. **IF** the extent of public nerve tweaking that seems to have been caused by the *horse dragging* case is truly representative of a societies priorities, then that is **profoundly** troublesome.

There **are** over-riding, pre-imminent **moral** **values** involving the *sanctity of HUMAN dignity and HUMAN life* that **are** crucial to the future of our species. These PRINCIPLES, necessarily, must be the fundamental PRIORITIES guiding the affairs of human society. The abuse of a *horse* is NOT remotely close to being equivalent to the serious abuse of a *human being*!

Sadly, the circus doesn't end when the introduction of evidence ends. The matter is argued and submitted to the Judge for decision. He takes the matter under submission. Two days later it's back on calendar, and the same boisterous crowd is back for the Court's findings. The culprit is on bail. The partisan crowd audibly hisses when he enters.

The Court is called to order. His Honor stiffly takes his seat on the Bench. The partisans anxiously lean forward in their seats. Straining to see the cowardly *horse owner*. Listening intently for the words of His Justiceship. As for him, he surveys the audience intently. Measuring their mood. When he speaks, he's opting to be a Court Jester rather than a Justice-maker. Probably sensing the absurdity of this primal fixation upon a *horse dragging* offense.

Says He, "What do **you** think? What should it be? You've heard the evidence too. What say Ye? Let's take a *head count*. ALL those who believe the **Defendant** IS GUILTY, let your feelings be known by raising your right hands in the air. [Probably 98% of the persons present raise their hands in the affirmative!] Very well! How many vote NOT

GUILTY? [**No one** – not a solitary soul is bold enough to raise his or her hand in the face of such consensus for GUILT.]

"The Ayes have it. Mr. Defendant, please stand. Sir, the Court hereby finds you GUILTY of the misdemeanor offense of **Abuse of an Animal**.. You are instructed to return in seven days for sentencing. The Court is in recess."

Great roaring rockets. If this Courtroom parody hadn't been so <u>pathetic</u>, it could have been mistaken for a mildly funny vaudeville act over on Glitter Gulch!

The penalty is imposed in a week's time. It's a little heavy-handed, I'd say. But that isn't pertinent. The Court is still performing his role as a vaudevillian buffoon by pandering to the partisans crowding his Courtroom. Shame on you, Your In-justice-ship.

"I never saw a Purple Cow, I never hope to see one;
But I can tell you, anyhow, I'd rather see than be one."
(Gelett Burgess, ibid)

Naturally, an Attorney who has daily Court-time should keep Court *happenings* in a proper perspective. He or she will **sleep** much better at night if eccentricities from the Bench are not taken <u>too</u> *seriously*. What I'm saying is, it's best to simply let them roll off your back like rain water rolls off a duck.

Oh, It's A Real Dog

(And other Courthouse Miscues)

"No brilliance is required in law, just *common sense* and relatively clean fingernails." (Sir John Mortimer)

Chapter 10

OH, IT'S A REAL DOG – GERTRUDE kills her husband with a knife, and she alleges SELF DEFENSE. However, her claim probably falls into the same category as Aunt Martha's proverbial remarks.

Defense Lawyer: "Aunt Martha, did you shoot that man in <u>self defense</u>? NO SIR! I shot him in the rump –– he jumped De fence." (Porter Lofton Larey)

Notwithstanding, Gertrude is sticking by her claim. She contends the physical abuse has existed through most of the marriage. She'd finally had enough. When he leaves around 10:00 p.m. for his usual round of boozing and carousing, she barricades the front door by hammering three 1x10 boards across the entrance. The lock is broken from past drunken re-entries –– according to Gertrude.

Then she retrieves a butcher knife from her kitchen drawer, sits down in her favorite chair, and waits. She hopes he won't get in, but if he does ––– she'll be ready. She <u>won't</u> let herself be subjected to further pummeling

She has a long time to stew. Hammerin **Hank** doesn't come home until 5:00 a.m. It's almost time for their rooster to crow as her husband reaches the door stoop. Immediately, every one of Gertrude's nerve endings is on *code red* alert. Will he or won't he? HE DOES!

He tries the door. The boards block entrance, of course. He pounds on the door, but Gertrude doesn't respond. So, Hank busts in! He smashes through the flimsy nail-job fashioned by his wife, splintering the boards into flying fragments of wood – and makes a bee-line for her –– according to Gertrude.

She steps forward and nails him with the knife as he staggers through the debris. The blade plunges into Hank's neck, severing a carotid artery. He drops to the floor in a bloody heap. He's gone quickly. There'll be no more binge drinking nor skirt chasing for ole Hank.

Gertrude calls the Police, and presents her version of the event substantially as described above. The nature of the crime basically limits fact finding to her one-sided recitation. The Police aren't privy to what happened, and Hank isn't around to rebut Gertrude's account.

There is a recognition in the DA's Office that this is a *thin* case. Yet, the boy's with the white hats don't want to play judge and jury by refusing to prosecute. Accordingly, Gertrude is charged with **Open Murder**. Perhaps, the Jury will find a comfort zone somewhere within the four crime options the pleading provides.

I'm given the privilege of working this one in <u>tandem</u> with Deputy Bill. He's an up and coming young lawyer with a wry wit. I remember the situation quite clearly still. A fifteen minute recess is ending, and the Court Bailiff has just summoned the Jury, Counsel, and other interested parties back to the Courtroom.

It's congested at the Courtroom doorway that leads to the Jury Box and Prosecutor's table. Thus, as luck has it, Bill and I are surrounded by the Ladies and Gentlemen of the Jury as we wait our turn to enter. Suddenly, a fellow lawyer spots Deputy Billy. They know each other very well. He threads his way through the maze and slaps my co-counsel on the back.

Much to my chagrin, the conversation that follows occurs in <u>full</u> **hearing** and in <u>plain</u> **view** of Jury members:

Fellow Lawyer: "How's it going, Bill?"

Deputy Bill: "I'm doing alright, how are you?"

Fellow Lawyer: "Fine, thanks. What are you doing here? Are you in Trial?"

Deputy Bill: "Yes I am."

Fellow Lawyer: "What kind of case is it?"
Deputy Bill: "OH, it's a **Murder Case**, but IT'S A REAL DOG."

To compound the damage, the flippant remark is preceded by Billy's trademark *chuckle*. A torrent of dark thoughts flood my mind. Things like, "What the hell, Bill. What are you doing? This Case is already tough enough. That jackass quip probably seals the deal. There's no way we can get a conviction now. Your backside needs to get personally acquainted with my shoe. How about a swift kick in the butt to bring you back to your senses." But I suppress the temptation to employ any *foot* patrol.

Really! Billy Boy has hit a nerve. I consider his conduct unconscionable. Once we're seated at Counsel table, the muffled words come tumbling out. Bill and I have a hasty, albeit, muted heart to heart. I'm doing most of the talking. The chastisement is explicit.

"Hey Bill, did you forget about the people milling around us? They're the MEMBERS of the Jury, **remember**! Your public expression of candor is mind boggling, Buddy. You and me may believe the Case is a dog, but we don't say it down here. Save the frank opinions for private time away from Juror's ears, please! We've worked hard preparing and presenting this case. And you send it to hell in a hat basket with one goofy remark. This isn't a strong case. It probably is A REAL DOG, but we don't have to tell the world. Apprising Jurors trying the Case of our personal view is hardly a productive strategy."

Deputy Bill is appropriately apologetic. "I'm sorry, Mel. I just didn't think. My head wasn't on straight. I opened my mouth and let things fly without thinking. It won't happen again."

But not to fret guys. It isn't a total disaster. As we learn later, the Jury is *either* hard of listening or they place little stock in the facetious opinion of a young Prosecutor, uttered to an acquaintance while the Court is in recess.

Despite Deputy Bill's **inadvertent** *advice to acquit*, vis-a-vis, "Oh, it's a Murder Case, but IT'S A REAL DOG," the Trial Jury steers an independent course. They've got a hard nosed attitude toward homicide, even if one of the Prosecutors isn't completely on board. They return with a **GUILTY** verdict for Involuntary Manslaughter. I tip my hat to the Jury. They're reflective and resolute. They weren't about to give Gertrude a *free ride* for a killing they consider mitigated, but <u>unjustified</u>. The husband-killer doesn't <u>totally</u> skate on their watch!

She's *waited* for him to come home. She could have left that night. Gertrude could have parted company with this man years ago. Instead, she elects to deal with the situation *outside* the legal process. It's <u>not</u> self defense in the legal sense, there's some vigilante justice here. What happens is of <u>her</u> choosing – sort of a preemptive strike. A killing that occurs during the commission of a preemptive act of violence <u>is</u> **Involuntary Manslaughter**, according to the Jury.

Sometimes a Prosecutor with a big mouth <u>can't</u> lose even when he *deserves* to lose! "No brilliance is required in law, just *common sense*, <u>and</u> relatively clean fingernails." (ibid.) Even **one** out of two may leave a Trial Lawyer in decent shape. Deputy Bill **did** have *clean* fingernails!

A TIME TO DIE? – Mary's husband has been gone <u>too</u> long – it's 1:00 a.m. He's told her he's just going for a carton of milk. The question being: how many cows is he having to milk to get the carton filled? Eldridge left two hours ago, and the Mrs. is fit to be tied. The convenience store is barely two blocks away. He could've crawled there and been back by now. She's thinking what he went for isn't milk. A carton of milk doesn't wear a skirt.

Mary's thinking Eldridge didn't go to no store, in fact, he never intended to go, unless the store is merely a way station for buying breath mints. Dear Mary knows her man's a womanizer and she believes he's gone down the road to the Colony Club for some boozing and dancing and necking.

So, with the passing of each late-night minute, Mary's suspicions rise in sync with her blood pressure. She's possessive of her man, and prone to nasty temper tantrums when he's on the prowl.

Mary makes a command decision. She decides he's not going to get away with his crap anymore – not tonight – not ever. She decides to retrieve her man if she can, but in case she can't, she's **not** going empty handed to the club. A loaded **pistol** is hidden in *her purse*, should ole Eldridge need some **un**friendly persuasion. He'll be leaving the club, whether he's dead or alive!

Jealousy steers her stride each step along the way. "Jealousy... [has] a human face." (William Blake, *A Divine Image*, Stanza 1)<u>Tonight</u>, jealousy's face is Mary's face. She stomps into the Colony Club about 1:20 a.m., *purse* in hand. Her eyes quickly scan the figures of those present in the dimly lit interior. She spies her two-timing man about 30 seconds later. There are several couples on the dance floor. Mister Milk Carton comprises one half of one of the tandems. Eldridge is locked into a clinch with some floozie wearing a slinky blue dress, oblivious to his wife's presence. Unaware of the brewing storm.

Mary threads her way through the swaying couples. The music blares forth its hedonistic refrain. Her husband continues to embrace a devil's handmaiden as she arrives on site. He seems to be nibbling on the neck of his partner. Searching for his carton of milk? Not likely. Making hickeys? Probably.

Dear Mary is infuriated. The shrillness of her voice brings him back from his undomesticated realm of bliss to the real world of a wife scorned. "Eldridge, it's **time** to go home!" He's obviously inebriated, and slurs his response. "Not yet, can't you see I'm busy?"

This time the wife's words are a spousal imperative, "Eldridge, **come home now**!" However, he ignores her sense of urgency. "Mary, I'll be home <u>when</u> I'm ready to come home. Beat it."

So, she grabs his arm, attempting to pull him away from the siren clutches of the enchantress his arms encircle. Eldridge abruptly pulls out of his dance floor belly-rub, and pushes his wife away – hard. Mary loses her balance, falling to the floor. The force of her fall dislodges *the purse* from her left hand. Sending part of the contents flying out. Scattering them on the floor.

The fracas causes uninvolved dancing couples and other nearby persons to hurriedly move away from the disturbance. They appear to sense the volatility of the tense exchange.

Mary gets up, bends over on one knee, and begins the chore of putting her personal items back into *the purse*. Methodically, she retrieves each item. However, the ITEM, **she came** to the club to retrieve, still stands nearby with his feet firmly planted on the hardwood dance floor. Eldridge ain't budging, it seems. But that will all change, momentarily.

Mary finishes gathering up the contents of *her purse* that were strewn on the floor. Then she stands. Simultaneously, her right hand darts into *the purse*. Her fingers clutch **the pistol**. It's a .32 caliber firearm. Small and compact and easily gripped. The butt of the gun fits nicely in the palm of her hand. Gun and wife being a perfect match, though not a match ordained by heaven. Furious Mary is on a frolic of her own.

Eldridge continues to stand less than five feet away. His expression is taunting and obstinate. The smooth, subtle lubrication of the liquor he's ingested has numbed his judgment. Though his Ms. Floozie in the slinky blue dress is more perceptive, she has wisely retreated to a more secure location.

Hey El, maybe you ought to duck, or hightail yourself to the other side of the dance floor – or something. "...[Your] Bird of Time has but a little way To Flutter – and the [dirty] Bird is on the Wing." (Edward Fitzgerald, *Rubaiyat of Omar Khayyam of Naishapur*)

The weapon is out. Mary takes a single step toward her man, extends the gun and fires. The bullet careens into his chest. Eldridge is stunned. The taunting obstinacy is gone now. He is shocked and in pain. A second round rips into his upper body. He clutches his chest, and collapses to the floor.

A club security officer and several male patrons rush up behind Mary. One of them grabs her arm. Another attempts to wrest the .32 from her hand. But Dear, Furious Mary is on a mission of retribution. She's *remembering* this night's humiliation, and <u>all</u> the other times. Dead or alive, Eldridge will be leaving the Colony Club **<u>tonight</u>** for the last time.

Her adrenalin rules. A wife scorned can be a pit bull. Though strong hands grapple her arm in a desperate effort to control her, she summons a burst of energy, leans slightly toward her fallen husband, and somehow, discharges **two** more bullets at his body as he lies convulsing, and even as defenders are forcing <u>her</u> to the floor. Afterward, some onlooker quips, "Man, this bitch was determined to fill this dude with lead."

Finally Mary is neutralized. Medics are summoned and Police are notified. The .32 ACP pistol is put in a safe place pending the arrival of Police. She is patted down for other weapons, and none is found. Then, the lady with the intolerant attitude toward philandering husbands is escorted to a bar stool to cool off.

An ambulance and emergency medical technicians arrive within minutes. They quickly cluster around poor Eldridge, attempting to administer to his urgent medical needs, and to provide whatever relief is within their power to employ.

A bartender has the responsibility to <u>tend</u> to Mary until Police get to the scene. He reports her reaction to EMT efforts to revive her husband. Mary surveys the clump of medics trying to resuscitate Eldridge. She has a solitary question for the bartender and it isn't, "Will you please pass me the phone so I can call my Lawyer?" The question on her mind is, "Hey bartender, what the hell they doin out on the dance floor?"

She is informed by her <u>tender</u> that paramedics are administering first aid treatment to the victim. Doing their best to <u>revive</u> him. And Mary says through clenched teeth, "Why they doin that? **Let him die**. Let the two-timing bastard **die!**"

Now, is that *icicles*, or what?

Well, Eldridge does die. The poor, skirt-chasing, dance floor habitue doesn't get to go back home that fatal night –– nor does Mary. He's hauled to the Morgue, and she becomes a compd. guest at the Clark County Detention Center.

Several days later, cold-hearted, Mary-Mary quite contrary, is charged with **Open Murder**. A Preliminary Hearing is conducted, and she's held to answer on the charge. The Public Defender invokes her right to a speedy trial, and Trial is expeditiously scheduled.

As luck has it, Deputy Bill and I are the Prosecutorial twosome assigned to this Trial also. And it has a few bumps along the road to verdict too! Subpoenas are issued. Bill and I hold pretrial conferences with crucial witnesses the week before Trial. A crucial witness includes anyone who's able to provide an eyewitness account of the shooting. Blinky [That's a nickname not his given name.] is such a witness.

We'd never laid eyes on Blinky until he appears in my office two days before the commencement of the Trial. But Bill and I form a specific set of opinions about him during the forty minute conference.

First and foremost, Blinky is a very pleasant, very nice, very <u>cooperative</u> young man who does <u>blink </u>with a certain degree of frequency. The cooperative attribute is definitely somewhat rare for a percipient witness in a Murder Case. I've previously documented the blanket of fear that typically short-circuits memories and verbalization by eye-witnesses in the context of Murder Proceedings. The prevailing mood being: see no evil, hear no evil, <u>speak</u> of no evil, and the destroying angel of retribution will pass you by.

However, Blinky <u>is</u> an exception to the rule. He wants to help. He's willing to do his best to help. He wants to be a responsible Citizen. In Blinky's case, "It's ask , and I'll give it my best shot to answer." Now, I realize that isn't a very good metaphor to use in a Murder By Firearm Case. But I'm sticking with it. I like this young man.

Deputy Bill and I take a few minutes attempting to put Blinky at ease and gain his confidence. We exchange introductory small talk and then get down to business. Our witness has provided a handwritten statement on the night of the offense to investigating Officers. He also has come down to the Station House the next day, providing a tape recorded statement. It's been typed by Metro and signed by him.

Innocently, we hand Blinky copies of both statements and ask him to read them. Trust me when I say, we are **not** prepared for the scene that *slowly* unfolds pursuant to our routine request.

Secondly, but not incidental to his performance on the witness stand, Blinky doesn't **read** very well and he doesn't **see** very well. His reading capabilities are plodding to say the least. Actually, he reads slow – very, very, very <u>slowly</u>. Which is connected, in part, to seeing the words he's reading very, very, very <u>poorly</u>.

The initial statement written by Blinky at the Colony Club the night of the shooting is only about **twelve** *lines*. He gets it in his hand and studiously stares at it. Methodically moving his head back and forth from line to line –– for about **ten** *minutes* or whenever it was we stopped him. He might still be reading if we hadn't taken the paper back.

We ask him why he's taking so long to read such a short statement. His reply, "I don't have my **reading** glasses on." So Bill asks, "Do you have your glasses with you?" Blinky: "Yes, I do." And we say almost in unison, "Well, **put** them on man."

Our witness reaches inside his sports jacket pocket, fumbles around for about twenty seconds, searching for the elusive **reading** glasses, I'd say. Finds them, pulls a primitive version of spectacles badly in need of repair out of his pocket, and painstakingly places them on his face.

Realistically, he probably needed <u>glue</u> to keep them perched on his face.

This is all dead serious to Blinky, but to the hard-core young Prosecutors it's funny and it's frustrating. Deputy Bill is chuckling over the process, but anxious to move this along. I'm finding it extremely difficult to suppress the grin that has become irrepressible, yet mindful that two other prospective witnesses wait in the lobby for their interviews.

Listen up. These so-called reading specs Blinky produces are truly vintage. Frankly, when the witness puts them on he's a caricature of himself. I won't beat around the bush, he looks goofy. The eyeglass frame resembles something made out of bailing wire. One of the lenses is missing, the left lense I believe. A thick wad of adhesive tape is wrapped around the section of the frame that rests on Blinky's nose. Presumably, it's positioned there to keep the frame from pulling apart in the middle. Completing the eyeglass ensemble, one of the side pieces that curves over an ear has gone AWOL. I think it's on the opposite side from the missing lense. Really, I'm putting it mildly when I say this pair of spectacles creates a spectacle!

But Bill and I persevere. We try to stay on course. Time is short. We have miles to go before we sleep and promises to keep. We ask Blinky to peruse his Metro statement. And oh my, if things were bad with a **twelve** *line* document in his own handwriting, imagine the challenge presented by having him read a **five** *page*

typewritten statement – with THIS PAIR of **reading** glasses. Well, **twenty** *minutes* later he's still reading. Brow furrowed, squinting slightly, beads of sweat forming below his eyes, periodically blinking, and moving his gaze back and forth from line to line as before – page after page. Blinky get's an **A** for effort, but he flunks out on speed reading. It's exasperating.

Ultimately, we take the typewritten statement from him. Thank him for his effort, a reading clinic it wasn't, and just have him TELL US what he remembers about the shooting.

So, we'll fast-forward this thing **five** days. The weekend is history. We've picked cold-hearted Mary-Mary's Trial Jury. We've gone through the foundational evidence. The first responding Emergency Technicians and Police have testified. The Medical Examiner details his autopsy findings. He finds evidence of two bullet tracks in the victim's body and two grazing wounds. He concludes the shooting involves **criminal agency**. We call three other percipient witnesses to the stand – with mixed results. However, they **all** read reasonably well – with or without glasses.

The STAGE IS SET for our man Blinky. And Deputy Bill and I are hoping, **NO** we're PRAYING, that Blinky has managed to get himself another set of specs for Trial. Mr.Blinky, come on down!

We conduct our Direct Examination, being careful he doesn't have to go for those awful glasses – if that's still all he's got. The approach is prompted by an abundance of caution. We ask for his eye-witness account, but we **do not**, I repeat, we DO NOT ask Blinky to **read** ANY documents during Direct. We've seen his performance during the Pretrial Conference. We know what to expect. To be fore-warned that we might be fore-armed with the ability to maintain a sober Prosecutorial persona – is our fervent wish.

However, the best laid plans of mice or Prosecutors often run amuck of Trial verities. Direct Examination is followed by **Cross Examination**. The Defense doesn't know what we know. And if they had known, their strategy wouldn't have changed. They're going to do **Cross** on this Guy come hell or high water. Let the chips fall where they land.

Counselor Devoe begins Cross. He's been probing Blinky's credibility for about ten minutes when he goes to the **five** *page* typewritten statement. He believes certain aspects of the witnesses' testimony are *contradicted* by what he's told the Police the morning after the offense. Esteemed Attorney for the Defense has **The Statement** marked as a proposed Exhibit by the Court Clerk. He walks to the

Witness Stand, passes **The Statement** to Blinky, asks him to **read** it to himself to determine if such a review refreshes his memory regarding his out of Court description of the Colony Club shooting, assumes a casual stance a bit behind and to the left of the witness, projects a smug, self assured demeanor to the Jury and the Gallery, then confidently **waits** for Blinky to complete his **reading** assignment.

Counselor Devoe doesn't know what's coming, but we do! This is deja vu. Blinky being himself – **Act II**. Mr. Blinky will be **reading** and **reading** and **reading** – as we wait and wait and wait. The process is going to seem interminable and *hilarious* to the Prosecutors. Indeed, the exercise may last until the next recess and beyond. How to keep a straight face is the sixty four million dollar question.

Deputy Bill and I begin to nervously fidget. Neither of us seriously believes we can *hang* on to a stoic bearing if this plays out the way we expect it to. It's high drama in the Eighth Judicial District Court for the Prosecutorial twosome. Once again, Blinky reaches into the **same** pocket of the **same** sports jacket, fumbles around for the **same** amount of time, and [aaargh] removes the **SAME** pitiful pair of ugly spectacles that look like they're made of recycled bailing wire.

We can't contain our mirth! This is simply too much. The Case be damned. If we lose, if we're demoted to Traffic Court, so be it. Ole Blinky's crude facsimile of **reading** glasses are out in the open for the <u>whole</u> world to see. He carefully fastens them to his face, and we stare into the jaws of the spectacle – **same** missing *lense*, **same** thick wad of adhesive tape resting on the bridge of Blinky's nose, **same** absentee side piece that is supposed to curve over the second ear, and the **SAME** effect upon the Prosecutors, only worse!

Deputy Bill is chuckling again – only it's <u>more</u> conspicuous. And Harmon is mindlessly grinning from ear to ear and <u>getting</u> spastic. Meanwhile, Blinky is doing his best. He continues to read, moving his head back and forth as he digests each line – in the **same** way as he did at the Pretrial. Billy and I look away. Laboring to think of sober thoughts that will divest us of the urge to laugh out loud at the subtle hilarity.

Nothing works. Our eyes inevitably return, as if Blinky is magnitized, to his unintended display of satire on the Witness Stand. I look down, trying hard to pull my professionalism together. <u>Every</u> time I think I have a handle on my emotions, I hear Deputy Bill give a **snort** that is only slightly muffled, and it sets me off again.

I shut my eyes. I attempt to say uplifting Poems in my mind. I think of Church and the words of traditional Hymns. I begin reciting the Lord's Prayer. I bite my lip. I pinch my thigh. I move my chair farther from my colleague. I try to remember some of Rhett Butler's memorable lines from "Gone With The Wind." It's all to no avail.

Deputy Bill's shoulders are shaking and his uncontrollable **snorts** are becoming more audible – though totally indecipherable. And of course, even with closed eyes, I'm still fixated on Blinky. I see him in my mind **reading** and **reading,** <u>squinting</u> as he peers through the single lense of those **awful** glasses. His head moving from side to side –line by line – page by page!

And it's so quiet, except for Bill and Me, you could hear pins drop if anyone was of a mind to scatter them. Counselor Devoe remains a bit behind and to the left of Blinky. He's looking ever more quizzically at the Prosecution. Wondering at first if his *fly is open*. He checks and rechecks the status of his zipper. He's proper. The zipper is not the source of merriment for these idiot Prosecutors.

The Jury is becoming aware of the jovial pair at Counsel Table. Several members of the Twelve Tried and True are looking rather askance at the twosome. Probably thinking, this is ridiculous. Telling <u>jokes</u> in the middle of a Murder Trial. You'd think these morons would have better things to do, uuuh, like listening and maybe taking a few notes?

Esteemed Counselor Devoe is a kind man and a patient one. He waits Blinky out. He doesn't try to rush him. He quickly grasps the situation. The Prosecution witness <u>doesn't</u> read well and he <u>can't</u> see well through those damnable spectacles. Devoe's eyes twinkle a smidgen, but he does **not** laugh. He just empathetically stands there with a nonplus expression clouding his distinguished face. He doesn't get it. Mel and Bill must have taken several juicy shots of laughing gas before they entered the Courtroom. Their behavior is bizarre.

And what of Deputies Mel and Bill? We think our giddiness agony will **never** end. But after **twenty two** *minutes* [who's counting] of torturous silence, disrupted only by Deputy Bill's frequent chuckling snorts and my court jester grins that are punctuated by paroxysmal shaking, mercifully it does end.

Blinky says he's finished **reading**, and he passes the document back to the esteemed Mr. Defense Counselor. Cross examination continues, and a state of normality returns to the two Prosecutors who'd experienced a form of temporary insanity. Brazenly **yuking** it up in open Court in reckless, but <u>unintended</u>, disregard of their professional duty as Officers of the Court.

And what of the Court? How does he view the ostensible demonstration of disrespect by two bumpkin Prosecutors? Well, He has NO OPINION. I haven't mentioned His Honor to this point for a reason. He is a non-factor. When things get slow, a Judge's head sometimes drops low. As it happens, His Honor is oblivious to the comedic comportment of the Two. He's fallen asleep. Sweet dreams, Sir.

How do we know? We know because His Honor has to be *roused* by the Court Clerk several minutes after Counselor Devoe resumes Cross. His Honor <u>fails</u> to *respond* to a Prosecution Objection that the Defense is being argumentative with Witness Blinky. [Devoe may be emphatic to the plight of the Witness, but his first duty is to his client – Ms. Cold-Hearted, Mary-Mary quite contrary.] When the Court does <u>not</u> react to the Objection, we **<u>all</u>** notice His Most Judicial's **eyes** are closed – and he's breathing the deep, rhythmic patterns we associate with *snoozing*. So, the Boy's with the white hats are off the hook with the Court. His ignorance is an act of grace to the <u>two</u> beleaguered ones.

"No brilliance is required in law, just [the] *common sense* [<u>not</u> to get tweaked into a public display of uncontrollable gaiety in the Courtroom] and relatively clean fingernails."(ibid)

The State completes its Case in Chief. The Defense calls a few witnesses and rests its Case. The decidedly **<u>un</u>**–brilliant tacticians representing the State of Nevada, decide to put on a Rebuttal Case. Not so <u>sensible</u> in retrospect, Guys. Bill and I call <u>five</u> rebuttal witnesses. The testimonial offensive *fails* in each instance.

These witnesses have either developed *cold feet* during their trip to the Courthouse **or** the presence of certain individuals in the gallery *tempers* their enthusiasm for telling the Jury what they've told Law Enforcement **or** they *crumple* under the erudite rhetoric of Defense Cross Examination. The whole **<u>Rebuttal</u>** thing backfires. They're <u>far</u> better Defense witnesses than Prosecution witnesses.

Cross Examination has been called "the greatest legal engine ever invented for the discovery of truth." (John Henry Wigmore as quoted in California v. Green, 399 US 149 at 158 – 1970) I'm not sure the ground Devoe plows during his Cross is a discovery of truth as it **<u>is</u>,** or merely witnesses presenting Mary's version of truth as it **<u>isn't</u>**. Adjusting the facts to justify the fact of Murder.

Regardless of what it is, esteemed Counselor for the Defense is stellar in his use of Cross Examination. <u>Each</u> rebuttal witness offers evidence during Cross about the relationship of Mary and Eldridge, that tends to mitigate her use of a .32 caliber firearm to kill her husband. Defense Counsel employs the wonderful **legal engine** of Cross Examination impeccably.

After the **<u>fifth</u>** rebuttal witness has been a Prosecutorial <u>flop</u>, Devoe leans toward the chastened twosome. He's wearing an expression that is both mischievous and triumphant. He gives us a verbal thrust and twists his parlance for effect. It's demoralizing. Devoe quips, "Hey Fellas, got any more witnesses like the *last five*? If you have, please bring it on. Don't stop the good stuff yet. Doug and I are licking our chops. Defense Lawyers don't often have this much fun in the Courtroom. We're <u>really</u> enjoying this!"

Actually, we did have more witnesses where those came from. But it would have taken an Act of Congress to get us to call them. Our **Rebuttal Evidence** <u>parade</u> had shifted our Prosecution into reverse. There was <u>no</u> up side, we were losing ground. We decided to cut our losses, submitting the Case to the Jury without introducing further ambiguity from the Witness Stand.

The smoke settles. The Jury is instructed. Closing arguments are made. The Jury deliberates. They agree on a verdict for Ms. Cold-Hearted Mary. It is **<u>guilty</u>** of MURDER TWO. Thus, we may infer that the Jury Tried and True forgave the Prosecutive Boys of their whimsical <u>indiscretions</u>, for the most part. Though the Court, who wasn't always sleeping during the Trial, has his own chaffing critique of the Proceedings. "When the Prosecution finished their Case in Chief [that would be <u>before</u> the Defense and Rebuttal Cases in the Trial Polemics], I thought the Case was going to be a *dead-bang* FIRST DEGREE MURDER **conviction**!"

There are a series of legitimate WHYS in the case. Why this? Why that? But the FIRST **<u>why do it</u>**, is the biggest puzzle? WHY, OH WHY – Mary-Mary did you do it? Weren't you accustomed to the behavior of your skirt-chasing Hubby? Was it really a huge surprise that the late night trip for a carton of milk is a ruse for late night dance floor feelies with the Babes at the Colony Club? It's happened before, why get so nutty on this particular night? Why take a loaded gun? Why **shoot** him with a stupid .32? You made him pay for his infraction, but does the punishment fit the offense? Killing for copping a few feels is heavy handed justice!

People do the damn-dest things for the silliest jughead reasons. He's **only** dancing, he isn't scr––ing. Why not walk away? Why not sleep it off? Why not get the hell out of his life if you can't take his crap anymore? Pack up his sh––t the next morning and dump the creep. There are sooooooooo many men, why give it ALL UP over this ONE two-timing stiff? Why allow a hair-trigger temper to control your destiny? The no-win, drag me down to purgatory futility of this course of action is astonishing. Dance hall *rage* just doesn't make sense. It's freaking ridiculous, Mary!

MOONLIGHTING, DEPUTY JOHN? – Cowboy Bandics is an alleged serial Bank Robber. A lone bandit wearing a cowboy hat has committed a rash of armed robberies in Las Vegas using the same Modus Operandi. His Cases are assigned to the DA's Office Major Violator Unit.

The morning of the Preliminary Hearing for <u>one</u> of the Cases, I put the **red** MVU folder under my arm and head to Court. I'm sharing the Prosecutorial honors in Justice Court this day with another Deputy DA. I **have** my <u>single</u>, high-profile in-custody case and my colleague, Deputy John, **has** a <u>stack</u> of folders that constitute **all** the other cases on the Court Docket.

He's a handsome man, and looks quite debonair in his tailor-made suit and red power tie. He's clean cut, neat, academic in manner, and professional in appearance. He wears glasses he's using to carefully peruse several files that are open on the table in front of him. Deputy John <u>isn't</u> holding his Badge in his hand and he doesn't have a *Deputy John* identifier pinned to his lapel, but probably <u>no</u> one in the Courtroom looks less like an in-custody bank robber than Johnny. He's hound dog tooth clean. Deputy John is a straight arrow. There's not a suspicious hair on his body.

The **Major Violator** Case is given a prioritized hearing by Judge Earl. My fellow Prosecutor sits in the next chair to my left still reviewing his <u>stack</u> of cases when my Case is called. Bandics sits in JAILHOUSE

BLUES to the immediate left of his Public Defender. They're situated about ten feet farther left from the Deputy DA, and at first they're whispering intently to each other.

Incidently, it's not a mystery that the BLUE jumpsuit the Defendant wears is a Detention Center issue. <u>Five</u> additional in-custody prisoners sit in the Jury Box to my right. They're in plain view of **every** person in the Courtroom and they **all** wear JAILHOUSE <u>BLUE</u>. Besides, Cowboy Bandics looks the part of a bank Bandito. It's like he's just stepped out of Central Casting. His hair is unkempt, a scruffy black stubble covers his face, tattoos can be seen on the prominent biceps of both arms – slightly below his sleeves, his facial features match the CRIME SCENE SKETCH prepared from the Victim's description of the Robber, he tries to do a **stare down** with the complaining witness, [Inexplicably, she **never** looks at him.] and naturally, the ATTIRE of the Defendant is a **dead-bang giveaway**. You'd think!

The Preliminary Hearing begins with the testimony of the Bank Teller who's been robbed. Direct Examination of the young lady proceeds smoothly as she describes the Crime and the Robber. Ms. Prissy Bank Teller details the man, the six-shooter, the signature cowboy hat, and the cowboy boots. She testifies of the hard earned bank currency that passes from her to him at gunpoint. She emphasizes her lack of consent. Frankly, she's almost scared out of her wits. She's never been robbed before. The event is burned into her psyche, she says. She'll **never** forget this character. And I'm thinking, it's time. Ask the crucial question.

So, I fire away. Ms. Bank Teller, do you see the man in the Courtroom this morning, who used a gun to take the bank's money without your permission? And –– she ––– bless her heart. Ya gotta love your witnesses. This–is–precious! She doesn't *scan* the Courtroom. No Sir. She immediately glances down at **Deputy John**, busily turning the pages of a file he'll be prosecuting as soon as this Chick <u>identifies</u> the serial bank robber, and locks on **Johnny** like he's the <u>only</u> male on the planet. How nice. Whoopie! Goodbye case. It's poised to fly out the window.

No matter that **Deputy John** wears a designer suit and is clean as a whistle, the witness thinks <u>he's the man</u>. Evidently, she believes we play *hide and seek* games in the Courtroom. We want to make it really challenging for bank teller witnesses. We *camouflage* these robber characters, dressing them up in nice suits and flashy ties. We have them wear eye glasses. We put DA files in front of them and have them laboriously studying them when THE MOMENT arrives to make an IN COURT **identification**. The <u>culprits</u> are *hidden*, so naturally a victim has to *seek* them in hard to find places —— **NOT true!**

We don't do this. We <u>want</u> criminals to be **identified**. What happens here is frustration city. On such a morning, a guy's bound to have a stray second thought or two flash through his noggin concerning choice of a profession. Certainly, the witnesses' initial mind-set makes me want to rephrase my question. **TOO LATE!**

The witness utters a <u>firm</u> "YES, I **do** *see* the man. Thanks for asking." I'm trapped in a Prosecutorial Debacle the witness is thrusting upon me. Who would have thought it. But regardless of the end result, it's a dog and pony show that has to play out.

I say, "**Point** to the person who robbed you, and **describe** how he's dressed.

And the witness COMPLETES her in-court *faux pas*. She pushes a bony index finger forward, points it **directly** at DEPUTY JOHN, then confidently asserts, "HE'S right there. The ONE wearing the classy suit and the chic tie. HE'S wearing glasses and HE'S glancing down at folders somebody's put in front of him. Obviously, HE'S trying to avoid looking at me. That's the ROBBER. There's **no** doubt about it."

Mercy, I have to complete the scenario. "Your Honor, may the record show the witness has **identified** DEPUTY JOHN as the **Bank Robber**." It's as though Judge Earl is enjoying this. There's no hesitation. He doesn't miss a beat. "THE RECORD WILL SO REFLECT," reverberates through the Courtroom. Then Judge Earl smiles broadly, stares at the Deputy DA who's no longer reading his files, and deadpans, "MOONLIGHTING, MR. WATKINS?"

The consequences aren't monumental. DEPUTY JOHN has an airtight alibi on the date in question, and Cowboy Bandics has approximately six additional cases in the system where the witnesses are **not** so charitable in their identifications! He faces the music while John and I *fondly* face the memory.

I don't see him often. I've moved from Las Vegas, and he's long since gone into a lucrative private practice. However, whenever I do encounter John, I always remind him of the time HE was **identified** as the COWBOY BANDIT. We have a good laugh about the good old days, and I tell him he owes me. After all, I didn't push my advantage when I had a chance. I **didn't** ask JUDGE WHITE to **remand him to custody!**

Realistically, John's identification is one of many <u>misidentifications</u> I witnessed during my Courtroom years. Misinformed commentators often speak of the *strength* of **Direct Evidence** and of the inherent *weakness* of **Circumstantial Evidence.** These News Pundits will speak in a disparaging tone about the latter form of evidence with the quip, "It's only a Circumstantial Case." As if that is <u>insider</u> information and they're saying something profound. The truth is: IN COURT IDENTIFICATIONS are frequently **specious** and CIRCUMSTANTIAL EVIDENCE is often **powerful** and very **persuasive**! CIRCUMSTANTIAL EVIDENCE, ultimately, is the **<u>most</u> <u>compelling</u>** evidence available to an Advocate.

It's simple, as I've previously explained. DIRECT EVIDENCE is anything a witness perceives, as the **crime happens,** with any of his or her *physical senses.* The issue becomes, how correct are those *physical perceptions?* CIRCUMSTANTIAL EVIDENCE is **<u>everything</u> <u>else</u>**. Of course, that dichotomy makes FINGERPRINT MATCHES and FIREARM IDENTIFICATIONS and DNA MATCHES, **etcetera**, <u>circumstantial</u> <u>evidence</u>!

The misidentifications in Court are a source of merriment now, but not so funny as they happened. I've had witnesses **identify** Bailiffs, Corrections Officers who are escorts of in-custody Defendants, spectators in the gallery. And this one is really jolly. A Prosecutor knows he's in trouble when he asks for an identification and the witness begins to *<u>pan the Jury.</u>* I'm not kidding, I had *several* experiences where A JUROR, **one** of the Twelve Tried and True, is **identified** as the perpetrator of a Crime THE JUROR is sitting in judgement of.

RULE ONE when you're in Trial: **<u>Expect</u>** the UNEXPECTED!

SO, WHERE'S THE APPRECIATION FOR A WELL CRAFTED ARGUMENT? – I'm remembering one of the most lovable Attorney's in the Clark County Courthouse crowd. He is everybody's pal – Attorney Al. He's a rotund, happy-go-lucky, peanut-loving presence in the legal community. It's a rare day when Al isn't hanging out in the Courthouse lobby. Always jovial, always willing to talk about the latest scuttle-butt from the County Bar scene. Al keeps his ears to the ground. He's a constantly renewing gusher of Court gossip, and his friendly grin is often framed by a grainy paste in the corners of his mouth that represents the latest package of salted peanuts he's ingested.

On a certain lazy afternoon, Attorney Al becomes part of Courtroom folk lore in Las Vegas. He's in the third day of a Jury Trial, and it's time for Summation. The Deputy District Attorney presents his Opening Argument. Al believes he sees gaping holes in the logic of his opponent. His confidence soars. He jots down a few pertinent notes, but prefers reasoning to the Jury without being tied to a script. The best approach is a low-key folksy manner, according to Al. During his laid-back closing forensics he tries to bring law and fact down to the level of the lay persons serving on his Juries. In Attorney Al's play book, homespun charm produces more Defense Verdicts than the truculent sting of verbal vinegar.

Al rises to his feet, clears his throat, and begins to highlight some obvious shortfalls in the Prosecution's Case. He's feeling sharp today. The words slide easily and naturally off his lips. After thirty minutes of conversational tones and friendly discussion, he believes he's sold the Jury on the veracity of his Client's cause. Thinking he's got a winner waiting in the wings, he pauses for dramatic effect, and with a broad sweep of his arm urges the Jury to **Acquit**. Then shuffles back to Counsel Table, sits down, smiles broadly at no one in particular, clasps his hands behind his head, rocks back on the rear legs of his chair, and smugly closes his eyes.

It happens at that precise moment. **Juror #6** THROWS UP! The internal eruption sprays the shoulders of the Juror in front of him, and creates a slimy puddle on the floor below the offending party. Is the regurgitation an Act of God or an act of Juror kabitzing? Nobody knows if **it's** the *flu* or a touch of *food poisoning* –– **or** *AL*. But whatever IT is, **it's** not exactly a ringing, "I'll **second** those remarks, Sir.!" The DISGORGEMENT is more consistent with a **slam dunk** rejection of Defense Counsel's remarks. May the **record reflect** a Juror THREW

UP as the Defense finished it's case. Let the good times roll for the State's Attorney, Baby.

The **timing** of the UP-CHUCK is impeccable for the Prosecution, but embarrassing for poor Attorney Al. The Courtroom gallery *LAUGHS* at his expense, and there are those in the Jury Box who softly chuckle at the possibility A LAWYER'S WORDS are so ill-chosen they'd made a fellow member of the Jury SICK to his stomach. Sometimes a Guy with a <u>*sweating*</u> *tongue* doesn't get much traction from *his sweat*.

The **Juror in distress** quickly puts the lid on his mouth, wipes his face, resumes a more appropriate, albeit apologetic, demeanor – and the Court declares an immediate recess. However, the damage is done it seems. The–Verdict–is–guilty. The Prosecution wins! The Prosecution wins! The Prosecution wins! Hey Al, **<u>expect</u>** the UNEXPECTED in Trial work, Buddy.

Is the Jury Verdict the product of the puke **<u>or</u>** the product of the Prosecutor's Rebuttal – after the puke? No one knows but the Jury. And they refuse to shed any light on the actual effect, if any, of a Juror VOMITING as a Lawyer concludes his Closing Remarks.

PS: Attorney Al's Motion for a Mistrial is denied! The Judge finds the Verdict is supported by the evidence and declines to accept a Defense invitation to *speculate* over the process that brought the Jury to its Verdict. The Court suggests that doing so will take him down a <u>slippery slope</u> he will not navigate.

"No brilliance is required in law, just *common sense*...relatively clean fingernails...[and Jurors who are able to keep their <u>lunch</u> in their stomachs.]" (ibid.)

Prosecutorial Duty

"A **sense of duty** pursues us ever. It is omnipresent, like the deity. If we take to ourselves the wings of the morning, and dwell in the uttermost parts of the sea, duty performed, or duty violated, is still with us, for our happiness or our misery. If we say the darkness shall cover us, in the darkness as in the light our obligations are yet with us." (Quoted in <u>State v. Boyd</u>, 236 A.2d 476 at 478-479 [Conn. Cir. Ct. 1967] – from *The Murder of Captain Joseph White*, 6 Works of Daniel Webster 105, 118th Edition 1881) – emphasis added.

CHAPTER 11

I FIGURE THE LORD GAVE ME **STRONG** **PIPES** for a reason, but using them isn't always appreciated by those within earshot. I'm remembering the afternoon I was sternly chastised for speaking <u>too</u> loud. Accused of **shouting** by the <u>Complaining</u> <u>Party</u> from an adjacent Courtroom, who knows NOTHING concerning the **heinous** **matter** being ARGUED and the **weighty** **decision** twelve citizens are required to render. Falsely charged, I'd say. Being **forceful** in the PURSUIT OF MY DUTY is the Defense.

We're wrapping up A MURDER TRIAL. The Evidence is in, the Instructions have been given, and it's <u>time</u> for FINAL ARGUMENT. <u>Crowing</u> <u>Time</u> for a Deputy DA. I've been mostly a witness <u>interrogator</u> to this point in the proceeding, my case views unspoken. Now, the **Interrogator** becomes the **Advocate**. Now, my case views will be articulated on center stage. It's <u>time</u> to haul ass to the Lectern and let the Prosecutive rhetoric fly.

The **quintessential moment** of <u>every</u> Trial has arrived for me. I'm **more** than a **TRIAL LAWYER** , I'm **AN <u>ADVOCATE</u> FOR JUSTICE**. **<u>I'm</u> <u>a</u> <u>Deputy</u> <u>District</u> <u>Attorney</u>**. I have a SWORN DUTY to *speak* <u>out</u> for the People of the State of Nevada. So, I'm shifting into my *Debating Persona*, and I don't intend to be silenced or compromised in discharging my **duty**.

No one <u>and</u> **no circumstance** will diminish or suppress or orchestrate the words I've conscientiously chosen to deliver to the Jury, if I have the ability to confound my detractors. My entire **focus** has a <u>single</u> objective: **convince the Twelve** the charge is righteous! The **Anatomy of The Case** <u>evidence</u> has to be laid before the Jury <u>by</u> decisive **Argument**. The Jury <u>must</u> **SEE** the <u>facts</u> as they are.

The TIME it takes to do this <u>is</u> incidental to me. Nor is the DECIBEL LEVEL I employ a serious matter of concern. If <u>raising</u> my voice for emphasis is an effective tool, I'll be <u>RAISING</u> my voice. The GALLERY and the JUDGE and DEFENSE COUNSEL <u>are</u> only ornamental <u>now</u>, merely background props. **WHAT MATTERS <u>IS</u> PROPER COMMUNICATION AND PASSIONATE JURY PERSUASION!!** <u>Proper</u> communication <u>because</u> **Justice does <u>not</u> embellish <u>nor</u> distort. Justice <u>accepts</u> the facts as they are. <u>Because</u> Justice does <u>not</u> flaunt ethical and procedural rules. It abides by them. <u>Because</u> Justice <u>is</u> respectful and courteous toward the Court and Defense Counsel – at all times.** <u>Passionate</u> Jury persuasion <u>because</u> The Trier of Fact <u>must</u> know The Prosecutor believes his case IS **just**. They recognize, for the most part, that he's their representative in the Courtroom, and they will TRUST him if he gives them reason to TRUST him. They take the measure of their Prosecutor from his *professional* MANNER, his *case* PREPARATION, and his *passionate* COMMITMENT to the **cause of Justice**.

A PROSECUTOR *<u>OWES</u>* this to the VICTIM, the VICTIM'S FAMILY, and to the PEOPLE of the State of Nevada. IT'S A <u>MURDER CASE</u>. He lets the Jury *know* by the <u>tone</u> of his voice –– by his <u>words</u> –– by his <u>manner</u> –– by his <u>gestures</u>, that this is **not** just a stroll in the park. It **isn't** a casual bull session. It's **not** party time. It's **not** theater. It's **not** a classroom lecture. This **IS** gut-wrenching REALITY. What their Prosecutor is doing is **not** conversational oratory! He's discharging his **Prosecutorial Duty**!

A **Murder Trial** is *raw* and *real*. The crimes are solemn events with *actual* **consequences.** There are **dead victims** in the cemetery and **charged Defendants** in the Courtroom. There is **bereavement** and **shock.** A **Murder Trial** is unique. Like punishment, the *passion* of the Prosecutor's *rhetoric* should FIT **the Crime!**

If my *adrenalin* isn't pumped in a **MURDER PROSECUTION** it's never going to be energized. A Deputy District Attorney who has the *Spirit of Prosecution* surging through his arteries is going to leave it ALL AT THE JURY RAIL as he argues **A MURDER**! A **Prosecutor's** highest duty in the context of CLOSING ARGUMENT is to be a **dynamic advocate for justice**, and he is **never**, **ever** *diverted* from **HIS TASK!**

But someone TRIES to *divert* me. Someone TRIES to *orchestrate* my delivery. Someone TRIES to get me to *tone* things down, to speak more *quietly*, to *lower* the noise level!

I'm about half way through my OPENING ARGUMENT. It's my sense that things are going well. The Jurors appear attentive. My vocal **pipes** feel strong as I recite the **evidentiary points** that connect the Accused to the *DESPICABLE UGLINESS* of MURDER. There is an ebb and flow to the rhetoric. The more measured, restrained tones introducing pivotal links of proof are followed by a swelling crescendo of **impassioned** argument nailing down the I GOT YA links that connect the CHAIN OF GUILT – point by point! To borrow a smidgen of musical vernacular, the ebb and flow is *a pattern* ranging in volume from pianissimo to fortissimo. Repeated as often as the **connecting evidentiary points** DICTATE.

Not staged, but spoken from the heart. A manifestation of the SPIRIT OF PROSECUTION and of the Prosecutor. It's a signature trait of my **arguments**. A guy has to do something to KEEP Jurors on message and to convey the **TRUTH of the message**. Furthermore, it's a natural expression of **passionate commitment** to the Prosecutorial Profession! And so the decibel level swings from *quiet* to, shall we say – *thunderous*.

I've found a nice rhythm as I argue the meat of the State's Case. I believe my words were persuasive and, at times, eloquent. I'd worked up quiet a head of steam when a door leading to the Chambers of

six members of the Eighth Judicial District Court Bench OPENS – *surprisingly*. A word that accurately describes existing circumstances. The **door** is immediately to the right of the Jury Box. That door RARELY **opens** when Attorney's are delivering their FINAL ARGUMENTS.

It's a DISTRACTION, and Lawyers who have invested long hours in the preparation of their Final Arguments <u>don't</u> like distractions – nor does the Trial Judge, who has invested <u>a</u> <u>week</u> out of his busy Court Calendar, want an untimely interruption during this crucial juncture of the Trial.

It's the Court Bailiff from next door. He has a NOTE from his Judge. I see him enter through my peripheral vision. He passes directly in front of several Jurors, separated from them only by the railing to the Jury Box. Strides up the steps to the Bench, leans over in cursory conversation with the Trial Judge, and passes him a NOTE.

And I'm thinking, "What the hell. I'm *in the process* of trying to hit a <u>home</u> <u>run</u> in **Final Argument**, and a fellow who **isn't** even in the lineup has the EYES of <u>every</u> Juror in the Courtroom fastened <u>on</u> <u>him</u> – NOT ME. Where's the logic to this? Couldn't this wait a few minutes? It has be some kind of emergency. Maybe there's a bomb threat and we'll have to vacate the whole damn building. What a tough break. This couldn't have happened at a worse time."

Well –– no, it isn't anything like that. The Bailiff exits the way he entered. The Judge quickly reads the NOTE, and pauses briefly as he reflects upon what he's read. Then exclaims: "Excuse me, Mr. Harmon. Will Counsel for both sides approach the Bench?" We comply. I <u>stop</u> in mid sentence. It doesn't matter what you're doing when the Court says, "Approach the Bench." A Trial Lawyer knows who butters his bread when he's in Trial. You get your fanny over to the Bench with all the alacrity you can muster.

When we've gathered in front of the Bench, His Honor passes the NOTE to me – with an injunction to read it. I hastily scan the scribbled words that appear on the piece of paper, suddenly fearful that one of my family members has suffered an accident.

Well –– no, it **isn't** anything like that neither. The NOTE is a **plea for relief** from the *booming elocution* that is carrying from us to them. Allegedly, piercing the wall that separates us. Disrupting the Hearing they're attempting to conduct in the adjacent Courtroom. The NOTE asks the Trial Judge to instruct the Deputy DA (that would be me) to ratchet down his oratory. Perhaps, the hot air being emitted could be given a slight temperature inversion – and so forth. Succinctly stated, "Have Harmon **pipe down**, please. We can't hear ourselves think."

So, the Trial Judge sort of gives me an innocent shrug that says, "Sorry. It's not me saying this. **I'm** completely okay with your argument, but let's humor The Man next door by *turning down* your volume."

Look, I'm not insensitive to the needs of another Court to conduct business in an orderly fashion. I understand we have to co-exist. There's a lot going on in the Courthouse. **However**, EVERY CASE IS UNIQUE. **A human life has been taken.** NOW is the time for **Justice** in this cause. NOW is the time to *impose* **personal responsibility** upon the Offender. This is a **MURDER TRIAL**, for gosh sake. FINAL ARGUMENT IS IMPORTANT.

"A **word**, once sent abroad, flies irrevocably." (Horace, *Epistles*, Book I, xviii, Line 70) Likewise, **words of argument** sent abroad by the Prosecutor fly irrevocably. They can't be retracted, nor amended after he's finished – and **words** spoken to the Jury can **change** results. Possibly, the MANNER of delivering those **words** to the Jury will irrevocably **change** the results! Jeopardy has attached. We don't get **second and third** chances, and we don't get SUMMATION **do overs**. IT'S NOW OR NEVER.

Isn't the NOTE rather presumptuous? Does the other Judge realize we're at a critical phase in resolving a MURDER IN COLD BLOOD? What's going on next door? Is it a Murder Trial too? Or is it Civil? A Landlord-Tenant dispute or a Hearing on a Breach of Contract or a Petition to Quash service of process or a Motion for Summary Judgement, to catalog a few possibilities?

We don't know. We only know that the JUDGE NEXT DOOR wants to *rein in* the rhetoric on A CASE he knows nothing about in A COURTROOM where he has **no standing** to adjudicate!

Everything that happens in Open Court has consequences for the Parties, but is the Action before the JUDGE NEXT DOOR so **monumental** that it requires him to meddle in MURDER TRIAL SUMMATION? **That's–the–issue!** Wherein lies the *inherent* authority or the *innate* wisdom of the JUDGE NEXT DOOR to **mute** the voice of the Prosecutor?

It's <u>not</u> the Prosecutor's fault if Courthouse acoustics are flawed, and the ringing sound of his voice is not strictly confined to the Courtroom where he stands. A Deputy DA <u>isn't</u> the building architect, nor the sound man, nor the *patsy* of the JUDGE NEXT DOOR.

<u>**HE'S**</u> – <u>**THE**</u> – <u>**PEOPLE'S**</u> – <u>**MAN**</u>! He's an Officer of the Court, but **everything** is subordinate to his <u>role</u> as OFFICER OF THE PEOPLE. So, **Most** Honorable JUDGE NEXT DOOR, *stick* your "Hush little Prosecutor" NOTE in your back pocket or make an airplane out of it or shit-can it or eat it if you have to. I'm trying my case MY WAY, and MY WAY is continuing to be <u>zealous</u> in MY SUMMATION!

I completed my Opening Argument. The Defense argued, and I breezed through my REBUTTAL, which I'll say — was **strongly audible!** I remained <u>steadfast</u> in the performance of my **DUTY**, as I saw it. Luckily, there was **no** second NOTE from the JUDGE NEXT DOOR. Actually, I'm <u>twice</u> lucky, the Jury listened. The Jury deliberated — and the Jury returned with a GUILTY VERDICT for **Murder** <u>in</u> <u>**the**</u> <u>**First**</u> <u>**Degree**</u>. A form of vindication for the <u>Victim</u> and for <u>strong</u> <u>jawed</u> <u>Prosecution</u>.

"Song's but solace for a day; Wine's a traitor not to trust;
Love's a kiss and then away; Time's a peddler deals in dust."
(Robert Underwood Johnson, *Hearth-Song*. Stanza 2)

But DUTY is solace for three hundred sixty five days <u>times</u> twenty nine, and <u>never</u> a traitor to trust. DUTY's <u>not</u> a kiss and then away, nor a peddler dealing dust. "A **sense of duty** pursues us ever. It is omnipresent...If we take to ourselves the wings of the morning, and dwell in the uttermost parts of the sea, **duty performed**, or **duty violated**, is STILL WITH US...If we say the darkness shall cover us, in **the darkness as in the light** <u>OUR</u> <u>OBLIGATIONS</u> ARE YET WITH US." (Daniel Webster, ibid. – emphasis added)

I'm inspired by Webster's words. They eloquently convey the **moral imperative** that guides the path of the Deputy District Attorney who <u>truly</u> possesses the **Spirit of his Profession**. A **sense of duty** carries such a Prosecutor. NOTHING fazes him. NOTHING trumps his focus. NOT snoozing Jurors; NOT a torrent of frivolous Defense Objections; NOT Judicial Advisory Instructions Of Acquittal; NOT Judges from next door complaining about loud arguments; NOT tapping pencils from the Bench; NOT recalcitrant witnesses; NOT obstreperous Defendant's who break chairs and kick over Counsel tables – sending pitchers of water spraying across the room; NOT a Deviate offering a glass of wine and rough sex as quid pro quo for an "A"; NOT a callous, <u>uncharged</u> Killer still an unrepentant braggart after ten years; NOT the <u>absence</u> of bodies of Murder Victims; NOT the devastation of night-time residential fire bombs; NOT fatigue born of sixteen hour days; NOT feelings of hopelessness that a Case can't be won – tomorrow's a new day with new circumstances; NOT the Judicial suppression of evidence; NOT the failure of key witnesses to make in-court identifications; NOT intimidating stares from family and friends of Defendants; NOT falling air conditioning vents on the third floor that shake Courtrooms ceilings and Final Arguments; NOT cases with extraordinary publicity; NOT television cameras in Court; NOT power ball threats of Judicial contempt; NOT acquittals; NOT convictions reversed –––

    <u>NOTHING</u> confounds nor stays the **sense of duty** of the Deputy District Attorney who <u>truly</u> possesses the **Spirit of his Profession.** Wherever he dwells – in the darkness as in the light, HIS OBLIGATIONS <u>**stay**</u> with him. He remains a DYNAMIC ADVOCATE <u>**for**</u> <u>**Justice**</u> until *the curtain* comes down on his LAST CASE.

About the Author

He is a retired Trial Lawyer. Employed by the Clark County District Attorney's Office in Las Vegas, Nevada for twenty nine years. Serving as Chief Deputy in charge of the Major Violator"s Unit for sixteen years. During his career he handled nearly 300 felony trials, which includes 136 Murder Trials. Probably, no Prosecutor in the United States has exceeded this number. He is uniquely qualified to discuss the prosecution of murder cases. He is well known in the State of Nevada, particularly in the Las Vegas area. He has participated over the years in many high-profile cases that received extensive news coverage. The Governor proclaimed both March 1, 1989 and October 26 1996 as Mel Harmon Days in recognition of his professional stature. He also received the State Bar of Nevada Distinguished Public Lawyer Award for "expertise, dedication and extraordinary service to the people of Nevada as a Public Lawyer" in November, 1992. Moreover, he was awarded the William J. Raggio outstanding Prosecutor in the State Award on September 23, 2004.

LaVergne, TN USA
10 September 2010
196564LV00004B/8/P